Black Social Dance
in Television Advertising

ALSO BY CARLA STALLING HUNTINGTON

Hip Hop Dance: Meanings and Messages
(McFarland, 2007)

Black Social Dance in Television Advertising

An Analytical History

CARLA STALLING HUNTINGTON

McFarland & Company, Inc., Publishers
Jefferson, North Carolina, and London

LIBRARY OF CONGRESS CATALOGUING-IN-PUBLICATION DATA

Huntington, Carla Stalling, 1961–
   Black social dance in television advertising : an analytical history / Carla Stalling Huntington.
      p.   cm.
   Includes bibliographical references and index.

   ISBN 978-0-7864-5944-5
   softcover : 50# alkaline paper ∞

   1. African American dance — History. 2. African Americans — Social life and customs. 3. Dance — Social aspects — United States — History. 4. Dance — Anthropological aspects — United States — History. 5. Television advertising — Social aspects — United States. 6. Popular culture — United States — History. 7. United States — Civilization — African American influences. I. Title.
   GV1624.7.A34H86   2011
   793.3089'96073 — dc23   2011022257

BRITISH LIBRARY CATALOGUING DATA ARE AVAILABLE

© 2011 Carla Stalling Huntington. All rights reserved

No part of this book may be reproduced or transmitted in any form or by any means, electronic or mechanical, including photocopying or recording, or by any information storage and retrieval system, without permission in writing from the publisher.

Front cover images © 2011 Shutterstock

Manufactured in the United States of America

McFarland & Company, Inc., Publishers
   Box 611, Jefferson, North Carolina 28640
   www.mcfarlandpub.com

For Mother Louise and Mother Lucille

Acknowledgments

Portions of this research were funded by research and travel grants received from the Association for Consumer Research, North America, and Missouri Southern State University, Joplin, Missouri. Research was also supported via IREGE, a department of the University of Savoy, Institute of Management, Annecy, France.

I credit the University of Chicago Press for allowing me to utilize Judith Hanna's model of dance communication, which appeared in *To Dance Is Human: A Theory of Nonverbal Communication* in 1987.

My appreciation is extended to Larry Blagg, senior vice president of marketing, and Dori Rothweiler, marketing project coordinator, at the California Raisins Marketing Board.

My gratitude is given for the respondents who spent their time in interviews for this research.

I would also like to thank my colleagues Jean Moscarola, PhD, University of Savoy, Institute of Management, IREGE, Annecy, France; and Loay Altimini, PhD, Management Information Systems, Assistant Professor of Business Computer Applications, Al-Isra University, Faculty of Management & Financial Sciences, Department of Management Information Systems, Amman, Jordan. Both of them were extremely supportive and helpful with the research and reviewing drafts of my writing.

For access to archived advertisements, I would like to thank the Paley Center, Beverly Hills, California, and, in particular, Martin Gostanian. At the UCLA Library Media Archive I thank the numerous student workers and Mark Quigley for their help in gathering sources for use in this work.

I thank the Association for Consumer Research North American Conference along with the HCR colleagues for allowing certain aspects of this work to be included in the 2009 Pittsburgh, Pennsylvania, conference, and the anonymous reviewers for drafts of certain chapters. In addition, special thanks are in order for the opportunity to present my work at the Consumer Culture Theory 4 Conference, held in 2009 at Ann Arbor, Michigan.

Sources of research material were available to me by assistance from the African American History Library in Los Angeles, California; the University of California, San Diego Library, San Diego, California; and the Huntington Library in San Marino, California. Elizabeth Dunn, research services librarian at Duke University Rare Book, Manuscript, and Special Collections Library, and David Strader, RBMSCL research services, Duke University Library were particularly helpful.

I would also like to thank David Geeting, former advertising executive with Leo Burnett, for his time and expertise.

Special thanks are sent to Jeff Murray, Steve Smith, Lisa Penaloza, and Jonathan Schroeder, for their encouragement and inspiration.

I especially thank Erik Walter.

Table of Contents

Acknowledgments — vii
Preface — 1
Introduction — 5

Section One: Literature and Theory

1. Dance Theory — 23
2. Marketing, Advertising, and Dance — 48

Section Two: The Research Study

3. A History of Black Social Dance in Commercials — 77
4. On Black Social Dance in Commercials in 2010 — 101
5. Interpretations — 129

Section Three: Conclusions and Future Directions

Conclusion and Future Research — 159

Chapter Notes — 169
Bibliography — 177
Index — 189

Preface

I love dance: doing it, watching it, teaching it. Simply stated, I have a passion for it. My life has been filled with dance as far back as I can remember. My home life growing up included dancing all the time: when people were visiting, for a special occasion, when we went to visit people, or for no reason at all except to have a good time, enjoy and let go. It was fascinating to watch, and most of the time I wanted to be right in the middle of the dance floor. I felt connected to people, and I realized, at some point, that people who danced at these gatherings had their own signatures and styles.

But my passion for dance included many varieties of dance, not just black social dance, and I have spent time in my life dancing in some form or fashion. I learned ballet and performed whenever I could, as some may say, semi-professionally, but I have continued to believe I did it just for the beauty, the enveloping of my mind and body in another world with classical music, and fully taking advantage of its meditative aspects. And it turned out, through my doctoral program of study and founding a professional ballet company, that I got the opportunity to teach and choreograph. As such, dance for me has been very fulfilling, as well as giving me behaviors that carry over into other areas of my life. These include the creative processes required to conduct business, disciplinary ability that dance affords me, and the confidence I receive from being part of a dance ensemble.

Importantly, there is exhilaration and a feeling of freedom that comes from dancing. If you are "really into it," you can escape from your present state of mental worry or anxiety or whatever may be on your mind and have a flow experience where you are completely in the moment. At that point the mind/body connection is complete. In this regard I find dance to be spiritual. When doing black social dance in a group where the group is in flow, there is a feeling of transcendence — from the history and the struggle. Look across

Ebony Echoes. Rare Book, Manuscript, and Special Collections Library, Duke University Press, Durham, NC).

the room and you see faces not as they were, filled with anguish, but rather faces that say, "I'm having a *good* time," in all that this particular phrase means.

This aspect of dance study seemed to me, in my opinion and view, to be left out of the scholarly discussion, especially as social dance found a categorically marginal place in the conversation.

My world not only has included dance, but business has been a large aspect of it, especially the disciplines of marketing and management in terms of professional experience and teaching. For this work the focus is on the marketing discipline, especially consumer behavior and advertising. My interest in dance as it relates to consumer behavior really started when, with my doctorate in dance history and theory from the University of California in hand, I was in post-doctoral study at the University of Arkansas, in Fayetteville. There I discovered the ways in which consumers are both a subject of study and treated by certain producers of goods and services as objects aimed at. The degree to which marketers try to get into consumers' heads was fascinating to me. So was the critical aspect of consumer culture theory.

Consumer behavior focused on how to get consumers' attention, and how to use that information in advertising and other marketing approaches. One of the areas pointed to in this regard was how music affects consumers and consumption. But there was nothing in that discussion about dance. Over the course of time, I came to understand how consumers were influenced with placements of products, how the body can be an influence on consumption. But still, nothing about dance.

This was odd because I saw commercials with dance in them. With this heightened awareness, the commercials using dance in them seemed to multiply as I watched television. Many of them used black social dance, but other dance forms as well. So, naturally, I started looking at the consumer research literature to see if there were studies on dance and consumption. There were none. The body was dealt with, but dance per se was not. Music was dealt with and images were considered in their abilities to attract consumers and help them remember products and brands, but dance was not addressed.

Something was wrong with that picture, in my opinion.

These were the motivators of this work. The fact was that due to my experience with dance I theorized that when people watched advertisements with dancing, they were affected by it. I just did not know what *the affect* was. And of course, I started wondering how long ago dance began to show up in commercials, and then what kind of dance and there I was, off on a new research path.

From a critical perspective, I wanted to know if there was any connection between what was happening in culture and what was happening in commercials. And while I could not examine the effect that the commercials with dance in them had on people back in the day, I could examine what effect were they having on consumers in the present day. Was it positive or negative? Did it not matter one way or another? What about aesthetics? How did that come into play?

In terms of developing a research stream, it was important to me that *at least the question of* **dance** in television advertisement as an influence on consumers be raised if for no other reason than to say that it has been looked at. It had not been, and I assumed that this was because it was just dismissed as not being seen, not being important, what some would call residing in feminine silence. That could not remain the case. Researchers in consumer behavior and advertising at least would now be able to consider dance as a message carrier within a television advertisement. And dance theory would have expanded its scope from its boundaries of being descriptive to being explanatory.

These concerns and others are covered in the following chapters.

Introduction

The typical advertisement or commercial is the professional product of highly skilled and exacting crafts people, and as such, presents a perfectly polished, opaque surface to the reader or viewer. Yet such perfection is only an illusion, a camouflage so well wrought that it deflects scrutiny of the churning dynamics lying below and beyond.[1]

BACKGROUND

As I sat one evening engaging in what used to be a normal practice for me to wind down from a hectic workday, I noticed a trend in television ads. Increasingly, they seemed to utilize dance in them. Moreover, I recognized the dances as dances done in cultural and social milieus, borrowed from theater or social dances. Because of my exposure to both the cultural study of dance and consumer research, it had occurred to me that dance in television commercials may be a significant vehicle for carrying meaning relative to consumption, markets, and culture, by concerning itself with the "contemporary moral, social, political and emotional issues" that dance addresses.[2] After an extensive search of the literature, I found that there were no studies on the effects of dance on consumers in television commercials. On this virtual stage where the dance occurs in our post postmodern theater,[3] meanings are derived from race, gender, and body image, both currently and historically situated for the audience. Why was that? What did it mean? What was the effect this was having or did it have historically on consumers if any? What about society as a whole?

The purpose of this work is to seek answers to those questions through examining the historical use and frequency of black social dance in television advertisements relative to changing marketing approaches from the advent of television to 2010. As I watched contemporary commercials with dance in

South Car'lina Tickle. Rare Book, Manuscript, and Special Collections Library, Duke University Press, Durham, NC.

them, I began to theorize that the consumption of certain brands and their related products had been connected to dance but was increasingly linked to black social dance. Except sometimes the dances were not performed by black people.

When I was reviewing television commercials at the media archives at UCLA, I realized that companies had been using dance in their advertisements for nearly the entire time television has been in existence. Knowing what I know about dance, I concluded that this was an area of scholarship needing to be researched. As a result, this book, along with other supporting research, is the first to evaluate dance and advertising, particularly black social dance and television advertising.

In this volume, I contribute to the historical dance and marketing scholarship fields by demonstrating that dance is important for meaning transfer and brand loyalty through commercial advertising, that it works in tandem with social issues, and that it is used perhaps unknowingly as part of a historical consumer behavior mechanism that has escaped theorization. While most researchers have focused on images in print ads, and music in television and radio ads, this contribution theorizes that *dance* is a mechanism for communication in ads. I also argue that using dance in commercials serves both an aesthetic and an anthropological function for individuals and society in the United States.

What Is Dance?

When one starts to talk about dance, one walks on a shifting desert landscape, complete with a mirage in the distance that promises a clear definition. But it is constantly elusive. This is evident in the fact that there are a number of definitions of dance that have been discussed and debated. For example, when I say *dance*, I mean *dance*—what people recognize in everyday life as dance (Francis, 1996). I mean all dance—social and concert—so I do not engage in the argument of high versus low art forms (Charter, 2006). Dance is not sports. Not cheerleading. Not ice skating. Not a marching band. Not pantomime. So with these qualifiers in mind, we can begin to see how defining dance is a slippery slope. In order to facilitate setting a frame of reference for what dance is, I rely on a blended definition of dance adapted from three dance scholars.[4]

In her work on kinetic communication in dance, Smyth (1984) claimed that dance is organized and beautiful to watch; if it is, then dance prompts a response from the viewer. This means that dance is both a visual and kinesthetic communication vehicle such that "there is a special sense for which dance can provide aesthetic satisfaction."[5] Of course, not all people find every dance beautiful to watch and it may not appear to be organized by aesthetic satisfaction, meaning the known or unknown exchange, use or sign value that dance texts yield, either positively or negatively, and/or emotionally or cognitively for a consumer.[6] With exchange and use value, users modify/transform objects so that they become a sign. Next, mass culture capitalizes on the transfunctionalized objects.[7] Dance has a use and exchange value and users modify the dance so that it represents a subcultural sign (such as cool); and the culture industry uses the new sign (dance) to maintain capitalist production.

As a nonverbal communication device, dance creates moods and situations,[8] wherein the cognitive, sensory and motor systems are intertwined with emotions.[9] In a later study, Francis (1996) defined dance as having a purposed movement motif, such as entertainment or artistic expression that is executed with expressiveness, which necessarily occurs in a particular context. I suggest that these characterizations of dance are circulating in commercials that contain dance, and consumers are receiving nonverbal communications from them. What kind of communication is going to be discussed throughout the following pages. I began with a set of interpretive dance premises[10] through which to examine how consumers base their interpretations of black social dance — knowingly or not. Dance scholar Deidre Sklar (2001) arranged five interpretive premises in the following manner:

> Premise 1: Movement knowledge is a kind of cultural knowledge and
>
> Premise 2: Movement knowledge is conceptual, and emotional, as well as kinesthetic. The moves embody culture-specific ideas about nature, society, and the cosmos; beneath these feelings are involved so that movement is associated with emotion.
>
> Premise 3: Movement knowledge is intertwined with other kinds of cultural knowledge.
>
> Premise 4: One has to look beyond movement to get at its meaning; concepts embodied in the movement are not necessarily evident in the movement itself.
>
> Premise 5: Movement is always an immediate corporeal experience.

These premises contain notions of macro- and micro-dances embedded within the consumer's sphere of attention.[11] I take the position that dance as an aesthetic communication device in commercials simultaneously provides cultural knowledge. In this construct, the viewer does not need to know how to dance.[12] Dance is immediately corporeal. It is intertwined with other cultural knowledge and the meaning of the dance is not always obvious to an onlooker. The purpose for narrowing the analysis in this way is to arrive at an anthropological focus on black social dance as it is currently used in American television advertising,[13] and to theorize its value and power in conveying information to consumers.

I posit that dance, particularly black social dance, is used in television advertising precisely for two reasons. First dance communicates without words and advertisers borrow "tactics to convey messages by means other than or in addition to words ... and advertisers prefer a suggestion rather than a definite statement when promoting a product or an idea ... and influence and direct consumer behavior by using language that is slyly constructed."[14] Second, since dance, on the one hand, and television advertising,[15] on the other, both occur in cultural semiotic contexts,[16] when dance is used in television commercial advertising it communicates and signifies coded social and cultural information "through the linked process of semiosis,"[17] which also focuses instead on symbolic relationships in the context of consumption.

The marriage between black social dance and advertising is perfect since advertising, like dance, is itself a signifying system itself using other texts to accomplish its mission.[18] Using black social dance in advertising by connecting it with consumption facilitates and communicates transfers of meanings.[19] The communication is interpretive through an intertextually based arrangement.[20]

In viewing a television commercial, we can assume that the performance space is the viewer's personal space, wherever that may be.[21] In this way it can be likened to concert dance. Thus, the performance space could be the living room, the any-room, kitchen, office, automobile, work lunchroom, or a public space such as a movie theater or street corner, or, as our society moves into the increased use of technological apparatuses for personal connections to media, even one's palm. The choreographer is the advertiser working through a dance practitioner and the camera, and the performers are digitized representations of humanity in a cultural context. Viewers are consumers and audience in their lived spaces and as such they now may very well be defined as dancers. From such a perspective, dance in television advertising can also be categorized as social, one reason for not joining the argument of defining what is concert and what is social, or privileging one over the other.

Advertising

Approaches to evaluating advertisements have historically focused on both print and television advertising, and the volume of literature about these is overwhelming. By way of summarizing that which is relevant to this study, I provide the following. In print analysis, the historical methods have focused on content analysis,[22] suggesting that print advertising reflected consumers' desires rather than product functionality. To this end creative production of artistic and rhetorical styles began to have more of a central place in print advertisement over the period studied, particularly during and between 1950 and 1970. Belk and Pollay (1985) examined print advertisements and their relationship to the "good life" and materialism in postmodern America. Their work also documents an existential change in the focus of print advertising from "being and doing" to "having" material goods. Scott (1994) considered print advertising as rhetorically imbedded in copy theory in that an advertisement — the equivalent of a picture — resembles reality. However, only when a consumer has learned to correctly look at an advertisement can he or she interpret its meanings, based on "conventions of representations."[23] Spears and Germain (2007) extended the visual rhetorical model and utilized a visual imagery progression model in looking at changes in print advertisements that included animals. This extended model suggested that images in print advertising are "repositories of cultural meaning"[24] and that for consumers these meanings change over time.[25]

In terms of ads other than print, one study found that music was related to classical conditioning in television commercials.[26] Other authors, such as Alpert and Alpert (1990), have expanded the study of the use of music and other non verbal elements on consumers' moods in television commercials. Their study rests on the theoretical notion that there are central (cognitive involvement) and peripheral (classical conditioning, low involvement, feelings derived, based on musical nonstructure (liking) and structure (musical content)) routes that consumers use in information processing and that these routes have currency in effect and emotional influences on consumers' attitudes. What this means is that consumers are affected positively or negatively with music when it is associated with emotion and decision making.

Scott (1990) stated that even though, at that time, consumers were known to recite jingles learned through music in advertising, "scholars who study advertising seem confounded by it [music]. Few studies of the role of music in advertising exist."[27] Scott argued that the studies that had been completed evaluated music for its non-semantic stimulus feeling effects, rather than upon cognitive bases. She illustrated that music communicates meaning cognitively by "performing any number of rhetorical tasks"[28] as well as evoking feelings and emotions. As a result, several studies emerged which experimented with the use of music in advertisements. One was that of Macinnis and Park (1991), which suggested that the analysis of music in advertising along the lines of the central/peripheral route split was oversimplified. Rather than looking at meanings and classical conditioning, the indexicality (music that evoked memories) and fit (consumers' perceptions of whether the music was appropriate for the message) of music in advertisements influenced low and high involvement processing.

Hung (2000) acknowledged the literature achievements mentioned above and went further to suggest that music is "always accompanied by at least one other ad component."[29] Scott (1990) also stated that "music never appears in an advertising context without at least one other executional element."[30] Those components and elements include voice, dialog, copy and visual. In the classifications "visual" and "element," however, the direct mention of *dance* is absent. And while the study of dance in television advertisements has begun[31] indicating that it has rhetorical and culturally specific meaning, there is no explicit documentation of dance as an ad component. And like a similar point in time with music, little has been done to study the incidence of dance in television advertising, let alone either the feeling or cognitive affects upon consumers exposed to it.

Music has not only been studied in relation to advertising. Mick and Buhl (1992) presented a meaning-based model of advertising that occurred in socio-cultural contexts related to life projects and themes. Later this was expanded with a call for a theory of visual rhetoric in advertising[32] and a response to it by McQuarrie and Mick (1999). Phillips (1997) researched consumers' interpretations of meanings in complex advertising, while Hirschman, Scott and Wells (1998) used discourse theory to understand consumers and their interpretations of television commercials and their behavior. Hirschman and Thompson (1997) used a multidisciplinary framework to explore relationships between consumers and mass media.

Paralleling these studies, researchers in consumer behavior have set forth theoretical frames for interpreting meanings, consumer responses to advertisements, and embodiment. In the area of interpretive consumer research, McCracken (1986) developed an account of how goods carry cultural meaning for consumers, while Thompson, Locander and Pollio (1989) presented a method of existential phenomenology with regard to consumer experiences. Murray and Ozanne (1991) contributed critical theory for interpreting consumers and their emancipatory interests regarding consumption. Thompson (1997) brought a framework for gleaning insights into consumers through textual analysis of respondents' stories.

Embodiment and consumption relative to the socialized body were addressed in a study by Thompson and Hirschman (1995) where the body was the focus of self-perception. Joy and Venkatesh (1994) looked at the body from the point of view of post-modern feminism to give the body a particular agency. Joy and Sherry (2003) contributed a multi-sensory approach to understanding consumption of experiences: they connected the body to feelings and the unconscious mind with reference to consumption practices, drawing a picture of how interpretive approaches are limited. Dance on the screen was studied in relation to British television during the 1990s as choreographed and directed for such medium.[33] These studies, however, as important and relevant as their contributions are, have not addressed dancing, and particularly black social dance, and its impact on consumption or consumers in television advertising.

Therefore, I begin to fill this void with this volume.

SOCIAL CONTEXTS OF DANCE IN ADVERTISING

As discussed by Spears and Germain (2007) there are several societal elements to be considered during any time period. They include economic, political, social, and institutional contingencies that make goods available for consumption. These categorical elements are considered in light of the use of dance in television advertising. Later these categories will be paired along with the development of the three stages of ideological meanings to examine the nexus between dance as use and dance as mass-mediated cultural sign.

For example, the 1950s were characterized by the civil rights movement[34] and "cultural upheavals"[35] in the midst of a broader postmodern period of prosperity,[36] stability and peace.[37] Producers of television advertisements promoted whites to perform music that was germane to blacks. In television shows, blacks were presented in stereotypical ways through the end of the 1960s. In the 1970s, with an economic downturn, again with a period of cultural upheaval with regard to the Vietnam War, women's liberation, and forced integration, blacks were presented in segregated programming and then later in integrated situation comedies. Since the 1980s and the economic prosperity it brought, blacks have become culturally assimilated in television programs, and have moved from the background and only with other non-black characters to a commercial presence into the foreground with only black characters.[38] In the 1990s and into the 2000s there were ups and downs in the macro economy, an increasing mode of globalization, reduction in affirmative action, and an increase in consumer debt, not to leave aside the Great Recession. The point is that in each of these periods, black social dance has been used in advertising of brands. As we move through the research we will discover whether it has been a positive or negative outcome for the racial problems so prevalent in America.

Of course, I cannot give an exhaustive discussion of dance history or history in general during the period under study. On the other hand, the reader would benefit from a brief overview of dance history in order to situate the use of television commercials during the time period. As such, the discussion includes social and concert dances as they furthered agendas of social and political outcomes.

For example, dance scholars[39] have written about the Cold War which spanned a large portion of the 1940s through the 1990s. Prevots (1998) demonstrated some of the ways in which social dance was used during that time. During the 1950s McCarthyism, the beginnings of the civil rights movement, and fear of communism as a threat to the American way of life gripped the country and these images were being broadcasted around the world. To combat these representations of American behavior, professional dance companies were deployed — under the direction of President Eisenhower, and approved and appropriated by Congress — around the world to perform concert dances that would present an opposing but more flattering image of the United States. The dance companies that were sent were selected by the American National Theater and Academy dance panelists. Those panelists included the influential dance company leaders and wealthy patrons; they purposely selected black dance performers and ensembles to send abroad. The dance tours were promoted by the United States Information Agency, and represented the first integrated and successful marketing program that used dance to carry out its aims.[40]

By the early 1960s dance, as part of the larger push towards government funding and expanding private philanthropy of the performing arts and humanities, took center stage. The National Endowments for the Humanities and Arts were formed in 1965[41] and the United States witnessed a dance company boom into the 1980s.[42] The expansion included ballet and modern dance companies, including the American Ballet Theater, the New York City Ballet, and the Chicago Opera Ballet. Rudolf Nureyev, Ruth Page, Rebecca Harkness and George Balanchine were among the brand names in dance at this time.

BLACK SOCIAL AND CONCERT DANCE

African and African American social dance used within social contexts, for political stability, and consumption purposes has been firmly documented from the African Diaspora to the emancipation period.[43] Following this, the period from the 1800s to the 1950s produced a broad array of African American social and concert dance for entertainment within permitted segregated social settings ranging from private parties and cotillions to church gatherings. The development of African American social dance continued through honky-tonks and cabarets. Euro-Americans found these dances entertaining, as evidenced by their attendance at nightclubs. African American concert dance also found a great deal of acceptance during this period of time. It included black-face minstrelsy, ragtime, and tap dance performed by African Americans initially and then by Euro-Americans.[44] Most of the concert dance supported comedic acts and often ridiculed or at least subjugated African Americans, reinforcing the racial hierarchy prevalent in American society.

Towards the end of the 1950s and into the 1960s, growing awareness of social problems resulting from segregation sparked the civil rights movement. The twist, the jitterbug and the hitch-hike were social dances and Euro-Americans learned and performed them. At the same time movement played a large part in the civil rights era as the resistive means by which segregation was fought. Many changes in African American social dances occurred from the 1960s to the early 1970s. Michael Jackson and *The Jackson 5* began dancing on televised stages, giving new contexts to African American dance. The resistance and strength began to represent positive associations with blackness and African American movement. This period included the popular culture association of African American social dance with "cool."[45]

By the end of the 1970s, popular culture that supported the cool identity began additionally associating African American social dance with "street authenticity," e.g., in break dancing. This period of American history marked a rise in African American gains in education, employment, and equality, which continued through the early 1980s, resulting from the emerging economic freedoms and affirmative action policies of the mid–1970s.[46] Break dancing originated in the inner-city ghettos and represented the "break" from social structures and a cultural administration growing out of the African American experience.

Reversals in affirmative action policies began occurring in the late 1980s and lasted through the middle of the next decade. Policy changes were viewed by many as returning to American discrimination not only for African Americans but for all non–Euro-American men. It signaled a period of cultural contradiction, with the recession of the early 1990s developing at the same time as globalization was increasing. These events in social history ran parallel to the benchmark Rodney King and OJ Simpson verdicts in Los Angeles. Resistive African American hip-hop social dance grew out of this era.[47] Response to cultural contradictions and globalization begun in the late 1990s continues:[48] Layered over the cool, street, and break from social structures, African American social dance states individuality through resistance.

In terms of social dances in the 1960s, white American youth culture dominated and mimicked blacks while black American youth dictated dances in the nightclubs and on television. It was also the first time that black and white teenagers appeared together on national television for the purpose of dancing.[49] Chubby Checker and Dick Clark played a large role in facilitating the spotlight for social dance on television. There was also considerable relational information being provided between the social and concert dance venues so that their performances and nuances influenced each other as people consumed, choreographed, and performed dance in different genres. Such a meshing can be seen clearly in dances of the 1970s. This was the era of disco dancing and choreographed line dancing. At the same time Latin dances became popular, and by the end of the 1970s and into the 1980s, hip-hop dance came to the limelight[50] and continues to remain a dominant dance form in the United States and abroad well into second decade of the 21st century.

But in popular readings and assumptions about it, social dance is equated with freedom, fun, happiness, and carefree emancipation from hegemonic endeavors. We jump for joy and dance in the streets when things are great. People dance when they have succeeded in removing an obstacle or achieved a goal. Dance is celebratory and relaxing when people dance the night away or dance to their own drum. At least, these are some of the ways dance metaphors are used in television ads. However, it will be clear that a much more complex reality exists for consumers when dance is matched with brands and products.

With this brief history of the social contexts and the growth of dance in both concert and popular formats, the research question stands before us ready for examination. Was black social dance in television commercials aired in the United States over the period under study used for purposes of increasing brand usage and controlling cultural meanings? Expectations of findings included an affirmative answer to the question and an increasing use of the dance over time, with a shifting of dancer type to reflect the changing social environments affecting the United States.

Issues for Consumers

Figure 1, "Issues for Consumers," provides a graphical representation of the fluidity through which dance operates in society, and as I suggest, television ads.

First of all, does the use of dance in connection to brands provide a positive or negative consequence for consumers? Contrary to popular beliefs about it, dance performs a critical function in society, and so by extension, is it doing so in commercials? As an art form, we see dance created in an aesthetic vein and providing value to consumers. Does it also do this in commercials? Does it provide an escape from mass consumption? Dance consumption and performance are social. As dance portrayals increasingly become digitized and staged in the "any-room" with a mobile device or screen,[51] on a Wii or Nintendo or Xbox, so that a picture of dance substitutes the real, how does that

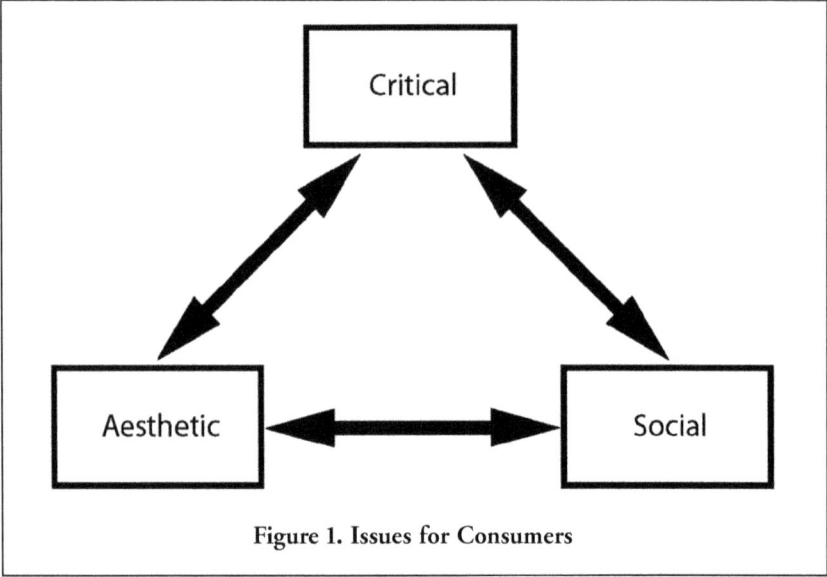

Figure 1. Issues for Consumers

impact the social signs and signifiers dance creates? These questions, along with those raised earlier, are addressed in the research.

THE RESEARCH

My writing about black social dance from this historical perspective places me on a critical edge. The beginning of dance history and theory was an attempt to look at dance as it occurred in different locations and forms, under the genesis of "What was dance anyway and where did it start?" Then the study of dance quickly moved into trying to assess what it signified and to whom. Nearly immediately or perhaps simultaneously, the discussion morphed into a conversation about its good[52] based on placement inside or outside a proscenium. Is it art or counted as aesthetic if it is staged elsewhere or done by the wrong people? Outside this conversation but in a parallel one, dance was viewed as something people wondered about paying for in terms of an academic discipline or a consumable good. All manner of arguments ensued about what dance is, categorizing it into movements and the study of bodies or things called performances in general, or ice skating, or cheerleading, or.... However, as a cultural artifact of study, *dance* has been marginalized.

I go out on a ledge in this book to talk about *dance*. Yes, I bring to this discussion some relevant literature on the body, certain arguments about aesthetics, and so on. However, my premise is *dance* is doing something for us in our society in advertisements just like it does something for us in reality. And in particular, black social dance does this something as an aesthetic art form transcending any categorical boundary of high versus low. As with music in advertising, one does not study individual notes but rather jingles and drops, according to Scott (1990), to find its affect; I suggest linking the dance with brands is also doing something.

Therefore, there are two aspects of this research. First, there is the archival data. Situated in a cultural studies theoretical frame, I used art historical[53] and print advertising[54] methods to document the use of black social dance in television advertising and the resultant social contexts and historical periods between 1950 and 2010. The UCLA Media Library television commercial archive covered a portion of the period under study, as did the Paley Center, and therefore these were my main sources of historical commercials to view. Of course, these resources, as extensive as they are, do not have *every* commercial produced over the last 70 years; they do, however, have thousands and thousands of them! The number of commercials viewed was cataloged and they number over 2,000. To facilitate locating commercials with dance in them I visually scanned each tape. For commercials in later periods, digital archives found through electronic online sources were examined. Each commercial in these cases are referenced within the text.

Of the total commercials viewed, dance was used in advertising in each year. Interestingly, within the archival materials, dance movement being employed in commercials increased in 1964, 1970, 1980, and 1982. Commercials before 1982 did not use dance in the foreground, but rather used it in the background; in 1983, the use of dance in the commercials changes from the background to the foreground. Interestingly, archived commercials before 1970 did not use African Americans.

In terms of analysis, I coupled critical semiosis[55] in television commercials with hermeneutic methods.[56]

The second aspect of the research includes interviewing respondents. I employed phenomenological interviews[57] based on Sklar's (2001) interpretive premises. I spent several years interviewing, recording, and transcribing African American and Euro-American respondents' interpretations of black social dance used in recent television advertisements, taking an anthropological viewpoint as an African American female participant observer.[58] I found that the two groups differ significantly in their interpretations. Blacks found the ads touched on their lives in ways that produced solidarity and were insulted by the ways in which black social dance was used in branding. Whites had a different relationship with the dance, but at the same time derived meanings from it in commercials that reinforced and maintained racial, gender, economic, and political social structures.[59]

Before going on, I would like to clarify what is meant by black and white. African American means black people in the United States in this book. Euro-American and/or Caucasian means white people in the United States in this book. What it means to be either one of these is what is recognized as a socially constructed binary opposition of race and color here in our capitalistic society, and the change over time that this represents. When talking about the dance, I will use black social dance to reference this.

ORGANIZATION OF THE BOOK

In chapter 1, dance literature is covered as background, showing it as a theoretical and communication construct. In chapter 2, I discuss the consumer, cultural, marketing, and advertising literatures as they relate to dance and commercials. Here I provide a review of the literature that focuses on bodily communications and classical conditioning in advertising, and in particular, persuasion routes and the nonverbal aspects of dance. In chapter 3, I provide documentation of black social dance over the 1950–2010 period, and give examples. I show its increased use in branding and products as we move into the post-postmodern period. Chapter 4 presents the interview data from respondents watching a Diet Pepsi commercial and that of a careered advertising agency executive as texts, and chapter 5 presents the interpretive findings. Here the informants' voices of blacks and whites from previous research (males and females), and their interpretations of black social dance and the meanings, connections, and affinity for the brand in commercials are shown. Blacks demonstrate a different relationship with black social dance than do whites when connected with consumption of branded products. However, both groups utilize their relationship with black social dance as the great cultural equalizer and identity constructor.

A grounded[60] "theory of black social dance in advertising" emerges:

> In a television ad, black social dance aesthetics communicates metaphorically historical and current socio-cultural behavior and knowledge regardless of which groups perform it, serving as a post-postmodern theatrical production. It works in the sphere of attention. Communicating and understanding black social dance in commercials occur in human beings through cognitive, emotional, and kinesthetic systems. Dance communicates imagined freedom and fun, through corporeal and non-verbal experience, setting up future expectations and drawing on memories or conditioned responses. Black social dance connected to brands portrays the increase over time, of the anthropology of consumption as immediately celebratory, fun, and freeing. These meanings are not necessarily evident to the consumer, but build brand equity for the producer. In tandem, black social dance in advertisements allows an ever-increasing, societal-level directive

of deflating power contained in dance. Instead of social commentary on the ground, people look on the screen and are mesmerized; on the ground people consume, either real or imagined consumption, *products* as social commentary.

Chapter 6 provides a conclusion and thoughts on future research directions. A call for experimental research is made.

I hope you find this work interesting, and that it will open your eyes to the power of black social dance, a silent yet most ephemeral historic communication device that has been undertheorized in both dance and consumer research in its critical nature in commercials — until now.

Section One

LITERATURE AND THEORY

1. Dance Theory

What sort of cultural object is a brand? ... It is a disposable object laced with associations and powers normally accredited to works of art.[1]

INTRODUCTION

People reading dance in television advertisements are consumers and television is an anthropologic phenomenon.[2] In other words those in the "anyroom" watching a television commercial have social identities and roles arising from the global self such that "I" and "me" are always present.[3] The self is an influence on how dance is read: i.e., social identity and individuality influence perception. In commercial advertising dance could be projecting a fulfilling *imagined* identity as if it were a "facilitating artifact ... that is important to people [and that gives them a reason to be a consumer]."[4] Therefore, before getting too far afield, it is useful to examine dance theories that inform the study at hand. While dance studies encompasses a broad field, ranging from choreographic development to critical assessment and many points in between, for this research I utilize the following nine theories of dance. These in turn inform dance in television advertising. Specifically, dance is educational. It conveys symbolic illusion and imagined power while being experiential and phenomenologic. Dance is functional, providing a vehicle for cultural anthropological knowledge transmission. As such, it is meaning-bearing and meaning-full, existing as a cultural text. Dance, additionally, is aesthetic while being kinesthetic and communicative.

In this chapter, I cover each of these areas to give background on the ways in which they inform dance in commercial advertisements. Next I discuss black social and concert dances as they have evolved over the study period, shrouded in the historically adversarial relationship dance has had with

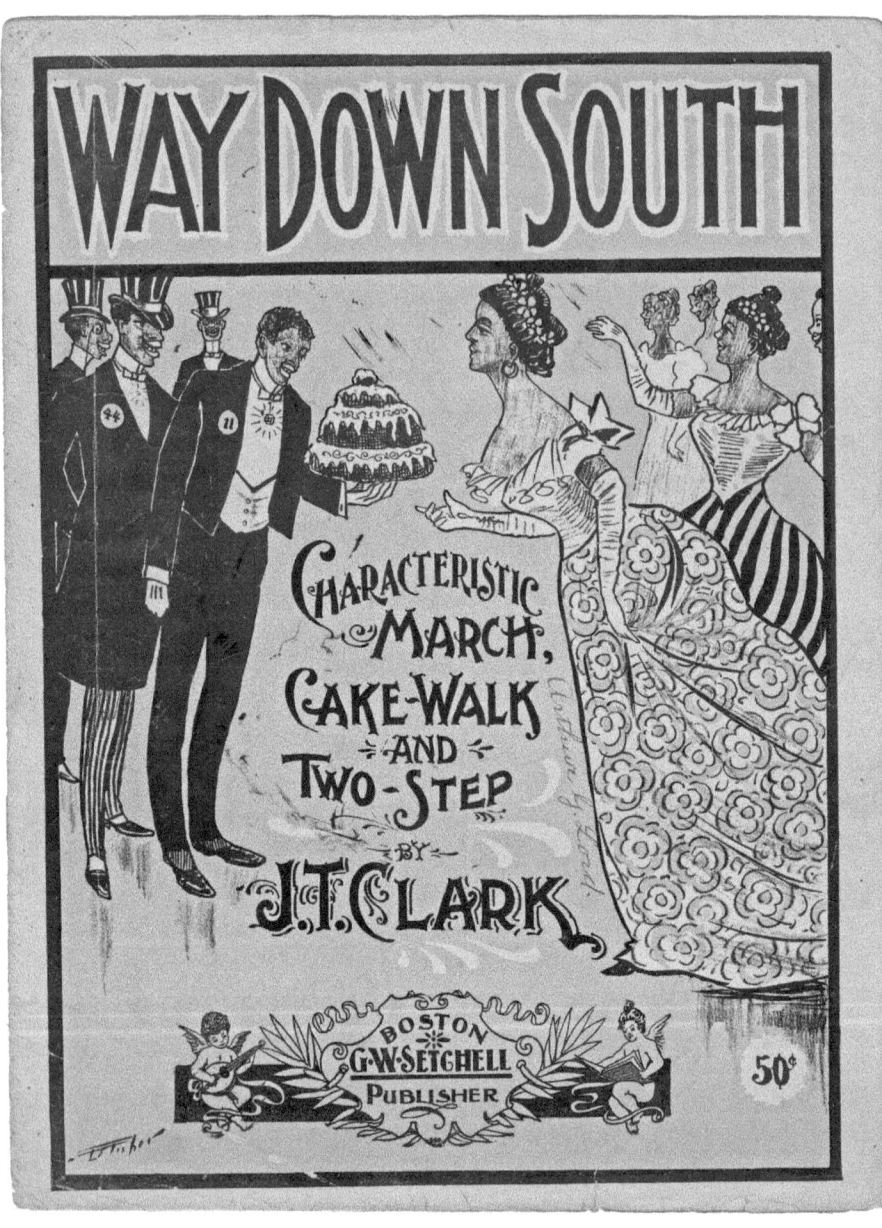

Way Down South. Rare Book, Manuscript, and Special Collections Library, Duke University, Durham, North Carolina.

humanity in this country. Finally, I discuss the use of black social dance as choreographed for television commercials, and show how it is linked to the effects of dance from a theoretical perspective. I will use this background in chapter 5 to demonstrate how black social dance is uniquely projected in commercials to teach, guide, and, some may argue, exert hegemonic control over the viewer in very important social, political, and economic arenas.

THEORIES OF DANCE

Theories of dance were born out of musings over questions such as why people dance, what exactly dance is, where it occurs, and what value[5] it holds. Without doubt, theorizing dance occurred in many historical contexts, from antiquity to the post–postmodern period.[6] Though many theories of dance were developed before the advent of technology, that does not limit their usefulness in understanding consumption. Dance then can further be divided into pre-television and pre-electronic or pre-digital segments. I make mention of periods in dance history mainly so that theories of dance can be contextualized. To understand the framework that surrounds dance, one must begin to evaluate when, where and why humanity danced, and the epistemological structures that defined dance at different points in time. Moreover, one has to comprehend the referential, socially constructed meanings associated with the body, its changing status relative to the mind and soul, and the political-social and secular-religious environments a given body danced or dances in. In addition, the issue of whether the terms "dance" and "movement" are interchangeable has to be addressed. Since this book is concerned specifically with dancing bodies and the interpretation of them, no arguments will be made for distinguishing dance and movement and what constitutes one or the other: they will be used interchangeably based on the definition from the prior chapter. The purpose for narrowing the analysis in this way is to arrive at a focus on dance as it is currently used in American television advertising, and to uncover its value in conveying information to consumers. With these boundaries established, let us turn to some historic ramifications and meanings of dance.

In Western culture, the mind has long been privileged over the body in the Cartesian method of scientific analysis.[7] This value came through historical, philosophical, and religious assumptions about the body. A shift in the emphasis on separation of the body from the mind, from viewing the body as something to be devalued and the mind as something to be worshipped to viewing the body as existential, occurred with such thinkers as Nietzsche and Sartre.[8] Later, the body, which at one time was considered to be private, emerged as a public entity to be managed and watched.[9] Being male or female also informed body status, with women's bodies being defined as less valuable than men's, and the privileging of white over black bodies is well documented.[10]

Regardless of the historical representations of the body, the consuming body[11] has its locus as a set of binary oppositions whereby one body is defined by another, and individuality is only sensible in relation to collectivity. The very purpose of such definitional arrangements is to construct social and personal identities.[12] Such construction of identities then forms a basis for consumption. For purposes of this book, bodies will be understood as both executing dance and consuming goods and services in individual and collective arrangements. Moreover, while Turner (1984) and Featherstone, Turner and Hepworth (1991) and their contributors have also studied bodies and society, and while each of these studies brings the body into the forefront, none of them addresses *dance* per se in the construct, or through the framework, of consumption. This volume does perform dance as a construct so that its theories are presented with an assumption that bodily representations underlie them.

Dance, whether religious or secular, aesthetic or sinful, historical or current in form, has been theorized and criticized as a creative art, as an anthropological phenomenon, evaluated as a social construct, and as a semiotic text to be read. Educator Margaret H'Doubler (1940) provided an analysis of dance that suggested that through dance that is performed "we discover the self through knowledge gained from the effects of our own acts ... but that the average person is kinesthetically unaware of movement as a source of self awareness and well being...."[13] She pressed the point that dance is an educational experience, both active and passive.

Historically, dance began with religious practices,[14] evolving from there to include secular dance as the social environment changed.[15] Over the course of time, attitudes towards dance have ranged back and forth across a continuum in social acceptance, from aesthetic to diabolic.[16] The political, economic and social structure of societies also determined the relative placement of dance on such a continuum, by identifying the social class of the dancers and audiences. Concert dances informed social status with royal classes while social dances informed other classes. In each of these cultural environments, social class, economic structure, and political influence was communicated and behaviors were reinforced through dancing.[17]

Education

Importantly, dance, though serving as an educational "medium for expressing and communicating,"[18] can yield multiple meanings. For example, in our current state of culture, consumers aspire to the abundant life and associate consumption with self and social identity,[19] though the possibility of arrival at an abundant life can be likened to a mirage.[20] Still, the myth of abundance through a consumer culture can be conveyed through dance, which in turn gives dance a certain social and political value. This is a conundrum, given that there exists so far "no accepted philosophy or agreement as to the value of dance."[21]

Rudolph Laban and F.C. Lawrence's (1947; 2nd ed., 1974) *Effort: Economy in Body Movement* was the first theoretical presentation of movement to evaluate it from both labor and artistic standpoints. Laban worked with industry, embarking on time and motion studies of workers of all levels, and developed a system of recording movements on paper, using a detailed set of symbols that had specific meanings. Laban's notation system (Labannotation) was adapted because of its fundamental ability to record not only the movement, but the *effort* involved in it:

> Few of us realize that our contentment in work and happiness in life, as well as any personal or collective success, is conditioned by the perfect development and use of our individual efforts. We speak about "industrial effort," or "cultural effort," without realizing that each collective action is built up from the mental and manual efforts of individual people.... Here ... is an attempt to penetrate to the core of man's efforts ... in two different fields of human activity — namely art [dance] and industry.[22]

Laban believed and demonstrated that effort can be shown in an individual's body motion. He also concluded that effort can be trained and through such training people can be educated in a variety of ideas and skills. For dance, "we can gather the meaning of a movement and though it seems to be difficult to express in exact words, it conveys something by which we are influenced: we may be excited, depressed, or tranquillised."[23] Such educational meaning conveyance is the very basis of dance.[24]

Symbolic Illusions

Philosopher Susanne K. Langer (1953) was so influential in the theoretical constructions of dance it is worth giving a relatively extensive overview of her work. Langer suggested a theory of dance that categorized it as artistic illusion and expression, starting from a reference point that "there are numberless misleading theories about what dancers do and what the doing signifies...."[25] That statement was in response to three widely accepted ideological assumptions that were circulating during this period of dance history. The first was the assumption that in social, professional dance creation and production, and in academic realms that evaluated dance, people danced to express *their emotional responses to music.* An alternative assumption about dance was that it was a series of pictures in motion, so to speak. That explanation was of course set forth as plausible before the advent of moving pictures.[26] If dance was not music brought to life, or pictures in motion, then it was thought to be pantomime, or part of the dramatic arts. What Langer argued was that these different historical theoretical notions of dance were merely the clay with which dance might be developed from and that "dance itself is something else"[27] entirely.

For Langer, dance was a form of gesture that consisted of a system of symbols congealing into a distinct language. Distinguished from dances of animals and inanimate objects that are often referred to as routine movements and metaphorical dancing, such as squirrels "dancing" up a tree, or a flag "dancing" in the wind, Langer postulated that dance-gesture becomes art when one can imagine the gesture. "Then [dance] becomes a free symbolic form, which may be used to convey *ideas* of emotion, of awareness and premonition, or may be combined with or incorporated in other virtual gestures to express other physical and mental tensions."[28] Theorized in this way, dance gives viewers agency while also influencing their sense of power. The self-consciousness of a person viewing dance with this theoretical framework in mind will be affected by "a sense of virtual power, ... to receive impressions, apprehend the environment, and meet changes"[29] that works in tandem with the individual's sense of free agency and will. "It is *imagined feeling* that governs the dance, not real emotional conditions."[30] Dance as an illusion to the viewer is a "representation of a world seen and imagined."[31] Understanding dance in this light also explains its use in television advertising, as will be discussed in chapter 5.

More than being the representation of imagined feeling that represents worlds, as an art form, dance uses the elements and symbols of culture to appeal to imagination and to reflexively "create a semblance of self-expression."[32] In other words, dance runs emotionally between what we see in reality and what we would like reality to be, how we are as human beings in reality and how we would like to be even if such desires are mythically derived symbols in culture and society.[33] The illusion created by dance encroaches on the spiritual, even in secular observations of dance, in that dance involves an illusory feeling built upon aesthetics that points to "some natural or supernatural power expressing itself"[34] in dance. In essence, Langer theorized dance as artistic, illusory, and expressive.

Dance Phenomenology

Phenomenologically, dance is descriptive as it is lived through time and space. Building from Langer's work, and that of epistemological inquiry begun by Edmund Husserl,[35] Maxine Sheets-Johnstone, a scholar who earned her doctorate in dance and philosophy, adopted a phenomenological approach; Sheets-Johnstone introduced the theory of dance as experiential, and therefore it must be understood descriptively both in time and space[36] and understood existentially as well. Understanding dance with reference to time allows for multiple layers of meanings that relate to a whole and include past, present and future. Such a referential time signature resides individually within each viewer's consciousness and awareness of self. With reference to space, we determine existence "in the midst of the world," the world as we have established understanding of it, or a "being hereness."[37] Dance is not only symbolic, then, as Langer theorized; it is also existential. Because symbolic and existential dance is immediately experiential, one must understand *dance as dance* when interpreting what is being danced and interpreting an individual viewer's exposure to a dance experience. Regarding dance as dance is giving it relevancy of its own; it is not dance as music manifested, or dancing to the music. Phenomenological dance theory yields "a systematic uncovering of the structure of these symbolic [dance] forms," exploring "how it is that symbolic [dance] forms are expressive"[38] in formulating structures of consciousness and, in turn, informing one's perceptions of the structures of the world.[39]

Anthropology and Function

Though *The Nature of Dance: An Anthropologic Perspective* by anthropologist Roderyck Lange appeared only in 1976, anthropological studies of dance in native societies were published as early as the 17th century. They "mainly mentioned [dance] in conjunction with customs and music. Additionally, dances appeared to many of the authors of that time as very 'exotic,' 'wild,' and 'indecent'.... Observers themselves would never have dreamt of performing such kinds of uninhibited movement."[40] Fortunately, anthropological perspectives on dance did not remain under-theorized, and in the 1920s many anthropology scholars, particularly German, wrote extensively on dance.[41]

Other anthropologists had written dance ethnologies, relying on semiotics to develop sign systems.[42] Before going on, it is important to talk a bit about semiotics and its relations to anthropology. Therefore, this section relies on Barthes' work (1964) to situate it within our cultural system. "Semiology, in the proper sense of the word, ... is ... a science comprising all systems of signs."[43] These systems, according to Barthes (1964), contain four elements: language and speech; signifer and signified; syntagm and system; denotation and connotation. The language (system) is composed of signs; speech (process) gives the rules for language but systems and processes are interdependent upon each other, according to Merleau-Ponty (1945). Levi-Strauss (1974) later extended this notion into anthropology. Barthes, however, described the clothing, food, car and furniture systems, showing them as complex, and importantly, treats advertising as a complex system, a subset of which resides in the category of mass communication. Before being able to determine which aspect of the advertisement is language or which is speech, it is necessary to know whether the system shown is original or compounded, and it is necessary that the system be analyzed. For example, right now we know music has its own language but no image language. With the press, there is the notion of connotation, making second-order meanings of things.[44] Here, I am therefore borrowing from this to talk about understanding the system and process of dance and what it connotes anthropologically through an advertisement. It is complex, unrestricted, and connotated.

Importantly, changes occur to these broad systems because of arbitrariness of signs, either by small or large groups ranging from communities to industries brought about by changes in needs, economic conditions, and ideologies. Meanings (signs) are attributed to systems based on the collective and adaptive imagination of the time they occur in and are therefore anthropological.[45] The signifier and the signified are the components of the sign, and acoustic images and concepts link to form a sign. It has both form and substance of expression and content. There is ease in separating these in semiology when the signifieds are substantiated in a substance other than that of their own system. Here I take this to mean, for example, when dance is substantiated in television advertising. Semiological systems such as dance (I call dance gestured image) have substances that were not meant for signifying but were first understood for their utility. When they are used for signs, they are sign-functions, which gives rise to a double meaning. Clothing is not only to protect, food is not only to nourish, but when there is a society developed, all usage becomes a sign of itself. This second-order language is not the same as the first one; the new "function that is re-presented does in fact correspond to a second (disguised) semantic institutionalization, which is the order of connotation. The sign-function therefore has (probably) an anthropological value, since it is the very unit where the relations of the technical and the significant are woven together."[46]

Semiologically, the signified mentally represents something, or is a concept, according to de Saussure. The person using the sign wants the sign to mean something. Gestures and images refer to something else but can only be expressed through those particular images and gestures, for example. Moreover, semiologically, signified and signifer are isologic when they cannot be separated and result in a metalanguage of their own even when mediated by the speech of the medium, for example, the television ad. The metalanguage develops as a result of asking people what the image or gesture means. Because

I attribute semiological application to the image and gesture, I will therefore begin to refer to it here as dance. Semiological signifieds of a system of dance form a large function, as does the system of advertising. Placing them together, they "not only communicate but also overlap" and so we have to look for a common ideology in the synchrony.[47] In terms of the systems of dance and advertising, consumers have multiple lexicons from which to read, different levels of knowledge based on their cultural position. Therefore, the same dance can be read differently in different contexts by an individual.

Signification has a value when viewed in economic terms. "For a sign (or an economic value) to exist, it must therefore be possible, on the one hand, to *exchange* dissimilar things (work and wage, signifier and signified), and on the other, to *compare* similar things with each other."[48] In this way, dance can be exchanged for products, and also compared with other dances; products can be compared with other products. Value attributes in relation to other things. Cutting dance out of the plane it was produced on and putting it on the plane of advertising gives it meaning, in relation to something else.

The aforementioned systems work in tandem with syntagms.[49] The dance system in advertising is composed of dance types which are not usually done at the same time and which are in the category of social or concert; the syntagms are the different types of dance steps (sign functions) borrowed from the system and strung together by the camera in the ad to signify meaning. The syntagmatic units have to be defined for both systems, the dance and the ad, then one has to identify the rules that determine their combination. Why are the signs combined the way they are? Why are they repeated the way they are? What does this combination do for aesthetics? These are questions that will be asked and applied to the commercials under study.

In terms of the systems of black social dance and advertising, what do they have in common? How are they opposite and how do we classify their oppositions? Here we are only concerned with what Barthes calls privative oppositions, "any opposition in which the signifer of a term is characterized by the presence of a significant element, or *mark*, which is missing in the signifier of the other."[50] That means an unmarked white person, more numerous in the system of advertising, dancing black social dance becomes a privative opposition. How many commercials show black people (marked) dancing white social dance or even white concert dance?

This brings us to the discussion on neutralization, "where by a relevant opposition loses its relevance, that is, ceases to be significant."[51] Neutralization occurs in response to a context, "the syntagm which cancels out the system."[52] Having whites create a dance syntagm of dance borrowed from black social dance neutralizes the power found in the system.

In the combination of dance and advertising, dance becomes an element of the advertising system, the plane of expression, a signifier of dance. Advertising is the larger of the two systems and has both a plane of expression and a plane of content; their intersection is significant based on the relation between the planes. As we suppose that dance becomes an element in the advertising system, this is the plane of connotation, developed through a metalanguage. "A metalanguage is a system whose plane of content is itself constituted by a signifying system."[53]

Or suppose that the system of black social dance has a plane of expression and a plane of content and their intersection is significant based on the relation between the two planes. Advertising becomes an element on the plane of expression within the system of black social dance. This is the plane of denotation.

Connotation is also a system of its own, complete with its own set of signs taken from the denoted system. The connoted system set of signs form a subset of the signs taken from the denoted system; "large fragments of the denoted discourse can constitute a single unit of the connoted system ... naturalized by the denoted language which carries them."[54] In functioning as a decipherer of the metalanguage of black social dance, dance signs produced within ads are a series of signs which have been neutralized.

In response to this semiotic treatment, Clifford Geertz (1983) remarked, "To be effective in the study of [dance or any art], semiotics must move beyond the consideration of signs as a means of communication, code to be deciphered, to a consideration of them as modes of thought, idiom to be interpreted."[55] Following that vein, Lange provided a very detailed history of dance and theoretical references supporting it, including that of economist Adam Smith and philosopher Herbert Smith. What comes to this work as important from Lange's contribution to dance theory is how dance functions, and understanding functionality can lead to understanding the value of dance in advertising.

Dance imitates something else "which would evoke in the spectator the impression of 'movement,' 'affect,' 'agitation.'"[56] Dance is concerned with inner attitudes, creating abstract expressions, and these become "connected with the accumulation of [a person's] inner experience"[57]; they are manifestations in the practice of life, and further, can be read and communicated. Dance is biological in that it has positive physiological results associated with pleasure, happiness, and a sense of relief.[58] Antonio Damasio (1999), for example, has shown the neurobiological aspects of emotion and how human consciousness is connected to it, as have Joy and Sherry (2003), who are moving in that direction with unconsciousness of consumption. Theorizing, dance is also a means of communication "which cannot be interchanged with verbal description. Movement conveys sophisticated meanings in a more compact and rapid manner than speech. In this way, it is closer to the biological existence of man than language with its code system already verbally externalized."[59] Dance transmits ideas: "The content may be very sophisticated, but it is instantly communicated to the receiver."[60] It is reasonable to consider it therefore, in playing a role in consumption.

Not only do the previous scholars discuss these functions; Anya Peterson Royce, in her 1977 *The Anthropology of Dance*, explains dance's function in terms of Western society.[61] I adapt this point of view, that dance functions anthropologically in television ads to take full advantage of a seamless focus of dance with respect to aesthetics; that is, I am looking to see where dance resides in human life in society, as it is presented in terms of human behavior. We cannot abstract away or ignore the fact that dance is televised in commercials, with television itself being an anthropological phenomenon.[62]

Royce arrives at the conclusion that dance provides functional aspects to cultural life in both literate and non-literate societies.[63] Rather than discuss a firm definition of dance, fearing the never-ending dilemma of a lack of a boundary as I already mentioned, she determined that "dance events"[64] are what need to be defined, such as those found in a television ad. Importantly, this conclusion is situated in the notion that dance is inseparable from culture.

Typologies of dance consist of four categories according to Royce. First, dance can be seen as pattern maintenance and tension management that includes macro level control of the masses. Next, dance can be placed in the category of observed adaptation, which concerns shifts in the social and non-social environment of people's roles and the attending economic forces. Thirdly, and simultaneously, dance provides integration through the mechanism of social intercourse. Finally, dance provides power through the structures that bind these societal elements at play.

While straddling these typologies, dance exerts a multiplicity of functions. They are either overt or covert, and either manifest or latent. Overt and manifest dances are used in ways that are acknowledged. Covert and latent functions are "those meanings and uses which lie beneath the surface and which are ascribed by the analyst,"[65] both points which will be evident in analysis of the respondents' texts later. In any event, functions change over time and from situation to situation. Many societies make up dances or call them by different names when they are to be displayed publicly, that is, out of context for which they originally functioned. In doing so, society believes these are different dances. As will be discussed in chapters 4 and 5, perhaps non-blacks doing black social dance or reading it in a commercial see it this way. Or the presentation of the dance with non-black groups of people make it palatable for non-blacks. However, Royce (1977, 98) suggests that regardless of who performs it or where black social dance is performed, given that we are viewing dance as one aspect of human behavior, ... from an anthropological perspective, then it follows that dance, like any other culture trait, can illuminate social and cultural history. Because it has not been used so frequently ... does not mean that it has less to contribute. There are situations where dance simply adds another piece to the puzzle of a particular historical analysis. However there are other cases ... where dance is unique in what it can tell us ... because the dance context is the only one in which that particular bit of information is to be found.

Moreover, dance has different purposes in complex society and one such purpose is its use as an identity marker resulting from social and cultural oppositional frictions between groups as the distance between cultures shrink. The result is the production of a collective consciousness and solidarity within the group(s). It is stored in the identity in symbolic form. Symbols are usually distinct and recognizable by each group, and in fact lead to stereotypes in many cases by picking out one or two features and emphasizing them.

Dance has the potential to communicate feelings, how people feel about themselves "particularly in situations where different peoples come into contact. This potential gives dance great power and at the same time makes it threatening."[66] It is often the case that dance is read as obscene when one culture looks at another's dance, and therefore it carries a great deal of power. Political response to dance has often been to ban it altogether, as shall be discussed in a moment. But dance *is* powerful expressive behavior, allowing things to be said which could not be said any other way. "Whether the response be one of enthusiastic approval or disgust or any emotion between the extremes, people always have some response to the body as it is used in dance."[67] I find this kind of response to be aesthetic as well.

Structurally, the anthropology of dance can contribute to aesthetics and creativity as culturally determined. As such, studying dance from an anthropologic point of view frees us from being concerned with judgments. Rather, we are concerned with speaking about "a culture's aesthetic values and a culture's determination of creativity."[68] In doing this comparatively, with two cultures, we are then in the position of being able to speak about "cross-cultural variation" in both their views on creativity and aesthetics. A structural approach looks at the pieces of a dance as a language, the grammar of the language that makes the movements culturally acceptable. When a society has more than one dance type, there is usually more than one aesthetic. In this study, then, we have at least two cultures and one cross-cultural variation.

Like Royce, Paul Spencer's 1985 *Society and the Dance* discusses dance in anthropological settings, and attempts to define dance in broad ways. His coverage of pertinent approaches to dance from an anthropological point of view include those such as dance as a catharsis, dance as an function of social control through education and the transmission of cultural behavioral norms, dance as a build up to release of emotions, dance as a competition, and dance as ritual drama. Importantly, Spencer concludes

> it then follows that dance may be defined in whatever way seems most appropriate to the study of any specific situation or society. Dance is not an entity in itself, but belongs rightfully to the wider analysis of ritual action, and it is in this context that one can approach it analytically and grant it the attention it demands. In a very important sense, society creates the dance, and it is to society that we must turn to understand it.[69]

It is this conclusion and Royce's positioning of dance in culture that leads me to the study of black social dance in American society as an anthropological function in television commercials.

Cultural Theory

Not only have anthropologists, sociologists and philosophers set forth theories of dance; scholars in literary and cultural studies have done so as well, beginning in the 1980s. At that point in time, bodies, the times they lived in, the ways they move and the forms they used became danced texts to be analyzed. Roland Barthes' *Image Music Text* (1977) informed much of this reading, through analysis of photographs and the use of signifiers and signs. Dance scholar Susan Foster penetrated a new area of theorizing dance by developing an array of writings that argued that dance was a culturally specific writing and writing was an act of culturally specific dance,[70] with syntax, style, vocabulary and mode of representation providing for meaning. For purposes of reading dance, it is important that

> during the course of the dance, the viewer repeatedly enacts, at the ever-increasing level of organization, the reciprocal process of interpreting how the dance represents the world in relation to how it is organized. The larger issues of the dance as a meaningful commentary of the world and its relation to other such commentaries begin to emerge as the various conventions in the dance inform and resonate against each other.[71]

Philosopher Graham McFee's important contribution *Understanding Dance* carefully and systematically exposes the aesthetic, linguistic, sociologic, anthropologic and kinesthetic theories about dance to much needed critical analytical rigor. Differing from those who argue against the claims about dance and its relevance and who are therefore dismissive of or remiss in recognizing its value, McFee (1992) aims at proving the value of dance and the contribution it makes to human life and emotional education. He devises "the theory of the understanding of dance."[72] Along with critical analysis of the theories of dance, he brings us to "the point of dance." The issue is that people have means and ends to achieving particular goals and outcomes. Goals can change conceptually with experiences that may not be easily put into words. Whether these goals change or not, ends are connected to wants and needs, arrived at through particular and/or multiple means. To define one's needs, wants, and goals, and to assess the outcome, one has to have the capacity to discriminate when change occurs and change occurs through emotion. Dance provides or provokes a "capacity to experience finely discriminated feelings" and so broaches consumers and their behaviors.[73]

Moreover, McFee (1992) postulated that dance is "concerned with contemporary moral, social, political and emotional issues."[75] In other words, the point of dance is to deal with the quality of individual and collective human life as these larger social issues bear upon them. Fallibility, failure, inhumanity, love, landscapes, and happiness are the issues of human life he refers to, and to our ability to cope with them in our lives and the lives of those around us. McFee defines dance as "meaningful or meaning-bearing" and he supposes that dance can be analogous to language. However, after getting a bit twisted in trying to categorize dance as either concert or social, he sets a boundary around dance: "what makes a movement sequence a piece of dance rather than something else depends on the context, and the context involves, for example, the use to which that activity is put in society."[75] What dance means in one cultural context may be different from what it means in others.[76]

Dance Aesthetics

Croce (1965), an Italian philosopher influenced by German thought, wrote during a time when it was believed that knowledge had to come from intellect and not intuition. Intellect was superior to intuition. Since aesthetics was believed to be concerned with man's creative imagination, at that time people argued that it was inferior. On the contrary, the philosopher insisted that an aesthetic approach to knowledge was just as valuable philosophically with intellect. The positivist and evolutionists dominated at the time, and these thinkers believed aesthetics was lowly, associated with the hedonic, sexual, animal, and visceral.

Aesthetics is both form and content in the abstract, according to Croce. He believed further that there are two forms of knowledge: intuitive and conceptual, simple and complex, respectively. Both of these forms have cognitive and theoretical value in their own rights. Against some points of view, one can see that these are not opposites because the emotional content of art is abstract only when it is viewed aesthetically, not viewed emotionally. Beginning in the 20th century, Croce, therefore, developed a logic of intuition alongside the logic of intellect.

Croce (1965) theorized that human beings have four co-existing forms of spirit, including the aesthetic, logical, economic, and ethical realms, which are endless, contained circles, not progressive and separated by lines. With this established, he also positioned human beings as both knower and doer. People have reason, but they also live by intuiting, that is, producing and enjoying images for the sake of enjoying them. Knowledge can be gained from images — which are art and products of intuition — or from concepts deduced from reason and logic. On the doer side, humanity is faced with economic realities in which they must satisfy needs, which is done though actions which arise through dissatisfaction. This is, I believe, one of the reasons that dance, or other art forms, are connected within ads that create needs. Croce insisted that intuition was a legitimate way of knowing, which is cognitively significant. "Croce really believes that artistic intuition, whose objects are particulars (images) as against universals (concepts), enjoys truth-value."[77]

The history of aesthetic theory began in the Greco-Roman world and is concerned with "the fact that art arouses pleasure."[78] Unmistakably, pleasure is not the only provocative issue with aesthetics. In fact aesthetics has been defined as something that causes an emotional response or reaction, be it either positive or negative. Moreover, along with provocation of emotion, awe must also be present in an aesthetic experience.[79] Awe is the experience that people feel when exposed to objects, nature, and certain social aspects of life, such as art and mystical people. Sociological and religious encounters can involve awe. People come away from religious experiences transformed, as they are also transformed through sociologically collective sentiments, like a political rally. The important aspect of this is that the experience affects whole groups, their well-being, and their collective interests.[80] It is the sociological and religious awe and aesthetic experience of dance that I believe is at work in commercials.

Awe is also felt in private, arising from sublime feelings: the expansion of felt thought as "greatness of mind" when exposed to aesthetic literature, poetry, painting,[81] and, I suggest in this case, dance. Sublime feelings are associated with beauty, admiration, and astonishment, such as when a viewer is astonished by what they see in dance on the screen. Moreover, "Objects the mind has difficulty grasping are more likely to produce the sublime experience.... [O]bscure images"[82] create sublime experiences more so than do clearly rendered images. And dance of course is obscure, fleeting, ephemeral. Often, dance can be considered astonishing, beautiful, and reverent, a peak experience, where we consider these as milder feelings associated with awe. My concern with these emotions as related to black social dance will become clear, as I will explain later. However, consider that astonishment includes "raised eyebrows, brighter eyes, gaping mouth, and in extreme cases, hair standing on end or goose bumps."[83] In addition, peak experience includes the feeling that certain polarities or dichotomies that were troublesome have been transcended, that one is lucky or fortunate.[84] Importantly, though, awe makes one feel like they are in the presence of something more powerful than they; there is a certain vastness included in the realization of human smallness next to it, which is sometimes accompanied by the Piagetian process of accommodation. That is to say that a given set of knowledge structures are interrupted and cause a change in the individual's view or understanding of some aspect of the world. According to Keltner and Haidt (2003), awe requires both of these conditions, vastness and accommodation. Moreover, awe occurs in many physically aesthetic situations,[85] and black social dance is of course physical, and has been defined as categorically aesthetic.[86] These are some of the same feelings and learning processes sometimes associated with watching something aesthetic that one would find impossible to do, such as black social dance for non-blacks. The bottom line is that the dance creates negative and positive emotions, sometimes to the extreme. For non-blacks the issue of accommodation plays a key role in shifting knowledge structures, a topic which is covered in an ensuing chapter.

Josephine Machon's *(Syn)aesthetics* (2009) takes the neurocognitive condition known as synaesthesia and adapts it to somatovisceral meanings. The physiology is something all humans are born with but diminishes as we learn to simplify incoming information in terms of awareness and perception as people mature[87]; the manifestation of it occurs when an individual experiences a sensation in one part of the body resulting from a stimulus applied to or received in another part of the body. For example, a word may conjure up a scent. Even though people are not always consciously aware of the synaesthetic experience, it persists within humans through holistic perception.[88] Moreover, synkinaesia demonstrates linkages of languages to the human body in terms of learning. These two facets are conjoined.

Machon's manipulation of the context of physiological processes to performance is useful to the study of dance in advertising because it marries aesthetic production processes and appreciation so that the viewer simultaneously receives and interprets the performance. It is both seen and felt "so as to fuse the somatic and the semantic in order to produce a visceral response in the audience."[89] There is a sensation being transmitted via corporeal memory to the audience in the synaesthethic approach, particularly with certain types of artwork.[90] Dance in ads, certain ads themselves that are deemed particularly creative, and anthropologic rituals come to mind here. Machon emphasizes the need to understand how a person recalls the experience through corporeal memory and bodily interpretations when theorizing artistic performance in the frame of contemporary aesthetics, such that we evaluate "the quality of experience undergone by the audience when appreciating the work in the immediate moment and in subsequent processes of recall and analysis."[91]

Synaesthetics allows the understanding of dance to be something that cannot be put into words, an experience that is in line with Husserl's noema, and to experience dance in this fashion is to perceive details corporeally. Moreover, the imagination is placed within the body and transcends the real and imaginary, so that the noetic process of engagement is undertaken as well. What we have is the lasting memory of an experience that is affective and ignited each time the movement is encountered. This is what the audience experiences, the perception and understanding without language[92] that cannot be articulated verbally.

Such an experience is brought forth through intangible ideas and emotions given in the performance physically that the viewer interprets through their imaginations. It should be pointed out here that the synaesthetic experience can be both positive or negative, in that we can be outraged by the performance or tranquilized. In essence then, the use of this theoretical framework removes the mind as a privileged interpreter of experiences and allows the body to have a say. Live performance, as well as television or other media-driven performance spaces where the viewer constructs his or her own "proscenium," are valid sites for synaesthetic experiences.[93]

Kinesthetic Communication and Dance

Between the textual and conceptual, dance also resides in the cognitive anthropological realm in that dance is a mechanism through which we learn culturally specific information and we as human beings are able to differentiate between dance and other types of movement. As such, ballet is the prototype of dance, with hip-hop positioned very closely to it. In terms of the purpose of dance, its function is complex and includes expressive and aesthetically pleasing actions.[94] In television advertising, it has been conjectured that dance is used to sell products.[95] I take dance in television advertising as the performance and the viewer as the audience,[96] along with the theories of dance covered here, and explore its affects on consumers in television advertisements.

There are two main levels of awareness for consumers: the conscious and unconscious.[97] At both levels there is of course affective and cognitive. In terms of communication with them, we have verbal and non-verbal. Consumers perceive dance as a sensory, nonverbal experience that occurs on both levels of consciousness, as well as on the corporeal level. In trying to isolate the neurological effects of dance on observers, one study found that in watching dance, a consumer may have his or her memory, extero-, intero- and proprioceptor systems activated.[98] At the same time, the excitement of dance sends communication directly to the neuro-muscular system. In this way, "[D]ance can have extremely powerful effects on those who watch it."[99] However, the

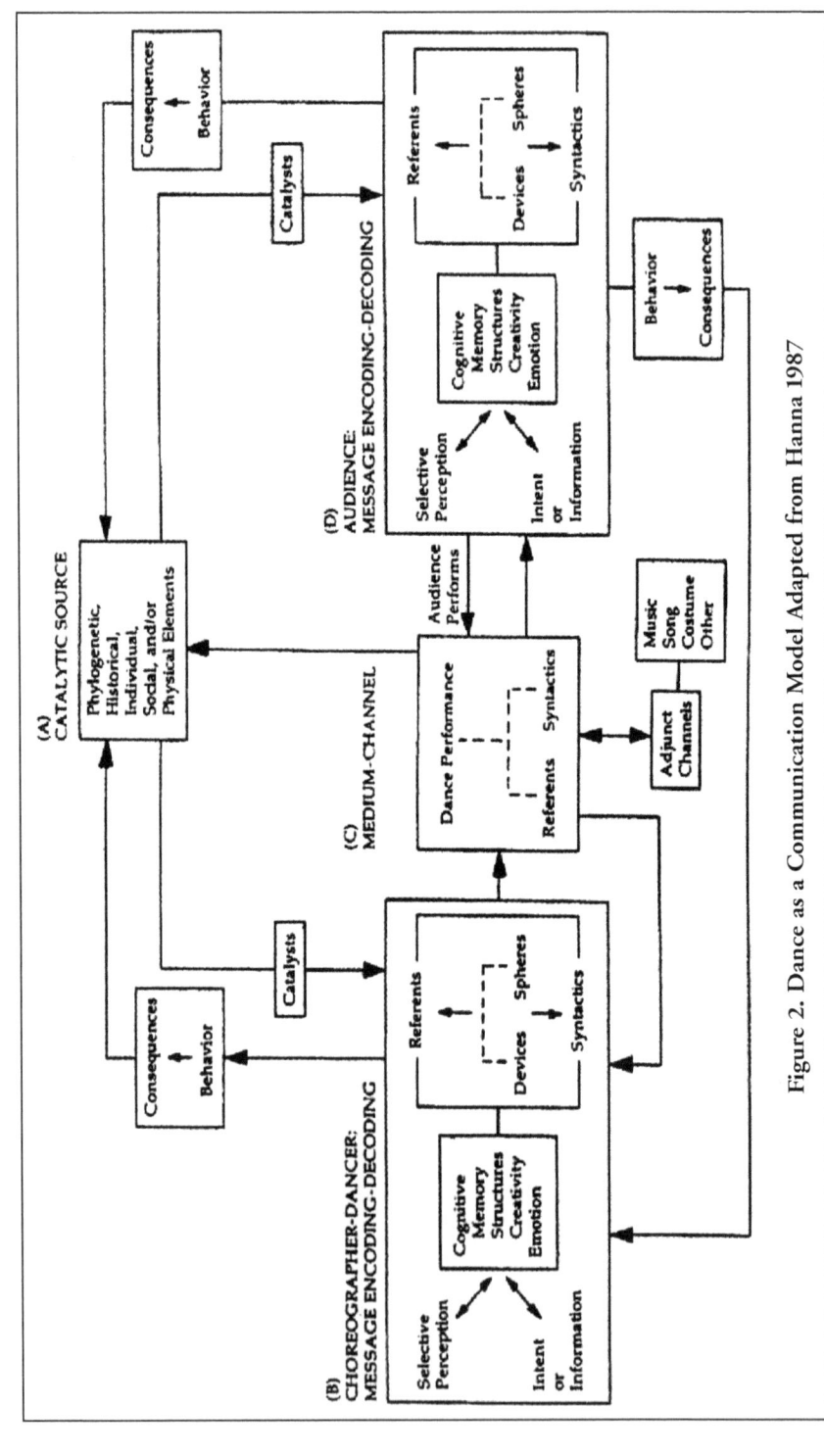

Figure 2. Dance as a Communication Model Adapted from Hanna 1987

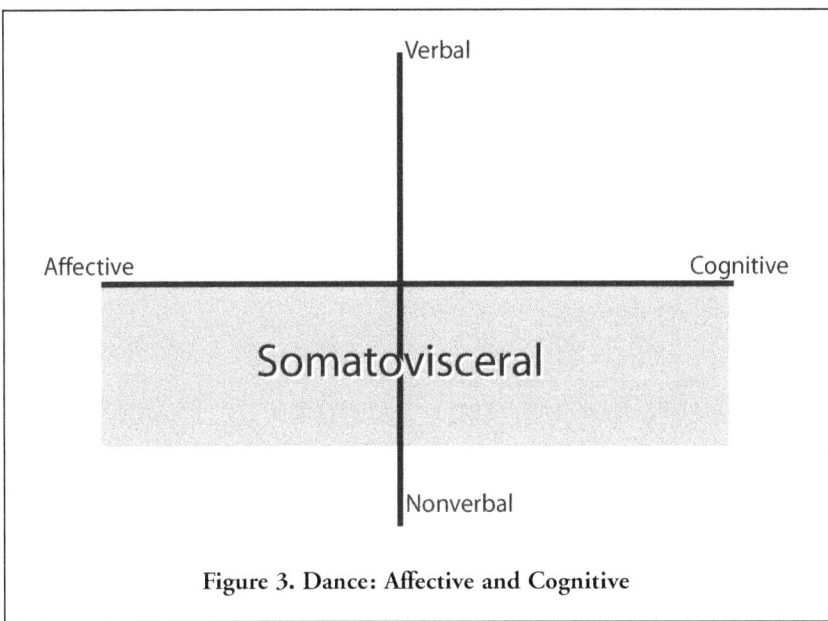

Figure 3. Dance: Affective and Cognitive

effect of the communication relies upon a feedback system of shared cultural knowledge that is stored in memory.[100] Figure 2, "Dance as a Communication Model," depicts a communication model of dance, while Figure 3, "Dance: Affective and Cognitive," displays dance on the verbal/nonverbal and affective/cognitive planes. The dance functions nonverbally but ranges in its somato-visceral effects from cognitive to affective.

Dance has been defined and explored as a human nonverbal communication device in several ways.[101] It is cognitive and sensory; dance and language are substitutes for each other; dance provides healthy outlets; and dance communication is affective. Moreover, the cognitive and affective aspects of dance are intertwined:

> The power of dance lies in its cognitive-sensorimotor and aesthetic capability to create moods and a sense of situation for performer and spectator alike.... What matters is not whether language or gesture is antecedent, but that both are conceptual vehicles and can reinforce and often substitute for each other.... In dance, affective and cognitive communication are intertwined ... and may be elicited for pleasure or coping with problematic aspects of social involvement."[102]

For adults, dancing may return them to childhood memories, while providing the excitement and experience of chaos without danger; it provides healthy outlets and distractions, reduces rage and crisis, and "thus allows more enduring personality patterns to regain ascendancy"[103] in reality and illusion.

Therefore, communication through dance semiotics can be conceptualized in a planar model, which we can apply to dance in television ads, as shown in figure 3.

For purposes of reading dance it is important that

> during the course of the dance, the viewer repeatedly enacts, at the ever-increasing level of organization, the reciprocal process of interpreting how the dance represents the world in relation to how it is organized. The larger issues of the dance as a meaningful commentary of the world and its relation to other such commentaries begin to emerge as the various conventions in the dance inform and resonate against each other.[104]

BLACK SOCIAL AND THEATRICAL DANCE CONTEXTUAL HISTORY

For the United States, any discussion about dance has to begin with its adversaries and how it was viewed from an early synchronic but panoptic overview. Dance was a popular amusement among whites in the middle and southern colonies,[105] either at the elite or regional levels, or when reflecting a newly emerging national style. Everyone danced regardless of station or ethnic category. However,

> blacks in the middle and southern colonies [in the 1790s] had their own dance traditions important for themselves but also for their influence on dancing of the non-black population.... A variety of dances for different kinds of occasions characterized the black repertoire. Several types of dances were done by blacks in contexts where whites were absent, or if present, were limited to a few spectators.[106]

Either way it is clear that blacks had the entertaining power while whites frowned on learning black dances and displaying them publicly, much like the genesis of anthropological study of dance. At the same time, blacks learning to do white social dance had to abstract away any semblance of blackness from their execution.[107] Even so, dance discourse begins much earlier and was heavily influenced by religion and politics.

To get a larger perspective on how black social dance has been perceived over time in the United States, we have to return to the thinking originating in the 15th century. In 1520, Martin Luther burned a reprinting of a theologian's publications (namely the Summa Angelica by Angelus Carletus de Clavasio) that classified dance and body movements as a sin. The publication had been circulating since at least 1411 with multiple reprints. However, the upshot of the arguments used at the time pointed to women as being culprits of sexual immorality and they steered men astray through dance. Wagner

(1997) carefully explained that dance has been a topic of debate since Plato's time, and within the debate exists the notion of dance's orderliness and disorderliness. Disorderliness was supposedly directly related to sexual immorality and vice versa. Many learned Protestant men in Europe wrote against dance. Even so, beginning in the 16th century, the Elizabethan era, new aesthetic ideals began to emerge around dance and its usefulness to society in terms of social class and social order. Around the turn of the 1500s, there was a notion of the "cosmic dance as the image of order and morality."[108] In addition, a well executed dance became the metaphor for a good marriage, with roles and positions clearly articulated. The issue, though, was that there was a disagreement between what constituted good social class value, and what the churches (Catholic and Protestant alike) dictated about dance. Each church was against it, and these ideas flowed to the United States when Europeans immigrated there.

By the 18th century, ideas were changing as dance became seen within a larger scope of culture and social class, gender, race, and morality. Dancing was to be seen as part of a cultured education, taught by a dancing master. Dancing in ballroom and jig was extremely popular, and whites in the southern colonies

> apparently borrowed from the blacks, these dances contributed elements of spontaneity to an evening of dancing. The fact that blacks usually served as attendants and the musicians at the assemblies in great houses suggests the likelihood of exchange and modification of dances and music between the races.[109]

The middle colonies of New York, Philadelphia and Boston had responses to dance and theater that ranged from apathetic to restrictive. Nonetheless, they had dancing masters and dancing assemblies, and dance as a cultured social practice was popular.

In 1778 a shift began, reverting back to an adversarial relationship with dance, through the preaching of Oliver Hart in Charleston, North Carolina. Hart was a follower of historical writers like Increase Mather, and they took up their old positions in the newly free America. He preached that dance was unclean and immodest, obscene and adapted to vulgar songs. And by the 1830s, dance had been characterized as not only immoral, but also unpatriotic. Just prior to that time, about ten years earlier, theater dance, i.e., ballet, was popular, and was advertised in newspapers and other publications. Nearly simultaneously, blackface minstrelsy took on popularity, and here is where a separation between high and low dance forms occurred, between the elite and the popular. In similar fashion, social dance for couples was popular. But the church leaders still found dance to be problematic from a moral point of view. Dance was animal, lustful, and categorically bad. Contrary to this point of view though, the Mormons and the Shakers were two religious sects that endorsed dancing based on biblical passages.[110]

The turn of the century to the 1900s saw both black preachers and white alike condemn dancing, and required congregants to select between the world and the church. A person could be cultured and a good dancer, which necessarily meant they were not Christian, but they had to choose. Dancing was evil, and stunted one's spiritual growth. On the other hand, Dr. Luther Halsey Gulick in 1910 contributed the idea that dance was a language and that it was expressive, and good for the soul. He supported the notion that social (folk) dance was important to people's well being, and that it constituted behavior of human beings since the beginning of time. Instead of thinking of whether dance was in and of itself worthwhile, he suggested that dance has value based on what it says. In short, he suggested that all dance was art.[111] At this point, he advocated the idea of dance as education, and dance education. It came to pass in 1918 that dance was included in physical education for both boys and girls.

It appears that, in my reading of this, there was a similar point in time as we saw with hip-hop dance,[112] when "[C]hanges in urban living and in class distinctions fostered the unprecedented popularity of dancing between 1910 and 1914."[113] In short, people demanded more places to dance, and society gave it to them, in bars, hotels, tea rooms, etc. Ragtime was popular, and blacks brought more hips, torso, head and shoulder moves. "Boundaries that had previously separated blacks from whites, men from women, and upper from lower classes began to erode as more women patronized public dances and the black population of northern cities rose dramatically."[114] But, evangelical ministers still preached against dance. By the 1920s, "energetic, rhythmic, vigorous, and sexy — the fad dances owed a debt to America's black heritage... American popular culture of the decade derived much from blacks.... The ... Cotton Club played to white audiences" while tap dancing became popular at this time.[115]

The adversaries of dance increased and intensified. Claims were made that little (white) girls were disappearing, and that high school delinquency and dropouts were increasing because of the diffusion of black dance and music. It was the great sin of the nation, and the blame was placed on women. With the inclusion of teaching evolution as a view of creation in the schools, the rhetoric claimed that "lunatics, blacks, and trained monkeys always proved to be the best dancers."[116] Only "overdeveloped animalism" creates the demand for dance as a social endeavor, it was claimed and directly pointed at blacks. "[A] racist attitude clearly was intertwined with the fear of dancing's alleged immorality in the early twentieth century."[117]

This position about dance did not stop the country from incorporating dance education in 36 states, and the establishment of the dance program at

University of Wisconsin at Madison. People had effectively changed and could not change back, particularly due to the technology of radio and cars, the shifts in population, and Prohibition. Still, after the 1930s, the arguments against dance came from the religious sectors, namely Lutherans and Baptists, with much of the lackluster stance against dance arising from concern over other more serious matters such as the stock market crash and the Great Depression on the one hand, and World War II's Hitler on the other. Moreover, it would not be until after 1969 that books specifically against dance stopped appearing.

During the war years, though, people flocked to movies with dance in them, such as those of Fred Astaire and Ginger Rogers, to get a break from the monotony of reality. Dance in movies was distributed beyond those who could afford to go see theater dance. In films people watched Busby Berkeley, Eleanor Powell and the Nicholas Brothers. Popularizing dance in films led to its popularity in social settings, with big bands and swing, evidenced by demand for dances and dance classes, such as those offered by Arthur Murray. It had become a craze; professional businessmen and doctors among other professions took dance lessons, and 16,000 dance schools existed in 1937. By 1943, black people dancing in the Savoy Ballroom in Harlem performed outrageous moves just for white spectators; such moves were at this point considered artistic and revolutionary by whites.

But, the Lutherans still put forth the idea that all social dancing was bad because of its sexual nature, having arisen from African jungles. The Baptists went a step further and convicted ballet in the same way, that it was immoral sexually. In fact one cleric said, "It does not take brains to dance. The negro in the back alley is often an expert in dancing. Those most often sent home from college ... are usually the best dancers."[118] Moreover, it was posited that dancing for blacks was "natural" due to their connection to Africa. In 1943, the Savoy Ballroom was closed for fear that the natural sexual tendency of blacks was going to rub off on or negatively impact white women. These women would lose their modesty and that would interfere with their ability to be good wives.

During World War II, ballroom and social dance were popular and the derision by the church declined. When the war was over, derision continued, but dancing's popularity declined more due to the return home of service men, and the fact that dancing was displayed on television, where people *watched* dance instead of *doing* dance. "New music, radio, phonograph records, and television were drawing people into different settings than the traditional dance hall."[119] It is, I argue, this cultural change that moved dance from an anthropologic activity that one participated in physically, to one that people watched remotely in order to participate. This shift still informs dance with television commercials and online ads.

Even as dance became more singular in nature, while being televised directly with dance shows or movies, into the present decade comes still the fact that "rural and small-town Americans have usually promoted the values held dear by conservative evangelical and fundamentalist Christians."[120] In fact, the town of Purdy, Missouri, had a case against dance in public schools supported by the Supreme Court in 1990 for these very reasons. Such attitudes persisted on many college campuses as well. Moreover, the attitude that blacks danced from natural and nasty and animal origins was infested with the 1850s ideology that blacks can dance better than whites.[121]

Other authors have suggested that black social dance in the 1960s was sexual depending on one's class more so than on one's race.[122] Moreover, lower-class whites were interested in outdoing blacks in their use of dialect and dance.[123] This was found not to be the case for middle or upper classes of

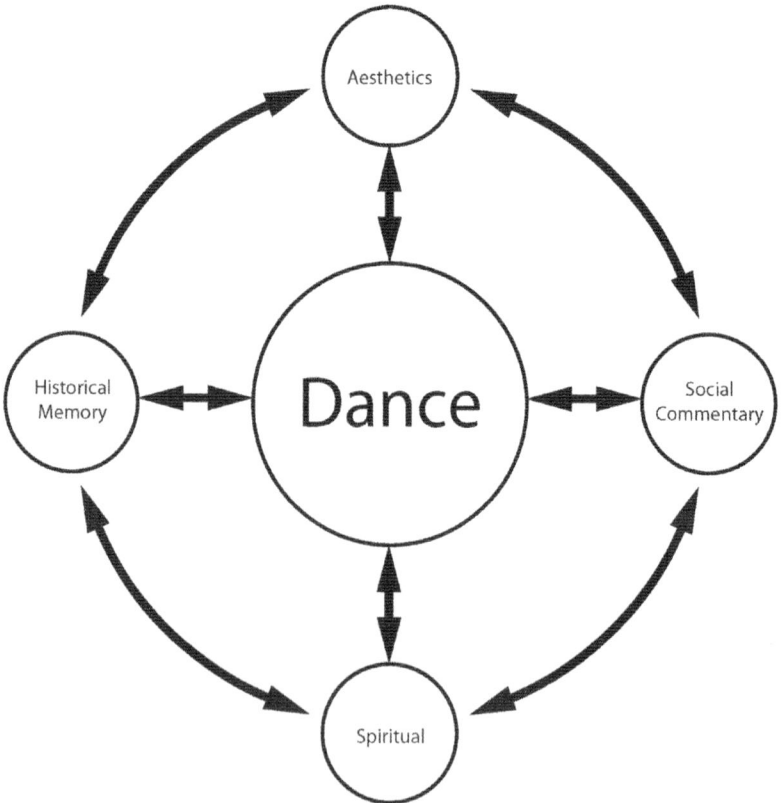

Figure 4. Dance Doing

either race. Interestingly, though, it was believed that "Lower class [black] dancers are the most innovative, introducing new techniques and conceptions directly into their own culture and indirectly into other cultures" through technological skill that creates the shift and transition of social dance forms.[124] At the same time, "elite" dancers were the opposite and possessed the least innovative dance skill set. Yet they derive gratification from having knowledge of the so-called sexually explicit black social dance and being somewhat competent at it on a shared class level. It is the kind of assumption many people may make about black social dance, even if they are not detractors of dance in general, and black social dance specifically.

To conclude this chapter and summarize the work it has done, dance involves reading cultural knowledge learned through social interaction based on one's positionality within the culture. These relationships can be seen in figure 4—"Dance Doing."

To conclude, dance is immediately experienced at the level of the body and consciousness simultaneously and the meaning carried by dance is not always immediately obvious. At the same time, dance carries meaning prediscursively, or that cannot be articulated with words. Several theories of dance and a historical look at how dance informs American culture in the current period of 2010 was given. These included dance theory as it is educational, and a form of educating. It has been theorized as symbolic with imagined power, phenomenologic; functional and functioning anthropologically. In addition, dance is meaning bearing, semiotic in its point of view. Along with garnering awe and being aesthetic, dance is a communication vehicle, silent and kinesthetic.

The next chapter provides a frame of reference for marketing and consumer behavior. That chapter, along with this one, projects the theoretical screen onto which black social dance in commercials will perform.

2. Marketing, Advertising, and Dance

So advertising is, and is about, what it is for something to be cultural. It has this resonance because so do objects when understood anthropologically.[1]

BACKGROUND

This chapter has only one aim. That is to elevate theories of dance so that they are considered as means to evaluate and understand consumers. I have been inspired to do this partly because over the last twenty years, the *Journal of Consumer Research* has published research that considered various approaches to understanding consumers. The voluminous increase in nontraditional, qualitative approaches resulted from the ideological view that "consumer researchers have a role to play in making society better by considering whether a program of consumer research can be developed to facilitate social awareness and change."[2] During consumer research's expansion into alternative methods of seeking knowledge, in the same period of time, dance studies as an academic category became firmly established itself. However, to date, it has not been evaluated in its capacity to theorize consumption behaviors or intentions of consumers. To address this and to contribute to the scholarship on consumption and dance theory, this chapter reviews and summarizes a body of relevant consumer research. Then it augments a framework of theoretical approaches to consumer behavior study introduced by Murray and Ozanne (1991) by adding dance approaches. These are arguably utilizable for consumer research to further understandings of consumers and facilitate awareness and change. In the end, the chapter sets the stage for utilizing and considering dance theory presented in chapter 1 as viable anchors for consumer

A Warmin' Up in Dixie. Rare Book, Manuscript, and Special Collections Library, Duke University, Durham, North Carolina.

research. Specifically, dance communicates meanings at the level of the body as well as the mind — emotionally and cognitively — but it has been overlooked within consumer studies. Therefore, first, a historical frame for what has become consumer culture theory in consumer research is presented. Following that, a discussion of how images and music in advertising have been studied *vis a vis* their affect on consumers is given to argue for dance theory's place and relevancy at the consumer research table. The chapter then embraces a discussion of blacks in advertising to set the stage for commercials that will be the subject matter of chapter 4.

A Historical Frame for Dance Theory in Consumer Research

Unifying and defining the field of consumer culture theory, Arnould and Thompson (2005) summarized the aims and perspectives of authors contributing to this interdisciplinary approach to consumer research. Within that synthesis, several presentations of research have relevancy for dance as a mode of consumer research.

McCracken (1986), for example, who modeled his arguments after Barthes (1976), a discussion of which was given in chapter 1, argued that the advertising system and the fashion systems transfer meanings to goods from the culturally constituted world. He claimed further that the systems provided instructions either through verbal or visual aspects, where the verbal text provides directions on reading the visual part of the ad. Danced texts also facilitate this transfer by providing nonverbal direction. Note that though dance, as was the case with the fashion system at one point, has not been fully studied relative to consumption, it participates in both the advertising and fashion systems providing meaning to viewers. Into his depiction of the mediating factors between the culturally constituted world and consumer goods, therefore, I add dance systems. The dancing body acts as a carrier of meanings through multiple and varied social constructions.[3]

Continuing with his theoretical approach to understanding consumers, McCracken (1986) described rituals that facilitated consumers' adaptation of goods into their individual possession, exchange, grooming and divestment activities. Dance in practice and performance has been evaluated by anthropologists as rituals across diverse cultures and societies as was already discussed in a previous chapter. Therefore, in terms of consumption, it could be said that dance moves between the culturally constituted world and the rituals that reinforce consumption activities. The dance carries information between the two.

"Alternative ways of seeking knowledge" was part of the title of an article published in 1988 by Hudson and Ozanne, which established that knowledge can come from different sources and "each form of knowledge is valuable"[4] in the Foucaultian and Marxian senses. Hudson and Ozanne (1988) were specifically addressing and juxtaposing positivist and interpretive approaches to consumer research. While the paper provided support for both approaches underlying assumptions and methods, its goal was to broaden the research that would be considered established knowledge, particularly understanding, in an ongoing and evolving manner, of consumer behavior. Specifically, "grasping the shared meanings with a culture of language, contexts, roles, rituals, gestures, arts, and so on"[5] and by extension, the historical and particularistic aspects related to the art, language, context, ritual, gesture, and so on of dance. And further, as the authors suggested of the shared meanings of other cultural manifestations, because dance is very complex, it could be deemed an impossibility to deal directly with positivistic causality. This is yet to be seen, though, as our abilities to research very cleverly with respondents who are selected for an empirical dance and consumption study continue to evolve, for example, in neurosciences and neuromarketing.[6] The outcome would lead to a possibly dynamic research process, nonetheless supported by research specific interpretive criteria[7] that illuminate culture and individual actors.[8] In the end, Hudson and Ozanne concluded "every approach to consumer research may have something to offer"[9] and based on this conclusion, I argue that dance theory applied in consumer research may as well.

Thompson, Locander and Pollio (1989) presented a paradigm encompassing the philosophy and method underlying existential phenomenology in consumer research. One of the purposes of that article was to bring to light the difficulty of seeing new paradigms when one is accustomed to one's own and at the same time nevertheless advocating for other consumer research methods outside the Cartesian one.[10] The authors concluded that using "existential-phenomenology employs a 'something different' ... putting consumer experience back into consumer research."[11] Dance theory as a consumer research paradigm offers "something different" to conduct and expand our understanding of people's consumptive experiences.

On the whole, Scott (1990) embraced the call for expanded theoretical approaches and set forth a rhetorical theoretical framework for studying music in advertising, building on the interpretive and culturally based methods published relatively previously to her article. In the findings, Scott proposed that consumers interpreted music in ads in more complex ways than at the simplistic levels of recall and persuasion. Actually, consumers interpreted the music based on stored cultural information and the interpretive process was a learned behavior. As such, music performed multiple rhetorical tasks,

Table 1. Position of Dance Theory within Consumer Research Assumption Structures (Adapted from Murray and Ozanne, 1991)

	Positivism	Interpretivism	Critical Theory	Dance Theory
Ontological Assumptions				
nature of reality	objective; tangible; single; ahistorical; fragmentable; divisible	socially constructed; multiple; holistic; contextual	"force-field" between subject and object; dynamic; historical totality	represented by individual and collective historical bodies
nature of social beings	deterministic; reactive	voluntaristic; proactive	suspend judgment; emphasize human potential	passive yet silently celebratory; aggressive: acted upon and acting back
Axiological Assumptions				
overriding goal	"explanation" via subsumption under general laws; prediction	"understanding" via interpretation	"emancipation" via social organization that facilitates reason, justice, and freedom	bodily manifestation of nonverbal aesthetics; explicative; interpretive; critical
Epistemological Assumptions				
knowledge generated	nomothetic; time-free; context-independent; value-free	idiographic; time-bound; context-dependent; value-laden	forward-looking; imaginative; critical/unmasking; practical	at the level of the individual body and collective bodies; ephemeral; first-order only
view of causality	real causes exist	multiple, simultaneous shaping	reflection; exposure of constraints through dialogue; reconstruction; reflection	bodies build multiple theories
research relationship metaphor	dualism; separation; detached observer	Interactive; cooperative; translator	continuing dialogue; liberator	expressive, indirect commentary

functioning as a language in a television ad through shared cultural meanings.[12] It was in this article that Scott again reflecting Barthes (1976), stated that, "music never appears in an advertising context without at least one other executional element,"[13] such as with an announcer or photography. And while Scott did not, nor did Barthes in his treatment of the subject, for that matter, directly state it as such, an executional element could be dance movement and dance is studied in theoretically rhetorical frameworks.[14]

Critical theory was introduced to consumer research in 1991 (Murray and Ozanne), as a way to provide exposure to social structures that constrain consumers, but at the same time, to evaluate how consumers emancipate themselves from that very structure. Underlying the premise was the connection between theory, practice and the critical nature of social contradictions. Building on the work of Hudson and Ozanne (1988), Murray and Ozanne (1991) delineated the relationships between worldviews and assumptions as they related to positivism and interpretivism, and extended this to include critical theory. I have extended their work to include the ontological, axiological and epistemological assumptions of dance theory.

Ontological assumptions about dance include representations of individuals and groups. Reality is understood by how dance impacts people in their communities and the way in which the world is explained and understood historically. In terms of expressiveness of being, dance provides what seems to be celebratory but resistive silent meanings. Axiologically, dance is aesthetically explicative, interpretive, and critical of social acts and comments on these issues. Dance generates knowledge at the level of the individual and collective bodies, but it is ephemeral and representational at the site of creation. Dancing creates theories about actions occurring in time and space and these theories are carried generationally and serve as a physical reference about the nature of causality. From a research aspect, dance is expressive and indirect with commentary. A rendering of these relationships is given in table 1, "Position of Dance Theory within Consumer Research Assumption Structures." I extend and position dance theory within it.

With the understanding of this bourgeoning canon about new approaches to understanding consumers, Mick and Buhl (1992) suggested a "meaning based model of [print] advertising experiences"[15] to explain how consumers use life themes and life projects that are informed by their personal history and current view of the world to derive meanings from advertisements. First-order interpretation of advertisements are commonsensical, whereas higher-order interpretations of advertisements are more "connotative, ... variable and less predeterminable"[16] for each consumer. Reminiscent of Barthes (1977) but using different terminology, and this will be raised again in the next section, the point is that while this research was shown with print advertisements, it serves to point out how dance could be considered in a personal history and current view of the world, and therefore used to build and support life themes and life projects in regard to consumption.

"A multitude of imaginary characters dance through situations" is how Scott (1994) opens the discussion of the usefulness of visual rhetorical theory in print advertising, which was expanded further in 1999 by McQuarrie and Mick. Both of these studies again illustrate new approaches to seeking knowledge about consumers and meanings they draw from print advertisements. And while these last three articles focus on print, they nonetheless provide space for dance to be considered as a viable meaning carrier in advertisements.

Bristor and Fischer's (1993) article on feminist approaches to consumption research considered the ways in which gender influences consumption. In that paper, the authors discussed feminist perspectives of research to demonstrate the ways in which research is carried out in masculine versus feminine constructs. Dance studies fits extremely well in the interstices of gendered research spaces, by using liberal feminism, women's voice/experience, and post-structuralist feminist perspectives to evaluate history and performance, and theorize and contextualize dance. Joy and Venkatesh (1994) provided further evidence of the cultural aspects of production and consumption through ritualized, gendered bodily representations in their discussion of postmodern feminist thought and consumption. Feminist perspectives on dance then can also be used in consumer research. That is to say, dance has been absent as a theoretical construct in this line of research for reasons that point to dance's silence and marginalization. Intentional or not, researchers just have not considered it.

The previous paragraphs have been given as introductory background to the acceptability of what had been considered nontraditional qualitative and interpretive research paradigms that have expanded the boundaries of consumer research. This has not been meant to be an exhaustive review of such contributions to the field. Rather, it was to allow that theories of dance are *as valuable*[17] as those aforementioned, and to point out that at one point in time, critical theory, rhetorical theory, and feminist theory, for examples, were not. It has to be suggested, though, that perhaps the reasons for dance theory's absence from consumer studies is basically because it is a silent communicator that circulates as a feminine construct: silent, sexual, ephemeral.

In dance studies, scholars moved dance out of its silence and theorized that dances "require attention to the ways in which dance is historically separated out from or linked to other forms of social practice, and to the ways in which the public display of the dancing body engenders and is engendered in its meanings."[18] Dance under this conception does not circulate as feminine, expressive, or emotional. As such, accepting that point of view, a shift has to occur in conceiving dance as a social fabric of production, consumption, and the generation of meanings representative of qualitative data.[19] This implicit blind spot with seeing dance as non-data is likely due to it being considered expressive and emotional, and has come about as a learned system within the practice of consumer research. However, the consumer research field itself dances and provides choreography[20] and its own performativity[21] in the "bodily enactment in the production and maintenance of ideologies of gendered subjects."[22]

If we enter into the dance class and performance space of consumer research, there are aspects of the dance construct. These include the ways in which technique and training are given (professor-student interaction, methods, theories); attendance, staging, and costuming at performances for papers, either on the main stages to be performed as presentations, or in the black box theaters *avant garde* commissioned choreography of abstracts and poster sessions; the current and historical choreography (the materials that are generated for the historical record through research methods and what is admitted to that record); and the critics (that editors of the consumer journals have historically been male and hold the power of admission to the research record).[23]

Women have been admitted to the space of consumer research dance class and performance with the caveat that their research follows the training and performance methods accepted by the critics.[24] As was pointed out earlier, consumer research has recently allowed new information into the historical record that was initially forged by men, however.

In effect, then, there are at least two feminist issues circulating. On the one hand, dance theory has not been examined as a viable basis for understanding consumers; on the other hand, consumer research practice and performance have not been seen as dance. Caught in the gendered "cognitive construct" of identity spheres,[25] researchers and resultant worlds exist in separate spaces. Helen Thomas (2003, 36), along with other scholars, reminds us that the differences between masculine/feminine are culturally constructed. Moreover, the differences may be implicit,[26] essentializing, and unintentional. However, it could be that it is always already[27] a constructed reality as the shift from one binary opposition creates yet others.

Perhaps the difficulty of admitting dance studies as a way to understand consumption and into the field is not only due to dominance or hegemony. Dance *is* elusive[28] and difficult to understand. It *is* fleeting, changing, communicating without words, ephemeral,[29] and therefore defined in our current constructions as *inherently* feminine. I aver that there are alternative understandings of dance, that these alternative understandings allow us to move beyond the created and bounded gendered spheres, and to use dance in ways that benefit our understanding of ourselves as researchers and consumers as dancers.

At the same time, one could argue that dance theorists themselves could have, and maybe should have, embarked on consumer-behavior research. Dance researchers contend that "there are relatively few theories in dance that are appropriate for testing"[30] in that the field concerns itself with characterization and descriptive theoretical methods.[31] If dance theorists construct this reality about themselves, it would stand to reason that dance studies did not make its way into consumer research until now. I could argue, therefore, that dance theorists also have a choreographed reality that accepts gendered study as implicitly natural, as have perhaps consumer researchers. The feminist postpostivist view of this phenomenon already exists, and it is not limited to a particular field of study or generated from a gendered naturalness.[32] In any event, using dance studies in consumer behavior research requires an underlying research protocol that acknowledges the boundaries between the two, and the effort to emerge from them.

Cultural Meaning and Dance in Television Ads

"A great limitation of present approaches to the study of cultural meaning of consumer goods is the failure to observe that this meaning is constantly in transit."[33] Advertisements are aesthetic events that are to be enjoyed as much as the cues that are used in them.[34] Post-structuralist, postmodern and feminist hermeneutical scholars of consumer-behavior research[35] and the body[36] are well aware that shifting cultural meanings are transferred through advertising and fashion systems onto consumer goods drawn from a culturally constituted world,[37] where consumers, even black consumers,[38] are supposedly *free to choose* an identity. This transfer is partially executed by advertising's "body postures and affective states displayed,"[39] and iterative reforming and recontextualizing of cultural meanings.

While the culturally constituted world moves into consumers' minds through goods placed in populists worlds,[40] the marketplace has evolved into imagined theatrical locations conducted on prosceniums to sell *experiences* to consumers bodily with products and services,[41] a decidedly "corporeal basis for marketing" and embodiment.[42] Further, because consumers' feelings are now seen as playing a central role in their behavior,[43] the conscious and unconscious mind *and* the body create consumer phenomenological experiences. Indeed, the body plays a role in the ways we think about aesthetic experiences.

And though there has been much ado about the body in consumption, there has been little attention focused on dance and what it means for consumption, particularly within the framework of television advertising.

As mentioned earlier, Mick and Buhl (1992) suggested that advertising is the communication method by which we mediate reality and meaning through life themes and life projects. Utilizing a hybridized, theoretical, methodological framework employing existential phenomenology, text reception and aesthetics, and semiotics and anthropology, they demonstrated how consumers understand and interpret their lives though advertising. Similarly, consumer culture theory has emerged as a full-fledged discipline to capture "culturally oriented consumer research" within a wide range of inquiry and theoretical constructs.[44] Dance and its influence on consumers and their behaviors would be situated in the symbolic, experiential and embodied aspects of the consumption cycle informing the consumer's identity. What I will evaluate are the emotional, affective, aesthetic and hedonic dimensions of dance relative to television advertising in a consumer culture theory frame. To wit, dance provides a basis for "the culture of origin [to be] socially reconstructed as something consumable,"[45] but as I suggest, through interpretive dance strategies reflected in or portrayed in advertising. Sherry (1987) has argued that

> advertising as a system of symbols synthesized from the entire range of culturally determined ways of knowing that is accessible through ritual and oriented toward both secular and sacred dimensions of transcendental experience in a hyperindustrialized society.[46]

Dance is used as one such symbol which is itself a culturally determined way of knowing.

The theory of visual rhetoric was used to examine advertising through a text-interpretive and reader-response approach.[47] In this construct, a rhetorical figure is artful, such as rhyme, or metaphor, or a figure of speech. These add interest to the advertisement and such that it "increase[s] elaboration and ... [provides] a greater degree of pleasure."[48] It has been shown already that dance is rhetorical in nature, and that it can function in an array of emotions, including hedonically. Now I contend that dance can be construed as rhetorical when displayed in a commercial.

Moving from cultural implications to interpretive understandings of ads, Phillips (1997), pulling from Scott's (1994) conception of visual rhetorical theory and the ideology of implicature established by Sperber and Wilson (1986), considered consumers' interpretations of meanings in complex advertising. Phillips (1997) suggested that information is conveyed implicitly through the visual, either as a strong- or weak-meaning carrier, or implicature.

In a weak implicature, consumers have to draw their own conclusions, and the opposite is true for strong implicatures. Dance could be construed as an implicature in an advertisement,[49] depending on how it is situated. In like manner, Brumbaugh (2002) has demonstrated the activation of cultural knowledge through source and non-source cues in television advertising. In this research I suggest that dance can be used as both a source and non-source cue as it activates cultural models and shared knowledge depending on context and target market. Drawing on Scott's 1994 work, Bulmer and Buchanan-Oliver (2006) defined television ads as visually complex using "fantastic imagery and other special effects"[50] as persuasive devises other than language, which can be interpreted differently depending on the culture of the reader. I consider dance as one such special effect in complex ads.

PHENOMENOLOGY AND CONSCIOUSNESS IN NONVERBAL COMMUNICATION THROUGH DANCE IN ADVERTISING

It is perhaps edifying to examine and incorporate some writings from Edmund Husserl (1933) to get our footing about cultural meaning created in consciousness and experience of a human being. From "The Fundamental Phenomenological Outlook," in the second section of *Ideas* (1931), in the first chapter, Husserl raises the philosophical view of a field of perception that we find ourselves in as humans. Included in this field is the co-present margin and a fringe of indeterminate reality which is infinite and dimly apprehended. Goods, practical affairs, situations in the world are just there, and Husserl considers that humanity exists as an object within the world as being in it. Other types of worlds exist, such as the arithmetic world, but one must go deliberately to that world; the natural world that humanity belongs to, however, one is always present in.

Husserl suggested that to doubt being or doubt everything is to bracket it away, and in particular it is to bracket away and suspend spatio-temporal existence. In other words, remove consciousness. Spatio-temporal existence, called Dasein, when bracketed and suspended, gives rise to the interpretive method of understanding the world in contrast to the positivist method.[51] Doing this allows one to suspend judgment and therefore experience, or come to phenomenology. At this point, consciousness is seen as a being of itself. It is important to do this because consciousness has its own Being, which is unique and unaffected by bracketing or suspending, and this is the field of science known as phenomenology. Phenomenology studies transcendental consciousness from the viewpoint of pure intuition — descriptively. It is an eidetic science, looking to study immanental essences.

In noesis and noema, Husserl explains that there is a difference between a real experience and the effect of the experience. He gives the example of being able to find pleasure in perceiving a real tree, and the related experience of seeing it. Something is perceived as such or remembered as such based on its perceptual meaning. It could be that the tree does not exist in reality but we can have the perception as in a hallucination. It is the *experience of the perception* and the *feeling of pleasure* that is *phenomenologic*, or noematic when all else is bracketed away, regardless of whether there is a real tree. Dance in television ads is such an experience and perception. The dance does not have to be there in reality, yet a real dance does exist somewhere, which has been bracketed away.

The dance in a commercial, plain and simple, is different from the perceived dance as such.[52] The dance in a commercial evades and disappears when the commercial ends, but the meaning of the dance in a person's consciousness does not.

> The object considered may be in every case a [dance] and in every case this [dance] may so appear that the faithful description of that which appears as such necessarily uses identical expressions. Yet the noematic correlates are for the very reason essentially different for perception, fancy, imaginative presentation, memory and so forth. At one time that which appears is characterized as corporal reality, at another as fiction, then again as recollection brought before the mind.[53]

According to Stewart (1988), nonverbal communication may be more important than verbal communication in advertising in getting into people's consciousness. That dance is a nonverbal system of communication is substantiated by the fact that it is a system of codes shared by a social system or systems. Meaning, therefore, is derived from context and situation.[54] In addition, both the dance and the bodies dancing serve as signs in that they convey information, evoke feelings, communicate a message. In terms of nonverbal communication, I already presented literature on dance as body movement and gesture.[55] As such, informing this part of the discussion are phenomenologic and metaphoric approaches to dance in advertising.

While approaches to advertising have changed over time, keeping pace with the ways in which production was designed in America, the purpose of advertising has been to sell, regardless of the ways in which a commercial is designed. Nowadays, though, advertising is used for much more — to permeate the consciousness of viewers to create relationships with customers, to give brands personalities, and to entertain viewers. People who watch ads know this is the case, and those who write ads know the viewer is keen on the purpose of ads. But, as a communication device, television ads lack feedback to the sender in any immediate sense. So the hope that ad producers link into is that of being able to hook into a field of the viewers' experience as they sit passively watching or ignoring a commercial.[56] The result is that they try to speak "with" the viewer, not "at" them. Within the field that the viewer experiences, there is more than the hard sell of the facts through speech. Ads are arranged in some instances where the viewer is able to participate, albeit in an imaginary manner. If they cannot participate, the ads become more of a passage of information. But this is not the goal; the goal is reciprocity and exchange as in interpersonal communication.

In the process of interpersonal communication with people, a space is created during communication, based on social and physical contexts. With a television ad, such a space is created but it is a virtual space which relies on "symbolic and substitute effects."[57] To create the illusion of an intimate communication, the ad will rely on aesthetics, such as story, drama, and other factors that create worlds the viewer imagines. The aim is to address the viewer bodily[58] as a participant in the discourse. As a result of the chosen aesthetic approach to the ad, the viewer is to be able to do something. To get the viewer to act in an exchange of goods and services, with monetary consequences for the product producer is the goal, and in order to do this the producer must get the viewers' attention. Mainly, ads make people "wish" for things, and these include escape from social stigmatization or other negative consequences from inaction.[59] "You wish you can dance" comes to mind here, especially in the context of television shows that are popular among amateur dancers. In my view, dance in an advertisement sets up wishes in viewers' minds.

Ads try to get into the consciousness of the viewer and doing so is done through meaning creation and symbolic desire that the viewer interprets from the ad's indirect appeal. Dance is an aesthetic mechanism used to create meaning. Because of this the ads have become more and more general and, at the same time, aesthetic.[60] They become mini dramas, according to Stigel (2001), where complete universes can be arranged, much like Holt's (2004) description of the cultural myth world. In creating the world the viewer is to become a part of it through their imagination, the senses are engaged, in visual and physical aspects, as with dance, "establishing a fellowship with the viewer around something virtual and imaginary, yet manifestly a visual experience which is being created on the screen."[61] This fellowship connection takes place in a virtual space between the television screen and the viewer.

While Stigal (2001) uses the voice-over narrative to make his point, the use of dance as a linguistic approach to communication with the audience is the point I make. Dance can be seen as a vehicle for creating virtual spaces, engaging the viewer to act, and creating meaning and desire.

METAPHORS AND DANCE

Metaphorical references to dance are used not infrequently in American parlance, and the use of them dates back to antiquity.[62] People tap dance around a topic, dance in the rain, have dancing eyes, watch stars dance across the sky. We dance the night away, dance with death, and hope in the dance of the cosmos. Then there are books published that play on the dance metaphor, such as *The Dance of Anger*, *The Dance of Leadership*, *The Dance of Change*, and a book about how capital makes talent dance. In American culture, dance is an oft-referenced metaphor that carries with it a myriad of meanings because metaphors make ideas dance. The purpose of using metaphors is to convey images and meanings that are not easy to communicate or to provide an aesthetic means to do so. And while metaphors hold within in them the ability to make comparisons, dance as a metaphor is not something that has been examined in regard to using it in advertising and so it should hardly be dismissed when used in working with consumers. Consider that "dance uses the body to speak, metaphorically ... though the cultural context will define the form of dance available ... [and] the conveyance yields a unity of body and mind."[63] So it is clear that dance has been metaphorically used over time and in different arenas to infer a variety of meanings, both positive and negative. It has been taken lightly in terms of its value in meaning creation.

At the same time, metaphors have often been discounted in and of themselves but some have resisted the urge to dismiss metaphoric power. Neisser (2003), for example, argues two points against the ideology of metaphor being "mere rhetorical flourish."[64] First he says that metaphoric interpretation relies on consciousness differently than does literal interpretation. Second, humans understand metaphoric thought through their embodiment and cognitive mental imagery, what he calls "the swaying form."[65] I take from this argument that there can exist a notion of dance cognition whereby dance is considered an important and meaningful metaphor, which cannot be interpreted literally. Neisser further pushed for understanding cognition as it is rooted in embodied experience. "Rooted in embodied experience, these images are value-laden for the interpreter in virtue of the worldly context ... we make sense of them [metaphors, i.e., dance] by drawing on the non propositional meanings of embodied experience."[66] Metaphoric seeing allows a comparative statement of "what it is like" in terms of us as "embodied agents."[67] The seeing takes place through commonplace association of images from which we make inferences. Imagination is sparked with the inferences as it relates to the perceiver's body image and schema. Here we are placed right back to Susan Langer's notion of imagined feeling, but at the level of the body. "In the embodied schematism ... imagination becomes the place where figurative meaning emerges from perception, and metaphor [i.e., dance] is the place in language where this embodiment can be seen."[68] The connection of the performed dance and the existential phenomenology of perception provides the noematic structure such that, "one's body scheme can be consciously manipulated via the image."[69] Here is what dance in advertising is doing.

However, while certain aspects of embodied experiences can be said to be humanly universal,[70] it is not true that all cultures experience attention and perception the same. Indeed, a metaphor in China is not the same metaphor in the United States; in fact one can argue that certain turns of phrase that are used routinely in one culture receive a quizzical, nonsensical response when used in another. One study suggested that white Americans are focal and tend to ignore the context, while Japanese are more contextually motivated in their perceptions.[71] Though the study did not specifically state it as such, I assume they were talking about white mainstream Americans and mainstream Japanese. My assumption is based on the fact that the authors did not specifically call out a race or ethnicity other than American and Japanese. In any event, it is difficult to imagine that *all* Japanese are this way, or that *all* Americans are that way. This becomes an essentializing characteristic, bordering on stereotypical, precisely the kind of labeling we need less of. That said, when dance is used in television ads, it can be seen in the sphere of attention in direct focus, or in the margin or on the horizon, but the message it portrays is contextual. As such, dance as a metaphor in television ads occupies multiple cognitive and affective, as well as embodied, imaginations.

Another study views metaphor as important to human understanding of art. Shiff (1979) suggested that artistic activity, including dance, is part of a metaphoric bridge between perfection and imperfection of life that also embodies the truth of the past and a newly evolving truth of existence and experience. In this view, art incorporates the artist's life and defines the culture or social group, linking its production to existential meaning. While Shiff distinguishes art as object from art as experience, he does claim that the experience of art, i.e., dance, reveals life and meaning in a way that is understandable metaphorically. "One senses the living force that lies within it[72] [and] "it conveys 'objective' meaning to all members of a society."[73] The point is that these artistic compositions do not necessarily provide meaning in an analytical sense; in fact, the dependence on understanding the meaning is so metaphorically taken for granted that it forms the foundation for the culture.[74] We have this exact bridge between black social dance and metaphor when we consider it to be an art form. Moreover, Ricoeur (1979) argued, and I extend and adapt his argument, that metaphorical understanding relies on semantic theory by inclusion of emotion and imagination. In other words, dance metaphors, like poetics, touch people's feelings and imaginations in their untranslatable role of providing truth and insight about reality to viewers.

Against the ideology of reason in point-blank opposition to it, Lakoff and Johnson (1999) state that the classical faculty of reason as separate from embodiment is wrong.[75] Rather, they provide "evidence for the view that reason is fundamentally embodied."[76] That means that reason is found in the body's understanding as well as in the brain. Moreover, the combination of the two types of understandings presents itself mainly unconsciously while providing a sense of reality. This is the perfect place for dance in advertising because it is silent, and not thought too much about in experience as artful social commentary. "Our sense of what is real begins with and depends crucially upon our bodies, especially our sensorimotor apparatus."[77] From this understanding I take it as given that there cannot any longer be the Cartesian mind/body split, that we must therefore throw that out from our consideration, bracket it away as Husserl (1933) suggested. And secondly, that from this we can clearly assert that people learn and understand concepts and information from inputs to their bodies, either by seeing the body do things, or by doing things with the body.[78] In short, people reason with their bodies and their minds.

With my thesis that dance in social situations and contexts is a freeing, spiritual, ritualistic experiential process, Lakoff and Johnson (1999) agree and suggest that spiritual experiences are embodied, and that people can imagine the spiritual experiences of other people when they see them.

> A major function of the embodied mind is empathetic. From birth we have the capacity to imitate others, to vividly imagine being the other person, doing what that person does, experiencing what that person experiences. The capacity for imaginative projection is a vital cognitive faculty. Experientially, it is a form of "transcendence." Through it, one can experience something akin to "getting out of our bodies"—yet it is very much a bodily capacity.[79]

This experience, I argue, is available in live or digital formats, and is recreated in the television commercial with dance in it.

Having argued the point that dance communicates in ads by way of phenomenologic and metaphoric means, in the next section I bring in the ways in which music has been analyzed in consumption behavior to give dance a space for similar application.

MUSIC AND ADVERTISING

Here, the discussion of music in television commercials begins with the work of Park and Young (1986), where the authors stated that music is a peripheral cue capable of affecting attitude toward the ad and therefore the brand under different levels of involvement. Their findings showed that the impact of music on consumption behavior occurred in both central and peripheral route processing, depending on the situation the consumer was in. In addition "attitude can be formed through pairing of a conditioned stimulus (e.g., a brand in a commercial) and an unconditioned stimulus such as a visual aspect of the commercial or emotionally charged music."[80] More, visual components are processed faster and generate feelings. For purposes of this research at this juncture, I assume dance in television advertising to be just such a visual, regardless of how the dance is being executed in the commercial. Future research will hopefully provide further elicitation of the role[81] that different forms of dance play in such communications.

Alpert and Alpert (1990) examined music and consumers' moods, attitudes and behaviors and found that musical structure in advertising influences emotional responses and behavioral intentions towards products. Dunbar (1990) pointed out that use of music in television commercials was more random than planned. This was unfortunate, since more commercials used music than not, and further, the study of music in such advertising was lacking. In his view, Dunbar asserted that music is a language that communicates on three levels: The sensual at the levels of both mind and body, the emotional as in meanings associated with moods and feelings which cannot be stated verbally, and the intellectual in terms of structure. Because of these aspects of music and its influence on human beings, it motivates one's interpretation and response to the ad. Scott's (1990) contribution advanced a rhetorical theoretical reader-response framework, applying it specifically to studying music in advertising. At that time few non-simplistic studies existed that evaluated the impact that music had on consumers watching television ads with music. These studies supposed a low-involvement, affective, and classical conditioning placement on consumer behavior.[82] Based on the work of Dowling and Harwood (1986), when processing symbolic components of ads such as music, and in our case dance, consumers have to retrieve cultural information. The premise is that "ads use a variety of symbolic forms to effect persuasion among culturally constructed beings.... Music ... contributes to the rhetorical task in ways as various as language."[83] In so doing, music is used to execute cognitive and affective tasks related to the message and content by shared cultural meaning. These views are not unlike that set forth by dance theorists Sklar (2001) and Hanna (1987), who claimed that transmission and absorption of dance knowledge is culturally informative somatically, cognitively, and affectively. It does not seem unreasonable to entertain the idea that such transmission and absorption is working through dance in advertisements. In addition, Macinnis and Park (1991) demonstrated that some executional elements in a television advertisement may affect both levels of involvement and attitude formation through indexicality such that connections with music form a conditioned response,[84] which negated studies that suggested that music was merely an influence on low-involvement message processing.[85]

As I mentioned earlier in relation to metaphorical usage and in addition to it, Scott's (1994) study addressed visual imagery in print ads as a carrier of rhetoric. Hung (2000) extended the semiotic rhetorical framework by working with both the musical and visual executional elements of television ads demonstrating that viewers read and create contextual and non-contextual cultural meanings from music and other visual cues in television ads. Drawing from this work, I consider dance to be a semiotic "other visual" signed and signified executional cue in ads.[86]

Allan (2006) researched the significance, that is, the degree of emotional meaning that popular music in radio advertising had on consumers with an eye toward expanding our understanding of how attention, memory and popular music affects it. He found that ads containing popular music with vocals were more effective than music alone. His work built upon other scholars who had shown that music stimulated attention and recall, but had not yet evaluated popular music on recall of the ad or the brand. His hypotheses were supported particularly when there was high personal significance for the consumer with the music. Oakes (2007), one of several researchers evaluating the technical aspects of ad effectiveness and music use, provides a detailed literature review and validates its use, pointing out that artful and incongruous music may have more influence on ad effectiveness.

Aside from making the case that dance's function in advertising is plausible with regard to consumers, the previous section points out that music is an important aspect of advertising that critically affects consumers. While many dance scholars oppose the notion that people dance to the music and music gives rise to dance, it would not be inconceivable that there is a relationship between them when it comes to consumers and their behaviors. In any event, it is clear that music once had no role in analyzing consumers until it was embraced by consumer theorists. The next section moves away from music and into motor processes and how consumers retain information based on body motions.

MOVEMENT AND MOTOR PROCESSES IN ADVERTISING

What makes a television advertisement likable in many different cultures and countries are six dimensions, which include ads that are entertaining, energetic, relevant, empathetic, irritating, and familiar, depending on the product category.[87] Advertising effectiveness can be evaluated through studying involvement and attitude formation and change, through central and peripheral routes to persuasion.[88] The central route relies on a cognitive model of attitude formation.[89] In the peripheral route, attitudes are changed within consumers not by extensive thought, but rather by associating an object with a particular positive or negative cue, or because of an inference, in the context of the advertisement.[90] These cues include utility of a product offering, classical conditioning, and secondary sources such as pleasant pictures and attractive sources. Music and body perception has been shown to fall within the category of peripheral cues.

Somatovisceral explanations for attitudes have been set forth by several scholars[91] demonstrating positive affective relationships between arm flexion and negative relationships between extensions, and similar findings for head nodding and shaking[92] within a self-validating process.[93] Dance may provide consumers with predominately positive thoughts and self-validation which in turn may increase positive attitude formations. Priester and colleagues (1996) showed that the positive relationship of attitude change was favorably associated with nonsensical words such that movement connects to veridical evaluations of the world[94] along a peripheral route to persuasion. These are physiologically manifested by human beings to make life easier "from the burden of considering the details of all relevant information each time a stimulus is encountered or a choice is required."[95] People change their attitudes in this way without conscious evaluation of centrally processed information. This is perhaps the role that dance plays in television ads, operating somatoviscerally. Stated differently, dance, i.e., "motion, affects attitudes."[96] This finding waltzes well with Loewenstein's (1996) findings that visceral factors influence consumption behavior in the present and within the self. Again dance being a present moment and self-involved cultural phenomenon works well with the idea of attitudes, nonvolitional behavior, and classical conditioning. Strack and Neuman (1996) further postulate that whether volitional or not, information processing is cognitive, which includes feelings. Moreover, "pleasant feelings may trigger approach behavior, whereas unpleasant feelings may lead to avoidance."[97] Associating a pleasant feeling with a movement toward the brand would likely benefit the advertiser.

In addition to this, Forester (2004), reviewing and extending the research on body feedback and consumer behavior found that "rather than merely reading attitudes from an internal meter, individuals' judgments can be influenced by subtle environmental and affective cues."[98] On the whole, the study was intended to flesh out more deeply the mechanisms behind the results of body feedback and consumer approach and avoidance. The significant finding for dance in advertising can be summed up in the following paraphrase:

> Given that people use their subjective bodily reactions for judgment formation, one might speculate that the conditioned reactions to body feedback and the reactions stimulus features have additive effects. If this were true, evaluations of a positively valenced stimulus should be increased by body feedback that signifies approach, whereas evaluations of a negatively valenced stimulus should be diminished by feedback that signifies avoidance.[99]

Dance in advertisements could be influencing valence for the product as well as positive body feedback by influencing the desire to buy. More research will be needed to fully tease these relationships out.

MARKETING CULTURE THROUGH DANCE IN ADVERTISING

Advertisements tell us who we are and how to deal with life, and they draw on aesthetics to do so. "Above all, they give us information about living ... in conditions of incessant change."[100] Television ads display problems we have in life, from race relations to employment behaviors. It is the medium whereby we see ourselves as we want to see ourselves, not as we really are, but in heroic terms when change is afoot. This is where people learn how to deal when there is no direction or user's manual for change.[101]

Varda Leymore's work *Hidden Myth* (1975) characterizes advertising as ritualistic and religious, where consumption constitutes the religious notion of triumph over death. Leymore's positionality is that of an anthropologist, relying heavily on the theoretical foundation laid by Levi-Strauss (1974). More than a solution to social change, Leymore contended that advertising is the myth-creating equivalent from primitive society used as such for our technologically advanced society. In short, we do not write on walls but we write on television commercials to support the social order and reduce human anxiety. It supports happiness, life, a feeling of belonging, and good over evil.[102]

Importantly, advertising gives people good feelings as they draw on outdated staged communities[103] and their projections of slices of life, or fictitious ones from projected future satisfactions. Berman (1975) informed us that because of mass consumption models for economic growth, these staged communities had to be the basis for the development of the middle class, whose consumption practices would differ from the wealthy classes. Wealthy people historically commissioned artisans to work for them, but their consumption practices were miniscule and unable to keep up with corporate development and capitalism. Therefore, in mass culture it would have to differ. Not only would it differ, consumption would be voluminous so as to support industrialization and growth. As such, it now rests on a mediocrity of goods and services that people are made to think are upscale, provided cheaply enough for the shrinking middle class to acquire, and to acquire through credit practices. Aesthetically speaking, the mass middle class views advertisements as objects of its imagination, presented in artistic formats that make them think they are seeing something of artistry. Wealthy classes do not confuse high cultural aesthetics such as books, symphonies, ballets and fine arts with the aesthetics of advertising. Here is where we can understand the "mass" consumer as an aesthetic subject, as advertisements and products take on the aesthetic appeal of self-reflection.[104] Importantly, advertisements reinforce the social system, economically and politically, in a democratic society.[105]

Arriving at such a mass-consumption model occurred through "proletarianization" which was particularly violent in America, where everyone was forced into it from another culture, and where Africans were more forced than any. The goal was to produce a homogeneous group of individuals who were attentive to production and time. In support of this, religion, education, military and political power has been utilized over humanity,[106] and to this list of institutions I would add "dance" or the absence of it as a way of controlling people in society. Many people were insulted with the imposition of the workday and work week, where the collective memory relied on movements of the sun, changing of seasons, and agrarian relations to mark or facilitate change. In many of these shifts, dance was an accompaniment.

But advertising's basic goal from inception was to give businessmen hegemonic control over consumption at the middle levels of society.[107] To do so, wages were adjusted higher so that middle-income earners could consume, installment credit was conceived and pedaled among them, and advertisements depicted the joy of consumption. Most importantly, workers were directed to want more, on mental and spiritual levels, of what companies produced, not more of the modes of production company's utilized.[108] And if people had more money to spend and it was a spiritual imperative, they needed time to spend it, and hence work weeks were reduced. They were to live, move and have their beings in spending.[109] "Modern advertising must be seen as a direct response to the needs of mass industrial capitalism."[110] Advertising must also have been connected to the direct need for the corporation to survive.[111] It has been such and continues to be through modernity, postmodernity and now post postmodernity.

The notion of being "free to spend" was a new, civilizing experience that developed in the 1920s, but clearly carries on in the current century. Moreover, the goal was to make it instinctual: "If advertising copy appealed to the right instincts, the urge to buy would surely be excited."[112] So you see the removal of any need for the product to be useful; instead there developed a "fancied need" in the consumer to be satisfied through consumption. And what better way to carry this out than through showing people doing a what humans have instinctually been doing for ages,[113] called dancing?

For corporations, consumption came to be linked with the need to be modern at the level of self-identity, and condemning messages of consumer ridicule and inferiority were widely disseminated, pointing shameful fingers to those who did not consume in modernity's wake. Consumption was constituted as self-preservation, which was in turn linked to the existential decision to put on the mass-produced. The transference of being a perfected Puritan was made when one consumed; the understanding and stability of a cosmos were had when products were used to create identities that defied the unstable and uncertain world of reality, as Ewen (1976, 37) pointed out. Desire, therefore, was created for better things, taking the focus off the deity.

To enact and carry out this new transference, people had to be placed at odds with their bodies, and to be told that it was the body's offenses and contingent self-esteem that stood in the way of happiness. Consumption of a product could solve it. It was, as Horkheimer (1941) stated, "a new form of command and obedience."[114] Art was enlisted to achieve these goals. Because of the degree of importance of this view, it is useful to quote Ewen (1976) at length:

> In the propagation of an aesthetic of mass industrialism, it was in the realm of artistic creativity itself that the organization of objects and the dissolution of the subject took perhaps the most obvious toll.... Advertising and marketing drew heavily on creative human resources in order to formulate its product.... Understanding the ways in which further use of the aesthetic dimension might enhance the social viability of capitalist mass production ... [resulted in] the enormous growth of the advertising industry and the commercialization of art ... to the depletion and demise of traditional sources and arenas of artistic expression and localized cultures. Artistic patronage, a province of the wealthy since ancient times, now was doled out through the economic avenues provided by advertising.... The effect on the graphic, literary, and performing arts in America was to be monumental.[115]

It is here that the new proscenium for dance developed alongside the crisis in the arts, which resulted from its co-optation to advertising.[116] Advertising itself became an artistic aesthetic endeavor. More importantly, it evolved into more of the anthropologic aspect of looking at ourselves, commenting on what we see. It was, according to Ewen (1976, 67), "the eradication of indigenous cultural expression and the elevation of the consumer marketplace" to a new god, a new truth.

Advertising happens within people's sphere of attention,[117] as commercial makers do what they can to get us to look at them, remember them, and associate a solved problem with a brand or product. Expanding upon Husserl's field of attention, as I explained earlier, Arvidson (2006) claimed that one's *sphere* of attention is broader than a field of attention and it contains a theme, context and margin, such that whenever someone pays attention to something, it is done so within a larger environment. Corporeity and existence as time passes, and other items outside the attention object context, are marginal and peripheral, existing on the horizon.

From the center of the sphere of attention, there is thematic attention, i.e., what we are to focus on directly; context of attention, that is, what the immediate surroundings are; and then the margin of attention, or what's happening on the horizon in terms of the larger existence of the world through the body's relationship with time and space. Adopting this kind of approach makes attention three dimensional, not two. Theme forms the activity in the sphere of attention; it is the focus or the target, separate from the background, but occurs in a gestalt-coherence whereby the whole object of focus is necessary for attention. Human beings "never stop attending thematically, some content is focal; it is central, consolidated, and segregated from the thematic context, or becoming so."[118]

Who we are and what we think of ourselves, our "essence," Arvidson says, is a function of attending. Our sphere of attention is developed by our existential style, achieved through habits and consistencies of attending. "We are identified in our human being by what we attend to and how we attend."[119] Our personalities come about through human existence, learned in cultural contexts. In short, human subjectivity is attending activity. Within the subjective attending activity, there are three phenomena that have to be taken into account which are very important to the effect of dance in television ads:

(a) the ever-present self i.e., the sense of self or subjectivity that is present with thematic attention, you are marginally aware of yourself, permanently;

(b) attentionality, or the difference between the object and the subject, or, as Arvidson says, "between the content attended to as theme and the process of allowing the content to be attended to as theme" (120). You are always already involved with the object outside of yourself. It takes this object/subject duality to create meaning. "Consciousness is defined by intentionality [attentionality, the author argues]. It is consciousness of an object on the one hand and an inner awareness of itself on the other hand";[120] and

(c) reflective attention, the sense of self, when the sphere becomes aware of itself in the world. Here the sphere presents itself both as focus and margin, where marginal and thematic content are connected. You have what is focused on and the focusing process in this category.

There are three different levels of reflection on each of the levels of attending, embodiment, and the environing world. They provide differentiation between them and the context, and the marginal halo with the horizon.[121]

(a) Distinction between the moment of the streaming and the marginal halo that gives the moment temporality;

(b) The distinction between the actual kinesthetic facts as thematic content within the indefinite context of corporeity, and the kinesthetic facts that are marginal in the halo giving a horizon of corporeity.[122]

(c) Distinction between the sector of the environing world as thematic content within the indefinite context of the environing world, and the marginal environing world represented in the halo that itself expands into the world in general.

Arvidson further distinguishes between authentic and inauthentic reflection. He gives an example of going to a party, where the self is focused outwardly, and you attend to changes in the environment but the self is not the theme, and so you are not reflecting. "This marginal self-consciousness is the presentation of temporality, embodiment, and the world, with reference to the body."[123] When you shift the focus from the external to the internal self, you become reflective, it is where the story of "you" develops and changes. With inauthentic reflection, the self-story is stable. If there are opportunities for self-reflection, the transformations replace one stable story with another stable one. Nothing about you changes with inauthentic reflection, even when the self becomes the theme.

The opposite is true for authentic reflection; that is to say, the context for the theme is not stable, and the context is unsettling, and changes to the self's story occur. *Here is where black social dance comes into play in advertisements.* For non-blacks, it changes the self's story from being presented with an unsolvable problem externally to an aesthetic experience of being happy and dancing around internally because of the proposed solution, which is a consumption and hegemonic requirement of capitalism. The reflection is an authentic one but is done somatoviscerally, liminally, silently, through dance. Between Arvidson (2006) and Ewen (1976), the consumer as an aesthetic subject[124] has emerged.

BLACKS IN ADVERTISING

Though it may seem surprising for people of a certain age in the United States, there was a time not long ago when advertisers did not use black people in their commercials.[125] In fact, they were slow to adopt the notion of segmentation of markets where blacks were concerned in spite of the strong spending power that blacks had within the proletarianization process.[126] Before the instillation of desegregation, African American–owned newspapers used to advertise to its segment. Of course advertisements at that time, in the 1820s, were aimed at informing consumers.

By the 1960s, though, blacks were still considered a conundrum for consumer scholars; blacks were seen as handicapped by drive and opportunity, were more likely to be below the poverty line, suffered from unequal education than whites, and so on.[127] The 1970s, in terms of marketing, was the time of the Negro Revolution wherein blacks were looking to be included in mainstream society, and wanted to consume name brands, in an effort to be accepted and demonstrate well being in American society. At that time, marketers considered the behavior of blacks to be either consumption for immediate gratification or inclusion into mainstream white America, skin color and native lands notwithstanding as privileges for other ethnic minorities.[128] Many stereotypes, most still familiar, circulated at the time, such as the status of the black woman and the black family, the motivation and self-image of men as compared to white men, as Nasir and colleagues (2009) described. None of that need be repeated here. What is important to take away from this is that the systematic approach to segmenting black markets (women, men, children) was, for all intents and purposes, nonexistent until after 1930. When blacks were finally advertised to, in the late 1960s and afterwards, it was with whitenized blacks, and with a hope that whites would not retaliate in a backlash for any ads that were integrated. While whites did not find it unpalatable, over time we have come to the understanding that whites are targetable with black social dance as long as that dance is presented in a contextual frame that allows indirect authentic reflecting.[129]

In the 1970s marketers of telecommunications products and services began targeting blacks with the "Reach out and touch someone" tag line, using black celebrities and realistic-looking black families, that is to say, non-whitenized people. This trend continued into the mid–1970s for other consumer goods, mainly food, beverages, body care, and cars. But still, the thought was that there were two categories of blacks, either poor or middle income, both with negative self images. That misconception changed for marketers by the 1980s, when a critical mass of blacks were considered to be upper middle and upper class. To their surprise, though, black people still enjoyed cultural products reflective of their heritage. It was the beginning of the use of black advertising consultants and firms to push products onto blacks. Even with that, into the mid–1980s blacks were not prime targets for marketers in general.[130]

In the 1970s, moreover, music began being used in ads in many different target groups, using whitenized versions of black music. But in the 1980s, music use turned to that performed by blacks,[131] and in particular popular individuals such as Michael Jackson, Lionel Richie, Whitney Houston, Natalie Cole, and others. Importantly, black social dance came to the advertisements in connection with use of black popular music. However, it should be remembered that many ads were used that only used black music as voice-over and background "while white models flashed across television screens."[132] A case in point for dance was the Pointer Sisters singing "Jump" for a dryer product while whites "jumped for joy" in the commercials. However, more and more commercials were aired that showed realistic portrayals of slices of life for African Americans as we moved into the next decade. Some of these approaches can be attributed to black owned advertising firms, many of which proliferated in the 1980s, but quickly saw their demise in the 1990s. Large non-black firms added special departments to their organizations that specialized in advertising to African Americans and other groups to capture newly identified market segments of different consumers.[133] Nevertheless, black people dancing wandered into white advertisers' spheres of attention as a focal point, in the contextual frame of promising more profits[134] both from the African American billion-dollar buying power and later white people's relationship with black social dance — the horizon of racism notwithstanding.

In looking back over this chapter, I find that it provided a broad brush and contextual reference for dance in advertising, moving from suggesting that dance has not been included in consumer research because it has never crossed anyone's mind. The reasons for this mainly point to the notion that dance is feminine. Then, I walked through research that explained several nontraditional qualitative additions to the consumer research literature, and argued that dance theory deserves an equal place alongside those approaches. I gave a view of dance theory's ontology, axiology and epistemology. From there, cultural meaning transfer in television ads was extended to include dance theory, and Husserl's phenomenology was regarded as a way to get into consumers' consciousnesses. Consciousness can be accessed in the use of metaphor, and clearly dance metaphors abound and have so since, well, for a long time. Rather than the dismiss the power of dance metaphor, it was suggested that it in fact carries meaning by comparisons.

Next, a brief history of the discovery and use of music in advertising was given, with the supposition that dance could be providing similar effects on consumers, either through conditioned or unconditioned responses, through connections with information processing, and through somatovisceral pathways. A review of the historical basis for advertising in the American capitalistic landscape was drawn, showing that advertising has conducted several missions over the course of its lifetime in connection with products and brands. In fact, I suggested that television ads use dance in them to gain access to people's spheres of attention to help them focus on the product or brand. And finally, I showed how black people were not advertised to with any earnest as a market segment, but that black social dance played a role in getting both blacks' and non-blacks' attention.

The next chapter turns to the data on black social dance in advertising. It is hoped that the information and background given in chapters 1 and 2 will provide the reader with the necessary backdrop to understand why it is important to evaluate the use of dance in television ads, and further, to establish it as a cultural meaning carrier in commercial, changing over time. What impact this has borne on the consumer in the face of technological advancement over the last sixty years will be the subject of chapter 6.

Section Two

THE RESEARCH STUDY

3. A History of Black Social Dance in Commercials

But most advertising is not that blunt. Advertisers are after more than wallets, they also want our custom.[1]

African American [social] dance embodies African American values. It reflects a way of looking at the world and provides a means of survival.[2]

ANTHROPOLOGICAL VIEW

In the previous chapters I have supplied the theoretical groundwork for what is to come in this chapter and the next: research into dance in television ads over the 1950-to-2010 time period and the effects of black social dance on consumers. In turn that will be used to build theory that accounts for, describes, and explains the phenomenon of black social dance in television ads.[3] This cultural and qualitative research design[4] is situated in an anthropological approach.[5] It employs an art historical method[6] to gather source materials as well as to provide a historic rendering of change over time. For interpretations, a semiotic analysis[7] of the commercials is utilized to get at meanings. An anthropologic view of dance allows the viewpoints of both the performers and audience members to be incorporated. Therefore, along with the examination of actual commercials, respondents were interviewed[8] who included African Americans and a retired Caucasian American advertising agency executive. The research also draws on Walter and colleagues (2009), Walter and Altimini (2010), and Walter (2011). Walter and colleagues (2009) provided a online research design using commercial clips with 101 respondents. Respondents resided in the United States and France. One of the findings was that most of the respondents indicated that they preferred ads with black social

Walking for Dat Cake. Rare Book, Manuscript, and Special Collections Library, Duke University, Durham, North Carolina.

dance in them. In Walter and Altimini (2010), the research revealed that black social dance was connected to the respondents' memories, and that ads with the dance in them could help them remember the brand. The respondents also suggested that they would buy brands that used dance in them if the brands were products they used without ethical objection. In Walter (2011), the author found that black social dance had a strong positive impact on Euro-Americans who felt their role as a dominant class had slipped away from them. Importantly, each of these contributions to research in black social dance in television ads used an anthropological framework based on Sklar's (2001) premises.

In addition, for a richer research result, ideally for an anthropological approach, the researcher should also know and be able to perform the dances, knowing how and in what order, as well as to get feedback from the community as to whether the researcher is doing them correctly. Performing dance as a researcher in this way acts as a storage device of sorts as well.[9] In this case, I do know black social dance in these varying degrees. Dance has a unique cultural function, which is not the same as language or any other phenomena. It is its own expressive and responsive behavior in and of itself, inseparable from people who do it. Therefore, it must be analyzed contextually. Approaching it this way ensures understanding.

The participant observer method of research is an oft-used technique, and I adapted this method by watching television commercials as they appeared in real time. The method requires that the researcher observe then describe what is observed. Next the researcher analyzes the descriptions based on reflections and "the interpretations offered by those native to the culture" on the descriptions. The researcher produces an analysis that considers phenomena on three levels: the actual behavior; natives' interpretation of the behavior; and the researcher's interpretation, with an expectation that there will be gaps between the three levels.[10] I will do exactly this over the course of this chapter, and the next two chapters, respectively.

Analysis of the structure and function of dance are the two paths that anthropological research can follow. Structure looks at the form of dance, while function takes the view of dance contextually and analyzes what it contributes to culture. Here the research focuses on the functional aspects of black social dance in commercials, since

> structural studies of dance traditionally have been concerned with producing "grammars" of dance styles. Functional studies, on the other hand, have concerned themselves with determining the contribution of dance to the continued well-being of a society or culture.[11]

Functional anthropological study is concerned with both the individual and the society, integrating these hierarchically. All aspects of a society contribute to its function or culture. An emphasis is placed on categorizing dance in terms of function — such as dance as a reflection and validation of social organization (i.e., black social dance versus ballroom dance as done by blacks or whites) — or functionally in terms of the ways in which men and women dance, within each form of dance as secular or religious ritual expression, dance as a social diversion or recreation, but only in their simplest forms so that the majority of the population can do them and enjoy them.[12] In this study, black social dance moves from complex to simple due to the presentation of the dance in commercials.

Other important functions at the level of the individual include dance as it provides a psychological outlet and release. "[D]ance is one of the most effective vehicles for psychological release because its instrument is the human body. Feedback is instantaneous and catharsis immediate for both the dancer and the observer."[13] Moreover, for the individual, dance provides a reflection of aesthetic values and a reflection of economic systems.

ART HISTORICAL VIEW

Schroder (2002) took an art historical approach to his study on photography in how it produces meaning in culture, adapting it to advertisements. In that work he concluded that advertisements were a subset of video and film. Looked at this way, commercials communicate as an engine of the economy and are major players in the political sphere. I add that, as others have already, it produces culture, or reflects it, or both. In addition, art is a part of this system, according to Schroder, and as such, I use this work to substantiate the claim that art is advertising,[14] dance is art, dance is used in advertising and therefore it communicates about the state of the economy, polity, and culture. As an image in advertising,[15] dance makes possible the articulation of historical cultural meanings and social directions that are often politically incorrect and impossible to state verbally. I claim that advertisements are anthropologic representations of our selves; much like the writing on the walls of historical societies, our commercials serve the same purpose. In other words, they are cultural artifacts.[16] And moreover, this approach "illuminates advertising representations infused with visual, historical, and rhetorical presence and power."[17]

Following Barthes' (1964) research methodology regarding semiotics, television commercials over the 1950-to-2010 period were studied, looking for black social dance within them and comparatively searching for change over time. For the 1990–2010 timeframe, commercials were mainly accessed through websites such as Adcritic.com or YouTube.com. I am very familiar

3. A History of Black Social Dance in Commercials   81

with the system of black social dance as an insider. As such, the commercials and my knowledge constituted what Barthes called the corpus. And, I only looked at commercials; that is, I did not search for commercials shown on tapes with particular television programming. I did take into account the racial and social history of the use of blacks in advertising over the years under study, as was discussed in an earlier chapter. However, diachronically, neither the systems of black social dance, nor television advertising, *per se*, have changed.

That said, the study is grouped synchronically, recognizing there has been change in what is projected through advertising with broadened demographic targeting and cultural change over the years. As such, I looked at ads for Pepsi and other consumer goods that were available via archives during a particular time frame that included dance. However, I also focused on the Pepsi brand as a definitive leader in staging cultural change in America through dance in television ads over the study period. Therefore, while this chapter does give a review of brands using dance in their television advertisements since the 1950s, Pepsi receives historical discussion as well to frame the respondents' interviews given in the next chapter.

It is, of course, impossible to consider every television ad that was created during the study period in the United States, but what I attempted to do was to look through each decade and see what television commercials depicted with respect to dance, and then in particular black social dance. At the same time, because I want to argue that dance in television ads is a reflection of culture, during the decades I sought to understand what dance television shows were popular and what dance movies were popular as well. As I will discuss in the next chapter, dance may appear in television ads to the extent that it appears in the larger culture. This point will be returned to in a subsequent chapter when I discuss cultural intermediaries. At least that was true before the 1990s; after that it has changed, as I argue that people look to commercials for their dance intake.

In the following sections, I present television commercials that used dance in them by decade. At the same time, I attempt to situate the commercials within the time period to show what was going on in the immediate cultural venues, such as movies, television shows, and theater dance. The goal of this section is to connect the ways in which dance was used in branding and product advertising, and to demonstrate the absence, the appearance, the rise of and the eventual sustained emergence of non-blacks doing representations of black social dance. I would like to include here one or two caveats. First, I do not try to analyze choreographic intent; I assume it is purely for the purpose of connecting dance with a brand, drawing on the aesthetic associated with dance. While this is true, I also do not comment on the camera work or the editing of the commercials, or whether the dance was imposed into the commercial by black or non-black creatives. My interest is only in the anthropological representation of dance as an aesthetic within the commercial and how it is connected historically to the linkages of dancing.

The 1940s

In a UCLA archival commercial collection, one from the 1940s included several television advertisements. Interestingly, they were very different from what we are used to by today's short 30-second standard spots. Good examples were the Pepsi Cola Cops advertisements. These were based on a comic strip, turned into a series of animated black and white films. One such film told the story of policemen coming to the rescue of a woman in distress and drinking Pepsi to quench their thirst once their mission was completed and the woman had been returned to safety. It was a mini-cartoon, lasting nearly three minutes. In another series of commercials from this time period, Alka Seltzer used a white woman dancer who performed classical ballet moves, such as *glissades* and *chinnée* turns, wearing a chiffon cocktail dress with matching dancing shoes. It was only 15 seconds, however.[18] Alka Seltzer produced two other ads, one showing the mid-sections of a ballerina in a tutu and the bare belly of a grass-skirted hula dancer, such that when the ballerina and the hula dancer turned or shook to signal stomach upset, if one took a packet of Alka Seltzer, it promised to calm the rumbles in the stomach that were arbitrarily connected with dancing. The other ad was an animated one, where the audience snooped on a man who somehow got "the blahs." The ad attempted to make the viewer connect the dots between the blahs and the onset of a cold or flu. However, once the man took the Alka Seltzer, the ad portrayed him dancing, doing *entrechacots* and fast dance footwork, along with a back flip. Dance was connected with the message that you could not be blah or sick if you dance, and one could dance after one's cured inexplicable blahs that preceded a cold or flu were managed.[19]

In a rare find that I came across in a commercial search online from this time period was a Jax Beer commercial. It included six African Americans and no Caucasians in a living room scene, with a piano and two side chairs and lamps as props. One of the men played the piano, and while the others swayed back and forth, dancing behind him, or sat in the chairs snapping their fingers and seat dancing. The women wore dresses with bodices and attached, wide ruffled skirts. The men wore dark suits, white dress shirts, and ties. The women sang a jingle about Jax Beer, and the other two men sat without speaking in the living room chairs, snapping their fingers.[20] It would seem that here African Americans were completely assimilated and happily accepted by whites into the American culture, wearing the clothing, owning the home, with the women having their hair straightened and the men dressed up in suits. Dancing was subdued and in fact the body movement was reminiscent of what may be acceptable in places where one was not supposed to be dancing. It was an advertisement that could evoke a surprise in that the six individuals' movements may have been considered inappropriate for them at the time. In other words, aside from the finger popping, they were hardly moving at all.

During this decade, the country came to the end of the worst economic depression it had ever seen, and it played its part in World War II. This is also the time period when black dance in theatrical productions were in the forefront. Many artists such as Katherine Dunham, Pearl Primus, and Wilson Williams staged and performed black dance in the United States and abroad. These three individuals in particular were also responsible for developing and leading dance companies, whose performances gained the attention of John Martin, an important Caucasian dance critic and cultural intermediary of the time.[21]

Though only a few commercials were accessible from this period for this research, that notwithstanding, it has been documented in this section that advertisers were using dance in television ads as early as the 1940s. And even as it was perhaps unusual, black people appeared in television ads with elements of black social dance which included body swaying and snapping fingers. The ads presented by Pepsi and Alka Seltzer were most likely presented for the general non-black population while the Jax Beer commercial was probably screened for blacks.

The 1950s

It is clear from extant marketing literature[22] that many ads from the 1950s represent a production-era approach to the consumer, and so ads typically pushed the benefits and features of products, like cars, appliances, and soaps, in support of postmodernity. However, Pepsi after a certain point in time never touted their benefits but rather early on *aimed for creating identity*. This is a theme that will be discussed in detail later on, as Pepsi is one of the products that is used in analyzing consumers' responses to black social dance, and Pepsi's commercial history over the time period. For now, though, it should be noted that a PepsiCo ad circa 1957 was done in black and white, with three men and one woman; all were Caucasian. The dancing was choreographed as if in a musical with "Be sociable, look smart, keep up to date, stay young and fair and debonair" as the jingle/tag line. These were "the Sociables,"[23] representing the industrialization craze the country was in. PepsiCo had another ad with Polly Bergen, emphasizing girls have to be thin to pick up men. "Pepsi cola is the light refreshment," and women's figures were held out as an important aspect of attracting a man. Clearly this ad was aired before the women's rights movement gained momentum; however, the relevant point is that the focus was on the body.

Dupont, the chemical company, circa 1958, aired a commercial valorizing and underwriting the American Dream, and how Dupont supplied chemical solutions emphasizing postmodernity and production. Women in these commercials were used to bring importance to fashion and beauty, and were all white. In other examples, there was a Viv Lipstick commercial with a man dancing, à la Fred Astaire, around a woman who did not dance. He twirled around her and she maintained that she nor her lipstick was moved by him. During this period, a Muriel Cigars commercial was done in black and white, and used soft shoe vaudeville with Caucasian men and women to press the enjoyment of smoking cigars.[24] Silvercup Bread circa 1955 used some dancing with a Caucasian boy in a cartoon commercial.[25]

A compilation entitled *Classic TV Commercials, Brooklyn College*, held in the UCLA media archive, showed an ad for Chevy automobiles circa 1959. It was a commercial with a Caucasian man and woman dancing, as if in a musical, in black and white, with a few simple side-to-side steps, nothing elaborate. The voice over in the ad explained the benefits and features of the car. Here is an example of a television ad for a high-involvement product using dance in it. Again, Alka Seltzer circa 1959 used a Caucasian woman who was under the pressure of a headache, dancing in a chiffon dress. Now she's alone, doing *bourrées, piqués,* and *chainnés,* the dance leading to a sparkle in her eyes, happy that her headache was gone from taking the product. In another commercial on this tape, Toni Trio Permanent circa 1959, used three Caucasian women dancing briefly, peeling off a staircased stage as if in a musical and singing. White Rain shampoo used a Caucasian woman dancing with an umbrella, also as in a musical. Tonette permanents for little girls used girl ballerinas on a human-sized music box, with toe shoes doing *passees*, and little ballet walks.[26] What can be seen from these commercials was the cultural emphasis on ballet during this period of time. As has been documented, at this point in America's history there was an increase in ballet companies and an expansion of teaching ballet technique.[27]

In a black and white Pepsi commercial circa 1950 with a tagline "more bounce to the ounce," Caucasian people were shown situated on merry-go-rounds having a good time. No doubt, this was a part of The Sociables" campaign.[28] From the merry-go-round, the commercial moved the viewer to perceive partnered social dancing at what appeared to be a formal dance scene, staged with a piano (auto playing). The humor of the commercial included men repeatedly cutting in on each other to dance with the only woman at the dance. All the men were dressed in black and white classic suits, all of them were young people, dancing around or near round tables with chairs in bistro style. Flowers decorated the tables as centerpieces. The voice-over said, "Come on, let's have some fun, let's join the Pepsi crowd"; and "Go get Pepsi for more bounce to the ounce" was the song jingle. Here Pepsi positioned dance as about popularity and fun.[29]

Old Gold Cigarettes, in 1952, advertised using "dancing boxes" resting on top of what appeared to be three Caucasian women's bare legs, whose feet were covered with calf-high cowboy boots. The boxes performed a tap dance.[30] This is an example of black dance performed by non-black women, that additionally once was categorized as a black man's dance, according to Emery (1988). Lucky Strike cigarettes used an anthropomorphic square dance as part of an advertisement. The scene was complete with the call-and-response formation of square dance, cowboy hats, and clothes, but used animated cigarettes that the consumer was to understand as people.

Not only was dance was growing in popularity in the 1950s, as noted through the social fabric, but also with the appearance of televised dance programs. Those representing the times included *The Milt Grant Show*, *The Art Laboe Show*, *Party Time*,[31] and *The Beech-Nut Show*.[32] These shows were usually sponsored by advertisements. For example, on *The Milt Grant Show*, he promoted Pepsi during the program, acting as a spokesperson.[33] *American Bandstand* came on the air during this period of time as well. But more importantly, African American performers sang and danced on these shows, which led to a spread of black social dance into living rooms across America. Broadcasted projections of dance were supported by Hollywood films, such as *Rock Around the Clock*, *Don't Knock the Rock*, and *Rock, Rock, Rock*.[34]

In addition, the decade recorded many "firsts" for African Americans. For example, African American films included *A Raisin in the Sun*, *Nothing but a Man*, and *Carmen Jones*.[35] Arthur Mitchell joined *The New York City Ballet* as the first African American male dancer and principle, while *Alvin Ailey American Dance Theater* was launched. To its credit, black people dancing had been center stage during the federal theater and dance projects, and perhaps this helped pave the way for the development of these important shifts for African Americans. On television, *The Nat King Cole Show* aired but was not able to sustain itself due to low sponsorships. Sponsors were afraid that white consumers would shun their products if they knew they were supporting the show.[36] In addition, *Beulah* had its place within the newly expanding frame of television, with an African American woman cast in the situation comedy. The list of great accomplishments goes on to include Marion Anderson's operatic singing, Gwendolyn Brooks' earning a Pulitzer Prize, and Althea Gibson's winning an Olympic gold medal.[37] As promising as these representations of change were, they did not seem to be included in the archived commercials. In addition, the commercials did not appear to impact in any visible way how blacks were shown in American culture. In fact, if one did not know about the history of racism in America, one would think all was well across the country. Unfortunately, because of that history, and, one may argue, as a result of advertising,[38] much of this positive change for African Americans was railed against in the ensuing decade.

The 1960s

The decade saw the ushering in of the Civil Rights Act in 1964, and Affirmative Action in the United States by the Kennedy and Johnson administrations in regard to African Americans and this was amended and broadened to cover a variety of other discriminatory practices. Many people were encouraged by the Executive Order to introduce affirmative action policies and what would come to fruition from it.[39]

Arthur Mitchell did not stop at his newly found success but went on to form *Dance Theater of Harlem*. Chubby Checker's *The Twist* was introduced in the 1960s. However, watching the ads of the decade revealed the apparent direction for Caucasian women's liberation. Ads with the ideology of freedom supported by desegregation and affirmative action policies did not appear until the 1970s.

In any event, it was a controversial and emotional decade complete with political and social unrest. For every step forward towards mitigation of racial divides, there seemed to be two steps backwards. In response to the passage of the Civil Rights Act, many were at the ready to overturn or challenge new initiatives. The Watts Riots occurred in 1965 in response to challenges to the act in California.[40] During the decade of the 1960s, however, I want to point out that there was a decrease in television programs that were derogatory or stereotypically negative towards African Americans, as, for example, *Amos and Andy* no longer aired.

It was a decade of despair and destruction, with the killings of Martin Luther King, Jr., and Malcolm X, along with an economic and emotional drain from the Vietnam war. Muhammad Ali emerged from his given identity of Cassius Clay, and *Hair* debuted on Broadway. At the same time it was the decade for instituting the National Endowment for the Arts and Humanities, and dance was an integral part of that effort.[41] Issues of race and violence in America were projected onto the Hollywood screen in this decade and continued in to the next. *In the Heat of the Night* was one of these, and was nominated for a Grammy Award.[42] Looking at the mainstream archived television ads, it would appear that there were still no African Americans in the United

States, and that there was complete bliss between the races if they existed; or worse that there were only Caucasian people living in America.[43]

During the 1960s, television commercials with dance in them were seen, with advertisers of Pepsi, Gillette Razors, the Lark Automobile, Contac, and Dial Soap. Apparently, along with the social unrest, the 1960s saw the emergence of baby boomers and their impact on the market. Pepsi claims it acknowledged this changing demographic and therefore positioned Pepsi as the brand belonging to the "new generation." Therefore, their ads referred to "the Pepsi Generation," and promised that one should "Come Alive! You're in the Pepsi Generation." Here we see evidence of advertisers moving away from discussing attributes as they switched into defining identity of Caucasian consumers' lifestyles and attitudes.

For Pepsi, there were several commercials with a theme where the ads emphasized outdoor fun and pleasure. In one Pepsi commercial, the dance was included in a fleeting shot of a Caucasian woman dancing in a ballet studio, mixed in with other scenes of outdoor activities encompassing Caucasian children, men and women. In a different commercial reliving a Jewish wedding, a man was coming off a boat to join his family and doing a dance in a circle to "catch that Pepsi spirit." In another ad, Caucasian children in a junior high school partnered dance proved that "Pepsi's got your taste for life." A Pepsi dance ad with Caucasian people dancing on the beach for the diet and regular soda promised now you must "come alive. You're in the Pepsi generation."[44] In other ads they showed people playing football on the beach using the tagline "taste that beats the others cold! Pepsi pours it on." In similar fashion, Pepsi is included in ads depicting men and women at a lake swinging with choreographed form off a suspended ring/rope and diving into a lake with somersaults and back flips. Clearly the so-called healthy and athletic body became the focus of the ads as people identified themselves as the Pepsi Generation. At this point in time, according to the data, there were no black people in these Pepsi ads, nor any others.

Pepsi introduced Diet Pepsi as a separate brand in 1964 and began focusing commercial advertising on that product as well. The first Diet Pepsi campaign was "Girlwatchers," and the ads emphasized how great a woman's body looked as a result of consuming fewer calories. However, by 1969, the campaign "You've Got a Lot to Live. Pepsi's Got a Lot to Give," was in line with a shift in the Pepsi Generation advertising strategy. The change was a direct result of working within the tumultuous times and the emotionally divisive aspects of the ways in which America was being pulled. As Pepsi has written on its website recently, its campaign was "a new awareness and a reflection of contemporary events and mood become integral parts of the advertising's texture."

Pepsi was not the only producer using dance in television ads.

In a Gillette commercial, tap dance was used in a vaudeville theme, with a Caucasian man and woman. Tap dance itself has come to be known as a conglomerate of dance styles but in the 1960s it was still associated with a black man's body, which was instilled in the collective American consciousness in the 1920s and 1930s.[45] The commercial in the 1960s, though, focused on the notion of giving the man a baby face after shaving if he used that particular brand of razor, and how happy that would make the woman.[46]

The 1962 Lark advertised its car with two Caucasian couples dancing a version of the Jitterbug mixing in the Twist.[47] Dial Soap touted its benefits by explaining how the Caucasian people on the dance floor dressed in after-five clothing could be worry free from perspiration. Apparently it was good to dance but not to sweat. And, Contac sinus used tap-dancing Caucasian women all dressed in white shorts-tuxedos, who danced in geometric formation on a clock to indicate the 12-hour relief available from the drug. The dance formation was reminiscent of the Rockettes, and while the women were all dressed in white, commercial was in color.[48]

The 1970s

Among stagflation and the oil crisis and the end of the Viet Nam War, and with feminism taking the center stage from black civil rights, remarkably some African American presence took hold in the movies. The movie *Shaft* was distributed in 1971, and other notable films such as *Super Fly*, *Cotton Comes to Harlem*, and *Farewell, Uncle Tom* were screened in movie theaters across America, mainly for African American consumption. Most movies, however, depicted negative and longstanding stereotypical portrayals of African Americans. On television, programs such as *All in the Family*, *Good Times*, and *Sanford and Son* aired and competed with *The Brady Bunch*, *The Mary Tyler Moore Show*, and *The Partridge Family*. *Soul Train*, a syndicated African American dance program, began broadcasting in 1971. In addition, *The Wiz*, a remake of the *Wizard of Oz* with an all-black cast, including Michael Jackson and his dancing, aired on television. In this decade, we began to see sprinklings of African Americans in commercials, but not many, and a few that contain only African Americans.

As for Pepsi Generation advertising, a new tagline emerged in 1973 which was "Join the Pepsi People, Feelin' Free." Its intent was to capture the mood of the country as people were involved in social and political upheaval. It envisioned and implied a "one-people" myth and stayed far away from staging any controversial themes. During the progress of the decade, Pepsi kept stride with cultural changes. In 1976, the campaign suggested that people should have a "Pepsi Day" with commercials that were supposedly upbeat, and by

1979 Americans were ready to "Catch that Pepsi Spirit," as a result of the changes that had taken place over the last 15 years. The 1976 bicentennial was also a major focal point helping to engage the image of freedom for all Americans.

In line with the ways in which the company engaged, capitalized on, and invoked culture, in circa 1974, Pepsi created a commercial called "Samantha," which contained only black actors, showing a girl whose nickname was "Sam" succeeding at softball as a girl. She is encouraged and supported by her father to press forward and pursue her dream to be a great softball player. As the sports scenes and the shots of Sam and her father play out on the screen, the viewer is exposed to music in the background, which was black gospel in nature. In another Pepsi commercial, again containing only black actors, a couple is shown bringing a new baby to a family cookout in what seems to be a large, upscale, well-furnished country house, to tunes that include black voices singing "have a Pepsi Day," circa 1974. Another commercial with all black actors showed a black boy receiving a scholarship based on his grades, emphasizing that the scholarship was not an athletic one. Here the viewer is shown some black social dancing mixed in with basketball playing to "Catch that Pepsi spirit, drink it in." Then, in another commercial, a black man was promoted to editor of a city newspaper; this ad contained whites as well as blacks, and all were celebrating his success since "Pepsi's got your taste for life." The "first love" commercial showed young people at a dance for preadolescent boys and girls again with "Pepsi's got your taste for life." [49] At the same time, Pepsi claimed to men "it's a thirsty world," with both white and black men as well as boys running, building buildings, and doing gymnastics and pushups. The men are told "you've got a lot to live and Pepsi's got a lot to give."[50] The point here is that Pepsi's ads in the 1970s were supportive of blacks and worked over the decade to include commercials that worked against stereotypical representations, creating messages of success and support within the black family. The company also characterized the achievements of blacks as normal in their depictions, and then worked to present an integrated face to the nation. Dance was included in these commercials, and so was black social dance. Pepsi contended that blacks and whites now had "a whole new way of living; if you're living, you belong; you've got a lot to live and Pepsi's got a lot to give." Proving this, the ads gave slices of life with blacks and whites, old and young men and women. Or, the Pepsi ad alternatively claimed the theme, "It's the Pepsi generation," showing outdoor activities, including dance, with blacks, whites, and children from both races, two young African American girls eating popcorn,[51] and concluded the commercial with "you've got a lot to live."[52]

Not only Pepsi worked this decade to people's advantage and used dance in their commercials. A collection of various advertisements presented an RC Cola ad, circa 1971, which opened with people doing ballroom dance, in black and white, with a black woman in the commercial but not dancing. Kool-Aid used a Caucasian woman dancer, showing only her torso, as she executed ballet moves with long unpinned hair.[53] Differently, Dr Pepper utilized black social dance in a dance club scene with whites.[54] Meanwhile, the brand also used tap dancing in a different ad, while still in another, one white woman and one black dance around Lee Travino doing ballet. Many Dr Pepper ads used choreographed stage dancing in scenes with all white dancers reminiscent of musicals, ranging from city streets to picnic settings.[55] The tagline was "Wouldn't you like to be a Pepper, too?"[56]

As mentioned in connection with the growth of dance in the 1960s, ballet had taken its hold in America and therefore *Time* magazine had a commercial about its telling of the whole story of the evolution of American ballet. In the ad we see a man in a ballet costume doing a *cabriolet*, with a voice-over informing the viewer that "it only took a leap to lift American Ballet to glory."[57] This dance form was underwritten for the population by the National Endowment for the Arts, and wealthy patrons who wished to hold classical ballet out as the exemplar of cultural refinement.[58] At the same time, Seiko watches linked the dance with time, earth, cosmos and the relation to humanity to time. Proving they could escape it by having such a watch, Caucasian couples waltzed in the starlight, dressed in evening clothes. Chemical Bank gave the viewers a *pas de deux* of classical ballet in a bank lobby, while wealthy people stood by reading the "chemistry" for each market.[59] Though it has not shown itself in commercials from this era, hip-hop dance as a black social dance form was growing in its capacity to comment on changing social, economic, and political structures that were affecting many neighborhoods in the United States.[60]

The 1980s

First Chicago Bank followed Chemical Bank's lead, with little Caucasian girls, but only in waist-up shots, doing *port de bras* ballet movements, which made the upper body move in that characteristic way that feet doing *bourrées* make it move, but camera did not show the foot movement to the viewer. From the data available, it seems that the use of dance picked up in this decade, especially black social dance with the advent of commercials employing Michael Jackson, Lionel Richie, Tina Turner, and other black entertainers and of course the California Raisins. This will be covered in a moment.

Sugar-free Dr Pepper, with all Caucasian men and women, staged an ad with a country farm square dance. It was complete with cowboy-cowgirl cos-

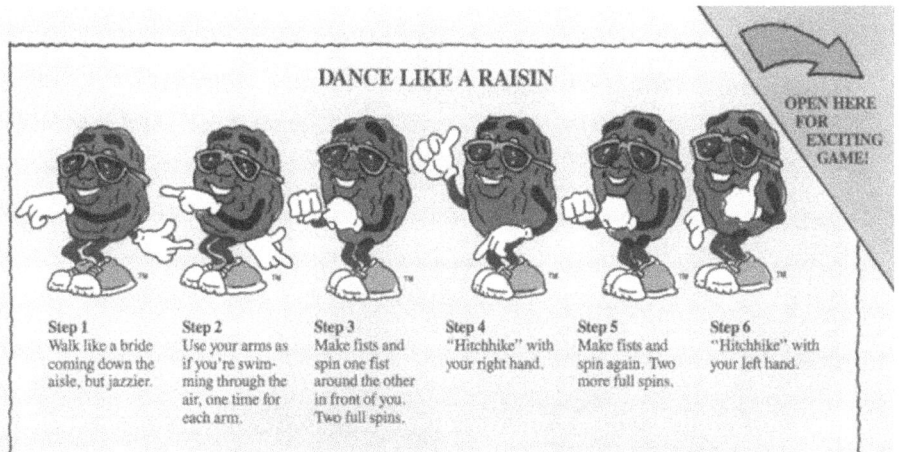

California Raisins. Courtesy California Raisins Marketing Board.

tuming—that is, men in cowboy hats and jeans, women in skirts and petticoats. One man got up on a bail of hay and did the hambone. Arwa Pantihose had an ad with a Caucasian woman doing splits and a little social dance, dressed in leotards, stockings, and a wraparound long skirt.[61] Fresca circa 1982 used two people waltzing, along with beach scenes and barbeques. Pepsi ads were prevalent with sports.[62] EF Hutton used a full *corps de ballet* dressed as *Swan Lake* on stage who moved off stage and "listen[ed] when EF Hutton says...." Again, this is an example of a high-involvement product placed with a dance commercial. The people are all Caucasian with the exception of one African American man in the background. Oscar Meyer wieners used little Caucasian ballerinas dancing happily for their brand.[63] A Hallmark greeting card dance ad connected ballet with a scholarship for a girl. In the commercial, she is taught by a male ballet master. The bigger scene includes professional women dancers only, in a school with a New York address. The studio is furnished with piano and mirrors, giving the viewer full access to the ballet world in New York. Meanwhile, a *Time* magazine dance ad used a man doing a *cabriole* but dressed as a gymnast as one scene showing slices of life.[64] It is interesting to note that ballet has been used with commercials pushing high-involvement products.

The small, spotty portrayals of African Americans continued with an increase in about 1982. Pepsi was a leader in this, such as in their ad showing an African American man teaching soccer to Caucasian boys.[65] But Pepsi also did a diverse ad with African Americans, Caucasians, men, women, youth, Asians and Africans. They said "Look, whose drinking Pepsi now ... the world is turning Pepsi ... a world of Pepsi people," in 145 countries. The ad included shots of fun had on beaches, with dance and elephants, with ethnic dancing in streets and in clubs, with brown-skinned men dressed in African garments doing cultural moves in Africa showing the pyramids, and other men doing moves like karate but their faces are not shown to the camera.[66] While Orangina had a dance ad with break dancing, at this point Michael Jackson danced a rendition of Billie Jean for the Diet Pepsi dance ad "You're the Pepsi Generation."[67] According to Pepsi, by 1984 a new generation emerged in the United States and around the world. "Pepsi, the Choice of a New Generation" pushed the change, and the most popular entertainer of the time, Michael Jackson, starred in the first two commercials of the new campaign. The two spots quickly become deemed "the most eagerly anticipated advertising of all time."[68]

It seems that, at this point, black social dance heated up in television ads, with 7-Up, L'eggs Pantihose, Canon Camera, Diet Rite Soda, and Pepsi "Goin' over the top."[69] Contac, Coke, and Coor's all followed suit.[70] Diet Coke used the Rockettes and stage dancing and Pepsi once again used Michael Jackson's music video to *Thriller*, transferring the dance and the words to the commercial.[71] They did the same kind of thing with concerts for Lionel Richie's "Running with the Night," "Pepsi feels so right," with multi-racial dancers,[72] and Tina Turner.[73]

Kodak produced an ad with a Caucasian woman with a boom box doing a solo jazz dance in a dance studio to Steve Wonder's "You Can Depend on Me." Kool Cigarettes staged a scene on a two-story airplane, and used a Caucasian man playing a saxophone, with another Caucasian man playing a trumpet. The scene cut to an African American woman smiling with approval at them as they passed down the aisle "enjoying the music." A Caucasian woman whose hair looked as if it had been crimped to mimic black hair, sang in a soulful rhythm and blues style, bellowing loudly. The Caucasian men and woman danced around the plane doing black social dance. Another ad for Body and Soul Beer had Caucasians dancing at a wedding with rhythm and blues music and what sounded like African American voice-overs accompanied by African drums.[74] Burger King used all African American people, children, teens, etc., break dancing. Hanes Pantyhose did an ad with all African American women and Donna Summer singing, all dressed in costume dresses, silver and long; "You got what you asked for" was the tagline for pantyhose for African American women.[75] Kentucky Fried Chicken also had a commercial with an African American woman and man dancing and singing with six other Caucasians, three men and three women.[76]

In 1986 we were introduced to the California Raisins. There were two different commercials from Foote Cone and Belding, San Francisco, and both won the Ad Age Award that year. One commercial was with two Caucasian people, a man and a woman watching TV with a commercial projected into their living room showing the dancing raisins, and the other was one with two Caucasian men at lunch at a construction site. The raisins provided them with dance entertainment.[77]

The 1980s was the decade of the advent of music video and Pepsi used Robert Palmer in a commercial using "This Kind of Love" sung as "Simply Irresistible" for the commercial, with all Caucasian women behind him dancing choreographed backup.[78] But a major turning point was when Pepsi did a commercial with all elderly Caucasian folks saying, "Rock and roll is okay but I prefer rap, and can you dance?" all the while drinking Pepsi and dancing to "Busta Move." The commercial lets the viewer know that the elderly segment was supposed to get Coke delivered for their picnic, but it inadvertently was delivered to a fraternity house. "They got the Pepsi, not the Coke." The Coke went to the Caucasian men at their fraternity house, showing them sitting around listening to elevator music and playing bingo. This was another Ad Age Best.[79]

Pepsi also signed with Madonna to use the "Make a Wish" commercial done to her "Like a Prayer" music video and song, with African American children in her home video of herself when she was a child. Many of the scenes in the "Like a Prayer" dance video, such as in the black church and with Madonna dancing with the choir, along with the commercial shots of her dancing as an adult and a child with African American people, show up in her commercial. In her music video, the audience sees an African American Jesus, and she kisses an African American man on the lips. Her choreographed dance scenes with other dancers behind her looked like Michael Jackson's commercials with Billie Jean, and the young and old Michael. Not insignificantly, the music video proved too controversial and therefore her $5 million contract with Pepsi for the commercial was pulled.[80] Not long after this, Coke did dance ads with Paula Abdul and Elton John.[81]

Out in the movie world, Spike Lee's *Do the Right Thing* was playing to audiences across the country. Blockbuster movies such as *ET, Star Wars, Beverly Hills Cop*, and Harrison Ford's various movies about Indiana Jones were also screened in this decade. *What's Happening, The Cosby Show* and *A Different World* began airing during the 1980s. While *What's Happening* still portrayed African Americans in a certain light, with the character Re-Run likely to dance at any given time, both of the other two programs gave a completely un-stereotypical view of African Americans. However, *The Cosby Show* always opened with scenes of the family doing different kinds of dance. Cosby himself usually did strange movements that were not representative of black social dance, while the other family members did. The television series *Fame*, based on the movie released early in 1980, also aired and in that show, of course, dance was a major theme.

Also in the late 1980s, the movie *Dirty Dancing* was a huge success. In that movie, mostly white couples, who are clearly socio-economically lower class as compared with the other characters in the movie, with a few black individuals, are shown doing "dirty dancing" to African American rhythms. While on the cultured stage, the two stars of the movie do a more formal dance. However, at the end of that scene, the whole crowd of upper class whites dressed in formal after-five clothing are shown to be doing their own form of dirty dancing to the degree that it is possible for them to let go of their hang-ups. In short, this decade staged and screened black social dance on many venues, and set the tone for moving the dance away from African Americans and onto non-blacks.

This decade marked what I would characterize as the pinnacle of portrayals of black social dance done by black people in television commercials, launched in tandem with MTV's appearance on the popular culture scene. The decade witnessed Ronald Regan's administration engaged in streamlining national funding for the arts, and Reganomics leading to a tremendous volume of production being off-shored to Asian countries. AIDS as a pandemic was drawing considerable attention, while affirmative action and civil rights policies had gone a long way to improve lifestyles of black people, as well as those of other groups suffering discrimination.

The 1990s

Pepsi's use of black social dance continued into the 1990s. Their MC Hammer commercial showed the dancer's Pepsi being secretly replaced with Coke, by nothing but the drop-in shot of a Caucasian hand conducting the switch. Mr. Hammer unknowingly drank the Coke, and as a result he started singing "Feelings" and sounding not like himself, but more like Barry Manilow. An African American young man, who apparently knew about the switch, secretly puts Mr. Hammer's Pepsi back, and the performer takes a sip and he immediately returns to dancing Hammer style. There are only African American people in this commercial staging an MC Hammer concert, except for the Caucasian voice-over saying they replaced his Pepsi with Coke, and the Caucasian hand that dropped into the shot from above and poured soda into the glass.[82]

But Pepsi soon had company in the use of black social dance, and the decade begins to show animated non-black humans and animals such as dogs and cats executing forms of dance, as for example when a group of disco-dancing bears dance to the beat of the Village People. Other companies — for example, Dreyer's Ice Cream — used black social dance with an animated

Caucasian baby, who moon-walked à la Michael Jackson and did James Brown–reminiscent turns and splits.[83]

YouTube's search on the commercials with the criteria of "commercials 1990 dance" returned more commercials than any other decade from the 1950s to the 1980s. That could be due to the way in which the growth of the internet allowed for this. However, it was more likely due to the growth of black social dance used in branding. Some exemplar brands include, in addition to Pepsi and Coke,[84] Duracell Batteries,[85] McDonalds,[86] AIDS dance4life.org,[87] Barbie,[88] Reebok with Paula Abdul,[89] and Sega Genesis with Michael Jackson.[90]

In this time period, changes in the social and cultural landscape were happening rapidly, deeply, and, in some instances, silently. As mentioned already, the Rodney King trial and the resulting riots, and the O.J. Simpson verdict were significant cultural markers and sent tremendous and significant commentary from one racial group to the other. At the same time in America, the Oklahoma City and the World Trade Center bombings took place, and the Columbine High School murders were major headlines under William Clinton's presidential leadership. Paralleling these events, Clarence Thomas was confirmed to the Supreme Court after Anita Hill spoke out against him. Here the country witnessed a black woman speaking out against a black man's sexuality not in a Hollywood film, mind you, but covered by broadcast televised media perhaps for the first time in history, which served only to be divisive in the end. America was in a giddily prosperous economic expansion by the mid–1990s that put reduction of welfare assistance on the table with a goal of increasing the work force and decreasing the welfare recipient pool. Not insignificantly, backward forces and backlashes were occurring to gains from affirmative action policies.[91]

On the big screen *The Bodyguard*, *Dances with Wolves*, and *The Lion King* were playing. African American films included *Boyz in the Hood* and *Malcolm X*, while *Martin* and *The Fresh Prince of Bel Air* were added to broadcast television, and *Rent* was staged on Broadway in New York City. *The Harlem Nutcracker* was performed at the New York City Ballet.[92]

The 2000s

The decade opened with George W. Bush defeating Al Gore on a recount of votes in the presidential race. That was followed by the tragic September 11, 2001, terrorist attack, destroying the Twin Towers in New York City, and hitting in Washington D.C., and Pennsylvania. Soon after, the United States staged the Iraq War, the Mexican drug war, and the war in Afghanistan, still ongoing at this writing. Many other wars raged around the world in third–

world nations.

China has become the major world exporter of goods, and a commander of currency. This has put the United States in a category it has not experienced since before the close of the World War II theater. The Great Recession occurred in the mid- to late 2000s, causing a long and protracted economic crisis touching on every corner of the globe.[93]

Eminem, a non-black rapper, was noted as the most successful rapper of the decade. And in 2009, Michael Jackson died as he prepared for a world tour. Many electronic media were produced as a result of his death to mourn and memorialize his contributions to humanity through his dancing and singing. On television, reality TV and shows like *So You Think You Can Dance?* and *Dancing with the Stars* aired regularly. Along with the video game *Grand Theft Auto*, *Dance Dance Revolution*, a computer-led exercise program, was released.

In the movies, *Hitch*, in which non-black people did black social dance, *The Original Kings of Comedy*, *Brown Sugar* and many other African American–cast films were produced,[94] satisfying the demand for more from the non-black hip-hop generation.[95] The three digitized *Alvin and the Chipmunks* "got their squeak on" and appeared in two major releases performing African American social dance.[96] In the creation of the *Alvin and the Chipmunks* movie, black people danced to choreographed scores and those performances were taped and processed so that they could be placed onto the animated chipmunks.

Additional brands, aside from and with the continued use by those already discussed, using dance in television advertising in this decade include, but are not limited to, those brands described in Table 2.[97]

There were also the Kibbles and Bits brand,[98] Bridgestone Tires,[99] MasterCard,[100] and T Mobile[101] that used black social dance in their commercials. What has occurred in this decade points to the widespread use of black social dance in advertising by and large with non-blacks doing more of the dancing. In 2010, Kia Soul has an integrated branding campaign with dancing hamsters doing black social dance.[102] The Kia Soul ad epitomizes integrated marketing communication and appeared on television, online, and on the company's website. This ad took the populist world[103] of the inner-city black neighborhood and removed both black and non-black bodies, and replaced them with caricatures of black men driving around in the neighborhood. Only now, the ad included the infused manufactured message of black athletes, bling, dance, rap music, and hip-hop culture.

In this expansion of black social dance with its linkage to brands, it was no longer limited to low-involvement products, such as soft drinks, food, and other beverages on a regular basis. High-involvement products including com-

Table 2. Examples of Commercials in the 2000s Using Dance

TV Commercial Product/Service	Summary of Commercial
Sierra Mist	Man wants a Sierra Mist soda and the clerk asks him to dance for it. After performing a movement the clerk informs him that there is none.
Volkswagen	Scenes from a dance club and driving acumen with the idea that it is safe to dance because Volkswagen cars are safe.
Volkswagen Jetta	A black man asks a white man to show him some dance moves because "all Jetta owners can dance."
Skechers	A man dances on a platform in what appears to be a gaming arcade with the caption of "finding your groove."
Pillsbury	Consumers log onto the site and design their own set of social dance moves, can learn to dance and can send an email to friends with the dances.
Dell	DJ Ditty does hip-hop dance and choreography.
Budweiser	Cedric the Entertainer is the designated driver.
Florida Department of Health	Dancing in an environment with cigarette smoke is a bad idea.
Cingular Wireless	Taxi cabs "dance" in choreographic formation.
Cingular Wireless	Football players are being taught ballet in a ballet studio, learning the joy of self expression.
Levi's	Stuffed animal rides alongside a male driver and "expresses" himself in the car.
CNet.com Technology	Two men on a rotating platform dance to the connectivity received from CNet.
Fox Television	Clay models of black sports announcers dance an end zone dance.
Tampax Tampons	Young girl dances on the tables at school cafeteria expressing happiness with her period.
Jet Blue	Testimony of customer that says Jet Blue made a bad situation good by having dancing in the airport terminal.
Hilton Hotels	Travel should be exhilarating; animated couple dancing.
Bell South Yellow Pages	Plumbers dance as if they were in a competition.
Nextel Communications	Men dance in an office showing the ease of work when using Nextel.
Docker's	African Americans in a dance club.
Apple	Animated person dances with the iPod.
Diet Pepsi	Diet Pepsi can dances while becoming a rap star.

(SOURCE: www.adcritic.com August 30, 2007)

puters, cars, cellular telephones, hospitals, and tires were now on board with dance. More importantly, the dance and culture as projected in television and media shifted almost completely onto non-blacks or "characters" of one type or another. Hip-hop cultural aesthetics by this point in time had become its own genre, complete with Wikipedia entries and pages, and an area of academic study, including theoretical notions of why it was attractive to non-black cultures. Popular books and magazines on the topic exploded, taking the once-black phenomenon into mainstream white culture in the United States.

Yet, black social dance continues to be a cultural manifestation for black people and perhaps something that "everybody knows" that black people do and it is expected. For example, on *The Ellen Show*, soon to be first African American president of the United States Barack Obama danced with Ellen DeGeneres,[104] and so did his wife, Michelle Obama.[105] The media coverage of Mr. Obama's dancing covered not only his as compared to George W. Bush's on the Jay Leno show, but the metaphors about dance and foreign and domestic politics flew across headlines like greased lightning.[106]

THE PEPSI BRAND[107]

Pepsi is a brand that creates and defines its own market segments, and they do not fit neatly into the categories developed by marketers based on geodemographics or lifestyle. Actually Pepsi creates segments such as the Pepsi Generation. Beginning with the heavy use of television advertising in the early 1960s, Pepsi became a product that reflected the cultural shifts and upheavals that defined directions for the next 50 years. Capitalizing on social unrest, Pepsi encouraged people to move away from the central thinking that dominated racism and sexism, both of which exercised hegemonic control. However, like all binary structures, Pepsi had to be defined in relation to Coca Cola, a company that dominated for decades before Pepsi came on the market. Still, the fact is that both products are basically the same, both originating as medicines and evolving into soft drinks, and it is the branding and product marketing that differentiate them, and deliver each company loyal customers.

Being a serious rival to Coca Cola since the 1930s, Pepsi's aggressive strategies in the 1960s were decidedly consumer oriented, and looked to create identity for consumers — even as Pepsi producers and consumers alike recognized that drinking soda is, for the most part, silly and serves no nutritional function. Therefore, it has always been about the consumer's personality and identity that is wrapped up in drinking Pepsi.[108] Moreover, it could not be about product benefits and therefore only could be about people's image.

Specifically, Pepsi was hip, young, sexy, and individualistic and created a point of view in the consumer about what it meant to live life to its fullest. Using images of dance and body movements in their commercials would be a serious way they did this beginning in the 1960s and carrying forward into the 2010s. The interesting point to note here is that these worlds of free and independent, life-grabbing, unafraid individuals are fictional. People watching them thought they were real, and they moved against racism, sexism, and anti-establishmentism.[109]

Pepsi and Coca Cola both started using celebrity stars in their ads, and Pepsi included black dancers and singers, as was already shown with Michael Jackson,[110] MC Hammer,[111] and Lionel Richie.[112] In the television ads featuring Madonna, the "Like a Prayer" ad included, we begin to see the shift of black social dance away from black bodies through the vehicle of MTV.[113] However, in the early 1980s, black social dance commentary was moved off the streets and onto the choreographed representation of the dance.[114] The shift was executed, in fact, by Pepsi when they employed MC Hammer. But even though MC Hammer's dance aesthetic was created on the ground in black culture, in

> his commercial association with dances like the Running Man through his PepsiCo campaigns for ... Pepsi..., MC Hammer's black body and those of his background dancers began to operate as an authentication of otherness. National mainstream media ... racialized all of hip-hop movement culture as "Black"[115]

and had nothing to do with the creative commentary of the dance. Using these people and black social dance in their television advertising campaigns dramatically increased Pepsi's sales.[116]

The purpose of this chapter was to demonstrate the increasing use and fascination with black social dance in television ads. The data show that its use has increased over the study period, with it being placed on non-black or animated bodies as it is connected with brands. At the close of 2010 there are more commercials using a form of black social dance than any time in the history of television. After all, the people demand it as part of their entertainment, down to and including watching the president and the first lady dance.

MOVING ON

The next chapter examines in close detail a Diet Pepsi television advertisement that aired as a Super Bowl commercial. It serves as the text that I used to interview respondents about black social dance in the context of the theoretical notions set forth in the beginning chapters of this book. Chapter 4 also presents interview material gathered from talking with an advertising executive who spent the 1960s through the 2000s creating television ads and working with people who created dance ads. In addition, the chapter will note the ways in which creative intermediaries have been characterized, and show that we have aesthetic forces at play in creating anthropological images and documents of ourselves. The fact is, though, that it is not a premeditated type of commentary but it manifests itself as it draws on individual people's experiences and values, as these are connected to the dollars appropriated for advertising results.

4. On Black Social Dance in Commercials in 2010

> *People have not stopped dancing; they have simply changed the form of the dances they do ... I take exception to those who argue that dance becomes less significant with increasing technological complexity ... dance in complex societies is significant for different reasons than it is in non literate societies.*[1]

The focus of this chapter is on African American respondents' views of the Diet Pepsi "Brown and Bubbly"[2] commercial, which was produced by Joe Pytka, DDB New York, and shown in the United States in 2006 during the Super Bowl.[3] This ad was chosen for analysis for a variety of reasons. First of all, it represents a point in time within the long line of Pepsi's advertising strategies for its sodas, as was discussed in the previous chapters. The commercial under study here carries the youth theme that Pepsi established back in the 1960s. The people in the commercial are, moreover, both male and female who visibly appear to be of different races, including African Americans and Caucasians. Additionally, the commercial features P Diddy as a celebrity and, most importantly, uses what has been defined in previous chapters of this book as black social dance contexts.

Using a semiotic approach to reading and analyzing the commercial,[4] I found many tropes relating to black culture running through this commercial. As the scenes of importance to this research are described, I note some tropes as I understand them; the reader should be warned, though, that space does not permit unpacking all the tropes, as interesting as that would be. Using five interpretive dance premises[5] as the framework for interviewing, between 2007 and 2009 I spoke with seven African Americans, who I will refer to as Todd, Jonathan, Kim, Alfonzo, Justin, Shiniqa, and Josh. I also interviewed seven non-black respondents during this time period, Michelle, Derek, Terri,

The Radium Dance. Rare Book, Manuscript, and Special Collections Library, Duke University, Durham, North Carolina.

Joey, Kenneth, Jessica, and Austin. All of the respondents were chosen from university students drawn from a general in-class announcement asking for undergraduate volunteers to participate in research interviews in exchange for course credit. Their identities are confidential.

Non-black respondents' interpretations to Diet Pepsi's "Brown and Bubbly" television advertisement has been discussed within the framework of the five premises.[6] What they experienced as a result of black social dance in this commercial was a sense of emancipation[7] from having been placed subordinate to African Americans during the hip-hop movement on the one hand, and the permission to enjoy being carefree and to have fun, on the other. They were able to express inherent cultural meanings as they related to the broader African American framework of success, achievement, and their relationship with the cosmos. They had a sense of being able to do black social dance while maintaining a hegemonic control that had historically been attributed to Caucasian Americans. Here, therefore, focus is placed on the African American respondents' views of the commercial. After that, I bring in the viewpoint from a Caucasian respondent who spent most of his career with the advertising agency Leo Burnett. In order to problematize the differences between the respondents' views and the literature on advertisers as cultural mediators (Cronin 2004), I draw on recent literature that blurs the lines between where the anthropology and aesthetics originate, to show that culture, consumption, and advertising are really symbiotically related in circular fashion. I discuss the advertiser's point of view of using black social dance in television ads over the study period, and compare and contrast that with interpretations of the African American respondents.

A caveat, or at least a reminder of the purpose of this work, is in order for this chapter. First, it is not meant to show any causal relationships between advertisements and culture. It is primarily used to point out the ways in which black social dance functions in black people's lives, and how it is removed from those contexts onto new ones. Mainly, it is to set forth support for a discourse or discourses about how dance, and, in this study, black social dance, should be taken seriously as a way to understand and communicate to consumers.

THE BROWN AND BUBBLY DIET PEPSI COMMERCIAL

When the commercial opens, a Caucasian American man sits at one end of a long conference table in a conference room that is furnished with contemporary decor in dim lighting. He is acting as an agent for the Diet Pepsi can. The Agent tells the Diet Pepsi can that he will do the talking. The agent, wearing a dark suit and tie, and the Diet Pepsi can meet with P Diddy, the producer wearing sunglasses and a white business suit. P Diddy is asking the agent to consider P Diddy's request to let the agent's client, the Diet Pepsi can, make a rap song because "he's fresh, he's new, the ladies love him, I got to have him signed to the label." The agent agrees with P Diddy's idea so long as P Diddy grants the Diet Pepsi can "mutual creative control." Here the issue of creative control signals perhaps ways in which African American artists were not given similar control[8] in certain artistic instances. At any rate the Diet Pepsi can is not going to fall victim to implicit abdication of artistic and creative control.

In the next scene important for this discussion, the Diet Pepsi can is wearing headphones, positioned before a large microphone in a recording studio. In the recording studio backup dancers and singers support the Diet Pepsi can with their movements and voices. The dancers and singers are dressed in popular clothing and wear headphones. Moreover, the recording studio appears very spacious with high-quality technical equipment. A record chart is cut in with the song "Brown and Bubbly" (with "D. Pepsi" as the singer) at the top, along with people dancing in night clubs, turntables ("wheels of steel") displaying the name of the song on the album being played, and DJs "scratching" the record. Wheels of steel and scratching are cues relating the Diet Pepsi can to black social dance. The viewer is shown the song title and the singer is positioned as number one on the record charts, reflecting the fact that many hip-hop songs — some controversial — topped the charts.

The Diet Pepsi can is next shown riding in the front seat of an automobile ("hoopty") with other African American men, one driving and the others in the backseat, wearing gold chains and baggy clothes, clearly marking the gender and race of the can as an African American male. Gold chains signal "bling" and gangster persona. The men are bobbing their heads, i.e., dancing in their seats and the Diet Pepsi can bobs, too. Together, these signal black social dance and culture and urban representations.

The commercial then moves to a scene showing P Diddy watching the Diet Pepsi can's "Brown and Bubbly" music video, implying success of the song and the decision to sign the artist. In the video, young Caucasian American women are seen dancing a form of black social dance in the sun at an outdoor activity wearing contemporary clothing. P Diddy is shown seated, watching his video creation on a flat-screen television in a personal space of some kind, dressed in a shirt and sunglasses; he throws his arms and hands in the air (a dance), smiles, and expresses, "Whhoooo." This frame could be a play on the interracial and gender issues that confront African American men and Caucasian American women. Finally, a full-screen display of the Diet Pepsi can is shown with the website address brownandbubbly.com. The viewer is delivered back to the agent, who is now dancing, snapping his fingers, and singing the lyrics to "Brown and Bubbly" ("Come and get you some") in his conference room chair, listening to the song on a portable personal music player.

The aforementioned tropes places this commercial so that it runs the gamut of black social dance with respect to hip-hop culture situated in American and African American history. In so doing, along with the associated media-generated cool identity for the consumer, it also epitomizes Diet Pepsi as cool against other soda brands, and allows the consumer to read that Pepsi as a company is also cool.[9]

African American Readings of the Commercial

Several cultural and emotional concepts are found from African American respondents' reading of dance in the Diet Pepsi can "Brown and Bubbly" commercial. When asked in general what they thought, respondents indicated that emotionally it was first of all, "funny."

> I thought it was pretty funny, that they, you know, they kinda depicted Pepsi as a singer, even though the Pepsi can't literally dance (Todd).
>
> It was funny, actually; the funny part was, like, seeing the Diet Pepsi with the ear phones on dancing, or he's not dancing, but moving, he's not a person, he's just a can (Kim).
>
> Well, I was thinking, [chuckles] ... I thought that was pretty funny throughout the commercial (Josh).
>
> The first time I watched the commercial, it was funny. You didn't pick up on a lot of things; you were just listening to the music; that was the first time (Alfonzo).

On the other hand some thought it was funny because the commercial took something that they owned culturally and placed it another cultural setting:

> Black people dance and white people can't, that's why it's funny. It just don't fit, it's wrong. White people don't like hip-hop and black people do. I mean, they say they do and they try but... (Jonathan).
>
> They're all like, "come and get you some," and I'm all "Really? Who would think of that?" [laughing hard]. That's funny (Kim).

One respondent saw it as continued stereotyping:

There is nothing new about the way African Americans are portrayed — reinforcing stereotypes. I cringe when I see these images (Justin).

The next premised concept that comes out of the respondents' views regarding black social dance in culture is emotionally having a good time in a social setting:

Everybody's having fun (Kim).

I was just thinking, they looked like they were having a good time, I mean, just the dancing and the um, ... you know, constitute as fun or happy times, uh, just everyone looked like they were happy, their smiles, everything, you know (Todd).

I felt basically it was interesting, it caught my attention, people having fun, yeah, like younger people having fun drinking Pepsi, and just going out and dancing (Josh).

You do this kind of dance at clubs, school events, to have fun (Shiniqa).

Cognitively, respondents' conceptualization of the dance in the commercial was that it was a *representation* of black social dance. It was not the "real" thing, it was too easy to execute, and the respondents suggested as much:

I mean it's definitely hip-hop culture dancing, *I* think. ["And ... why were they dancing like that?"] Mainly because I think they were getting paid to dance like that [laughing], trying to have a good time at the same time but I don't think it was merely off of emotion or anything (Todd).

It was more of a — it wasn't really black social dance.... It was just, I don't know (Kim).

I think the dance, was ... well, they were going for a hip-hop-type vibe with the dance (Josh).

The dancing? Actually, you know, it wasn't like a lot of hard dancing, I mean, it was more of things that are simple to do, easy. It was like nothing that was too hard for anybody [non-black] to go out and learn (Alfonzo).

At the same time, these *representations* of black social dance led the viewer, when asked what the dance in the commercial meant, to *see usurping of a valued cultural artifact* to portray gangsters and sexual motivations, as Nasir and colleagues (2009) suggested, driving a profit motive:

African Americans are still shown as dancing gangsters. [Agitated and there is impatience and anger in his voice and demeanor] African Americans don't own the distribution. Mainly Pepsi is making money. P Diddy may be. To make profit today, et cetra [as he pronounced it] (Justin).

It was very suggestive. I mean, there's a saying "sex sells," and a lot of the females were kissing up if you will, to the Pepsi can, and that's the kind of dancing really going on (Todd).

The females were doing some type of, I guess you can call it a sexy type dance [chuckle].... Basically [chuckle], I guess they were trying, I guess they was really dancing like they were in a club, dancing with a guy they wanted, but, I mean, they was dancing around a Pepsi can. So ... I guess the Pepsi can is like the player, that have, you know, the women all around him and stuff like that (Josh).

[The dance] had nothing to do with Diet Pepsi. [They were] selling themselves, selling sex — the girls. To find a guy or a girl (Shiniqa).

However, conceptually, black social dance *not* shown in the commercial *signified cultural meanings* for respondents. It is "laid back" or, in other words, relaxing and provides an escape. Black social dance involves a system of pleasure. The dance happens in tandem with and comes from liking the feelings arising from the music. Such feelings and meanings are mostly associated with social situations of black culturally based clubs or parties:

I mean the guys were cool and laid back, you know, kind of representing how, I guess from a guy's standpoint, how you would be in a club or at a party, just kind of laid back moving a little bit but.... That's pretty much what it looked like (Todd).

I thought it was kind of catchy ... using Puff Daddy and surrounding it with kind of a groovy feeling, like with all the dancing and everything.... Laid-back kind of thing (Kim).

The males, I mean, some of the guys were kinda bouncing, while ["What is bouncing?"] They was just kinda nodding they heads, you know, just kinda nodding they head, trying to, just feeling the music.... I mean, when someone nods their head or bounces to the beat, I mean, you can tell they kinda like the music (Jonathan).

'Cause, I mean, pretty much, most guys would love to be dancing around a lot of girls, a lot of beautiful women like that, ... you know, like women you'd see every day at a party or something like that (Josh).

In a way, it does represent a lot of, you know, because there's a lot of different styles of dancing, um, that a lot of African Americans do, I mean, so it was a lot of hip-hop, a little shoulder lean, little footwork, things like that so it's all incorporated in hip-hop music, as well as hip-hop dance (Alfonzo).

After getting respondents' impressions of the commercial, they were asked why they thought black social dance was used and to whom the ad was targeted. In their view, using black social dance in the commercial had several purposes, cognitive, emotional, and visceral, as they are linked to performing the dance socially. Those themes included engaging the viewers' curiosity, developing and drawing on historical connections of the dance to African Americans. Visceral memory for the product was developed by providing a feeling of freedom while giving an imagined sense of release from racial tensions and self-identity from fitting in.

[The dance] gets you from the get go.... It's young, fly, fresh and the ladies like it so you're gonna sit there and look at the commercial because you're wondering why.... I liked it because dancing itself always makes people wonder what kind of dancing they gonna be doing or you hear the music like so they might BE dancing, so you always gonna keep that commercial on and every time you hear that specific beat or song, you gonna think about that commercial (Alfonzo).

They *put the dance* [respondent's emphasis] in it because dancing kind of tweaks your interest, when you see people dance, you gotta have a mind set of what type of person are doing what kind of dance, so you have Caucasian people here and African Americans there and all together around this Pepsi everybody's doing the same dance. It's so funny. You just don't see commercials like that. You never see that, where everybody's on the same page, no shame in the dancing, just rockin' it out, I felt good, and I'm thinking I should be in that commercial, I want to be in that commercial, I don't even dance and that's the whole point of it. A lot of those people probably don't dance (anymore) so I liked it. ["So you imagine yourself in it?"] Yeah (Kim).

I liked the commercial. There's so much going on; you got a song, Diddy's in it, it's almost like too much for the soda, it's all people dancing, you know. Dancing has to do with fitting in. In St, Louis, there was a dance at a night club [where I dance all the time] called the Monastery, and that's what they started calling the dance. All the rappers in St. Louis, they were doing that dance. I come to college, people here from California and Louisiana, they know it. They done got crazy with the songs and the dances now [on television].... Some black people think because of history, you have to know how to dance, I mean, like a white person say, "I don't know how to dance," that's okay, you not supposed to be able to dance, but a black person has to know how to dance, but it's not the case, but it's what people think (Jonathan).

In addition, though the respondents thought the ad targeted African Americans, that using black social dance in this commercial painted a picture of Caucasian society's acceptance of a their understanding of a representation African American culture. The masses are moving towards hip-hop as a lifestyle as barriers change and minds open to the way African Americans do things for fun.

Well, it definitely targets, *I* think, African American culture but I kinda feel like us as a society is kinda moving towards that direction. Like, seems like every commercial from McDonald's to anything else is kinda going towards the hip-hop, African American music or beat or dancing or.... So generally it targeted African Americans but everyone else at the same time. You know what I mean? ["Why do you think the commercials are moving that direction?"] I don't know, I don't know if it is because, us as a people [blacks], you know, has come a long ways or as barriers change, there's more open minds to the way we do things or the way we think or ... you know, I think that over time, people, other than black people, they have come to find that our [black] culture is fun, and fun is attractive and that's why all the commercials are going towards that direction of hip-hop (Todd).

This commercial was mainly for blacks (Shiniqa). [Rolls her eyes]

Because today, it's 2009, African American dance, hip-hop dance is widely accepted. A lot of people, you don't even see; you see black people, but you see

4. On Black Social Dance in Commercials in 2010

white people, Spanish people, black people. I mean, they even have America's Best Dance Group. I mean, that's hip-hop dance so they use it in the commercial because it's accepted by most cultures. Why? I guess 'cause it's a different form of dance, it's more of a freedom of expression, guys spinning on they heads, girls dancing how they wanna dance, it's not the type of classical dance, the waltz, it's more freedom of—in hip-hop dance you can do what you want. ["Why is that? Why do you think it's so widespread? What does it give people?"] It gives people freedom of expression, I mean, basically, that's what they feel like doing at the time, there don't have to be a name or something for the dance as long as it's what you feel like doing. ["What does a person get from that? What's the benefit?"] They're just expressing their selves, you can relieve. I mean, I know some people, I know my brother, when he stress, he goes outside and break dances in the grass. That's how he gets rid of his stress. I know people dance, who for money, some for just to win, competitions, ... just to be the best. So ... [silence] (Josh).

While respondents seemed to be resolved to the notions about the use of black social dance in commercials, one did not. He felt the dance was used to keep the negative images alive and to cause emotional turmoil:

I just wish there were more commercials that portray African Americans more positively. They used dance because it's mainstream. At [non-black] clubs, there are mainly white people dancing hip-hop but let an argument come up and the white people will be the first ones to call out with the N word. Couple weeks back, Club 502, there was an altercation outside; white guy kicked a black guy, the police came, the black guy got arrested. Whites all blamed the black guy. You always have to watch your back (Justin).

Next, the respondents were asked to discuss their views and memories of the opening scene, with P Diddy and the agent for the Diet Pepsi can. When thinking about the interaction between the two men, several respondents remembered P Diddy as the initiator of the interchange, while others thought it was the agent approaching P Diddy. In the instance with P Diddy approaching the agent, respondents found it to be unusual in that, in their cultural knowledge, P Diddy does not ask for deals: On the contrary, he is asked to do deals. In any event, it was seen as *removing power* from P Diddy and showing him as in the position of having to ask a Caucasian man to represent what was interpreted as a "colored" representation of an African American in the form of a soda can. As such, it was further a muted representation of a black person who could not effectively negotiate the contract with the supposedly sly African American businessman. The agent was going to "protect" the colored can.

Pepsi and his agent was approaching P Diddy. It looked like they were negotiating a contract for Pepsi's deal. ["Who was asking who to do what?"] The white gentleman was telling Pepsi "I'm was going to do the talking," basically just negotiating, I suppose, I can't really remember. I think, uh, I was kinda taken by the whole him talking to the Pepsi can situation but, he was negotiating what he wanted, I guess, for Pepsi. That's what it looked like, anyway. It looked like a conference room, I mean, I think, just to kind of show, to make it look as if it was a real business deal, like a business deal, like more authentic as a contract situation (Todd).

It was racial, him being white [the agent], and the can was colored (Shiniqa).

It was like a business deal being made, gave a real business vibe, sitting across the table from each other, some type of deal was being made. P Diddy, I don't know his real name, but P Diddy [was asking for the deal]. ["Is this a normal flow?"] No, nah, it's not a normal flow, I mean most of the time with P Diddy people come to *him*, far as I know, with as far as reality shows, and making up, mostly people come to him and try to get him to promote *them* (emphasis the respondent's). ["So why is the commercial doing it in the other way?"] They just wanna promote Pepsi, I mean, they want people to see that P Diddy wants Pepsi to do this music video. They want people to think Pepsi is cool, because, I mean, P Diddy, everyone knows, he never approaches anyone, asks anyone, everyone comes to him; he never approaches anyone for anything so it was kind of different, I mean, I never seen him do something like that. ["What does that imply to you?"] I guess, it kind of implies, it can go both ways. I mean, even though you don't see people actually ask for stuff, or do certain things, eventually they did it, you don't see, eventually P Diddy had to ask someone to help him out with his business; the shoe's on the other foot now (Josh).

Diddy was approaching the soda and the agent for the contract. He's such a huge producer you gotta be a big deal to get his attention (Jonathan).

Diddy was asking, you know, he needed the Pepsi can because he was young, fresh and fly and the ladies love him [laughing], so and then I guess the Pepsi can's manager was like, we gotta have some controlled environment or something like that, then all a sudden it just went out of proportion (Alfonzo).

In two respondents' views, the intent of the interaction was to further separations between the races, symbolized by the conference table. In addition, the dialog and positions between the two men was meant to usurp valued aspects of African American culture. This was seen as being done by Pepsi merely for profit.

I guess that's how it is in the business world ... but I don't know why the table was so long, that it was set up like that (Alfonzo).

The white guy represents the separation of cultures. P Diddy equals the hip-hop culture and [black] stereotypes and the white guy represents white America, trying to use words like "yo, Dddiiidddy" trying to sound black. I hate when white people do this. Pepsi is just doing this to make money; they don't care about nothing else (Justin).

Because the white guy wanted to separate himself from P Diddy. They made it look like P Diddy had the power but this is reasonable to a point. Blacks don't have power, like in slavery there was no power. They are still trying to separate blacks and whites instead of being equal (Shiniqa).

In summary, the two concepts that arise from this scene are minimizing the dance's importance through deflation of power it carries and its separation from its culture by providing a representation of the dance.

In asking respondents to reflect upon the scene with the Diet Pepsi can in the front seat of the car, only one respondent had difficulty recalling it:

> No, I don't remember that.... I saw it three times and I didn't notice that [car scene] (Kim).

All the others remembered it without prompting, and were able to articulate meanings. They named two dances as head bobbing, and back and forth leaning, conceptualizing these as natural dances for African Americans in terms of cultural specificity. Moreover, in their own words, respondents suggest that people doing black social dance are interpreting music, and feeling relaxed and safe. It is a flow experience that provides an escape. Having people riding in a car together for the pleasure of relaxing and trusting friends was a frequent occurrence, and the person who rides in the front passenger seat enjoys a special relationship to the driver. The Diet Pepsi can earned this reputation as being one of the boys, due to his newfound success. He was cool and popular. Again, respondents expressed the notion of how the use of a head bob is now societally mainstream for youth who want to be seen as being cool, having fun, and most of all, having acquired rhythm, but it was a reflection of African American men as used by mainstream culture:

> ["Do you remember the car scene?"] I do, vaguely. ["Tell me what you think."] I think that scene right there is just a depiction of, you know, Pepsi with his boys [laughing]. ["Okay, so what are the boys?"] I mean, just somebody he can depend on, you know, somebody he can call, just talk to, people he hangs out with. ["What kind of dancing were they doing in the car?"] Just like bobbing, you know, you can't do that much dancing in the car. But you know it was definitely to the beat, just having a good time. ["Who does that kind of dancing in the car?"] Well *everybody* does *now*, but mostly, you know, our [black] culture [emphasis respondent's]; African Americans do that bobbing. ["Was Pepsi can doing it?"] Slightly, you know, but not as much [laughing]. No, it's just kind of this line going back and forth. ["When you say everybody does it now, what does that mean?"] Well it's just back to what I was saying earlier about the cultural acceptance, it's seen as cool, seen as fun, rhythm is fun, not having rhythm isn't [laughing] (Todd).

> ["What did you think about the men when they were in the car?"] I thought they were kinda going for, how can I say it, a urban look for that, you know how guys just ride around listen to music, nod their head, just kinda chill with the fellas. ["What do you mean 'urban'?"] More of a, you know, an African American community, area, yeah. ["Why do you think the can was sitting in the front seat?"] I guess the can was the, um, he was the HOMEboy [laughing] (respondent raised his voice); I mean, he was in the front seat, so he was in the front seat, I mean.... ["He became a homeboy because...?"] Because of the music,

because of the song, I mean, he was popular. ["Why do you think that particular scene with the guys, the 'hood, why that movement?"] Try to advertise to more of an African, I mean, more of a diverse community. You don't want advertise to, I mean, to white people or Spanish people. You want to advertise to everybody so, I mean, I guess they put that in there to try to relate to, you know, African American men. ["So you think the commercial was aimed at African American men?"] No, just that scene, yeah (Josh).

The commercial made it like it was a whole party, a huge party scene, and all they were doing is dancing and drinking. In the commercial when they were in the car, they weren't dancing real hard but they, when you driving you can only bob your head, you can't do all that while you driving. The can was in the front seat because he was the big dog, the hot new rapper, cool. So he gets chauffered (Jonathan).

["What did you think about the can riding in the car?"] With the seatbelt, and sometimes had head phones on like it could actually listen to music? [laughing] When the only thing it was doing was [laughing] popping the top, which makes a funny noise every time it did it, funny as it did [laughing]. ["So what did you think about the scene, with the people in the car?"] The guys just sitting there driving in the car, nodding their heads, well, it's not like a normal thing for the can to be strapped in, but I guess they felt like it was one of the boys so it chilled with them in the car. ["What kind of movement were the guys in the car doing?"] Mostly head nodding, and back and forth leaning side to side.... [laughing chuckle] ["And what does that mean, in terms of?"] Well, that's like a relax thing, more like a, just a natural, when you listening to music, just a natural head nod ... or something. ["Natural for whom?"] I guess, people of, I, African Americans? I mean, I never rode in the car with a lot of [other] different people, so I don't know how they exact, you know, their interpreting music, but a lot of African Americans do it just by head nodding, going with the beat, with the flow, it's just natural, I guess. ["If it was a different type of person, like when you ride in your car, and you have music on is that something you do?"] I do, it's not even, it's just naturally, that's what you do, I guess, go with the beat. ["Do other people who are not African American do they do that?"] I believe so, in their own way, if it's not the head nodding, maybe it's the hand, it's the leg, or tap your foot to the beat, but it's always something going to the beat. ["What about the guy who was dancing in the car and in front of the microphone?"] The big guy? ["Yes."] He was doing some type of dance, some names are different from others, but the same dance incorporated in his own way, his own style (Alfonzo).

The target market for this is youth and they are mainstream. Pepsi is trying to reinvent their image to tap into that market. The majority of the people that are in hip-hop culture nowadays are in the suburb anyway, and do it to make their daddy mad. I hate when they take one thing out of the culture and use it as a negative portrayal. Driving and head bobbing there's nothing wrong with it. But it makes it look like blacks only do that all day, listening to music and enjoying himself with head bobs (Justin).

Moving on to P Diddy's dance, according to the respondents, at the end of the commercial signaled his emotional approval of his choice to endorse the Diet Pepsi can. Cognitively, it was an outward expression his triumph and knowledge of success despite historical bounds. Indeed, the respondents conceptualized the dance as his "signature" movement, though he is not considered to be a good dancer. And if someone correctly adapts his dance, they are cool and fit in. Again, that theme of fitting in emerges, while at the same time P Diddy is exempt from the requirement of being able to dance well because of his way of being in the world — financially and racially free.

> ["At the end of the commercial, P Diddy did his arm movements. What does that mean?"] He was just happy. I mean, he was responsible for the actual production of the music video and the advertisement. I think it was something he created so he was happy to see it was successful and number one on the charts. ["When you move your arms like that does it mean the same thing?"] Well, it depends on the situation. There were times when I moved my hands like that and I was like, oh man, I didn't want that to happen, but he had a smile on his face, and you know, the tone in which he said yes, or something he said was happy (Todd).

> ["Do you remember the end of the commercial ... (P Diddy) threw his hands. What does that mean?"] Just a movement. I mean, he was happy because his song was a success. ["Does that mean the same thing, that sort of arm movement, in every case?"] Nah, sometime the arm movement can be, like going back to the guys bouncing in the car, I mean, it could be the same thing, maybe he was liking the song, feeling the music at the same time it could be a dance of some sort that he was doing. ["Would it mean the same thing, or in what situation would it mean something else and by whom?"] I never really looked at it, I mean, when he, he kinda put his hands up, and uh, I guess, when you're in a classroom putting your hands up to a teacher, but for the most part, the way he was moving his arms, that's more of a music thing. So ... I don't really know other situations where he can just put his hands up like that (Josh).

> I didn't pay too much attention to P Diddy, so when you see him dance you ignore him because I see him dance all the time, but a white guy in a suit makes you pay attention (Jonathan).

> ["Why does P Diddy throw his hands at the end?"] That's his signature. He's happy, the product is finished (Justin).

> ["The end of the commercial you have P Diddy doing an arm movement, remember that?"] Yes, isn't that one of his signature moves, the arm moves? ["What does it mean?"] I don't know, I guess it's more suggestive than anything, this is how we roll, I'm behind Diet Pepsi, kinda get you in the video. ["Do you ever do that movement?"] [laughing] Yeah, when I was younger I probably tried to pull that one off, it was a little lame, but I did try to pull that one off. ["And when you did it, what did in mean?"] Oh, nothing really, I was just having fun, it was a way of expressing how I felt at the moment, I was trying to be cool, everybody else was cool, so that's how I did it, that's what they did so I did it. ["So it's like fitting in?"] Uh huh, for most people I think it is. You have a few people who make up stuff on their own, but as far as dancing goes, it's one of those things where people follow after certain dance moves, and that kind of stuck with me for a while (Kim).

["At the end of the commercial, ... P Diddy threw his arms, what does that mean?"] That is his signature move that he does when, I guess, he feels like he accomplished something. Well, if you've seen any of his TV shows he does, when any of his artists do well, when he's on stage, and he does a good performance, or when he thinks he's done a good performance, he does that, so I guess it's like his signature. I've done it, I've completed it, type of deal. ["Is that something that he developed?"] Well, I, P Diddy is not known for his dancing, he's really not the type of dancer you would actually see.... [chuckle] ["Why not?"] He's just, he's not really, I don't know, he's never been the dancer. Ask everyone, you can ask anyone. He has his own way, but he doesn't care because it's his way, so it's just like that so.... ["Did you ever see anyone else do that type of arm movement?"] A lot people do, you know, some type of hand gesture, you know, I'm that, that was wack, you throw your hand out, it's a natural thing but his is more of a high fisted up in the air "I've got it." ["Do you think it means the same thing if anybody does it, or is it just that way if P Diddy does it?"] ... Well, it just depends. P Diddy is more ... of the business type, so you wouldn't actually see a business man throw his hands in the air too often but when he does that's when you know he's completed something well, normal people do it, you be like I'm not sure what that meant. ["When you say 'normal people,' what do you mean?"] People, that, everyday life, that aren't millionaires, aren't movie producers, record producers, stars, things like that, so you get average people walking down the street and you throw your hands up. You have no reason why. You come to the conclusion that maybe they're not all there (Alfonzo).

P Diddy wasn't sure if he agreed about [the Diet Pepsi can] being able to rap but when P Diddy liked it he threw his arms up in triumph (Shiniqa).

However, when the respondents were asked to consider the agent's dance at the end of the commercial, they saw it as reflecting historical memory, and the relationship of the dance with emotional release naturally, historically, and genetically done by African Americans. Black social dance and its relationship to consumption attracts attention and therefore associating it with the product leaves an indelible impression in people's memories of the dance association as fun and freeing. Having a non-black person execute the dance does this while at the same time pointing to non-blacks' desire to be considered insiders to black culture. In the respondents' views, though, it is always already an imitation of a representation of the dance with the imagination of execution related to consumption.

The agent dancing was one of the funniest parts to me (Jonathan).

["At the end of the commercial, the agent is sitting in his chair dancing, remember this?"] [Laughing], I do.... ["What were your thoughts about that?"] Honestly, it's kind of funny, I mean, I think whenever African Americans look at other cultures who are "acting like us," per se, it's kind of funny because it doesn't really look natural, but I thought it was fun, it was cool that he was doing it, he was partially glad he was making money, had a hit, something his client had produced. ["So his dancing meant what?"] That he was happy that his client was successful and he liked what he produced. ["So from your point of view, was he dancing well?"] I mean, he was dancing well for, I guess, a white guy [laughing].... I hope I can say that.... ["You can say anything in here...."] [laughing] I don't think that genetically he has the capability to dance the way we do.... ["When you say genetically what do you mean? Why do you say that?"] For one thing, the music he was moving to is not culturally based the way he was brought up, not passed down through generations so for him to move to something foreign is kind of like, you know, knowing how but not necessarily possessing the motor skills to do it correctly... does that make sense? ["Uh huh."] That's what I think. ["Is it just motor skills?"] I don't know what else you would call it ... motor skills, you know, rhythm. ["Let's just use me as an example.... If it was me dancing at the end of the commercial, would I be able to do it in a way that would be genetically correct?"] Possibly.... I think you would be more apt to do it than he would because you are African American? ["What does that mean, I'm African American, I am — I mean, I do dance...."] Good! [laughing]. ["So what does that mean in your mind? That I'm African American and I can dance, he's not, he can't and you're saying it's genetic."] I just, you know, really believe that it's just foreign to him, I believe, but you belong in that situation as far as your capabilities to execute the moves whereas him, he doesn't really belong in that situation; he doesn't even look like he would do that on a regular basis, like if he wasn't in his suit just in a normal setting he doesn't even look like that's something he would do. ["So.... Okay, what does it mean in terms of consumption? How do you think that affects people's desire or lack of desire when it comes to consumption of a product? You talk about the genetics of being able to dance in a certain way. How does that affect the viewer?"] I don't think that someone's ability to dance necessarily affects the consumption per se because I mean if it was another product, like a car that someone put in a hip-hop commercial, if they like the car, they like the car, okay, so they're gonna get it. If anything, so with Pepsi, if someone likes it they're gonna drink it. If anything, the hip-hop commercial does is kind of make it more attractive so maybe it'll make the consumption go up because, you know, the advertisement drew someone's attention, and make them "You know I think I'm going to try that because it looks like it's fun." I think a lot of selling and consumption has to do with mental (Todd).

I haven't seen a non-black person actually dance hip-hop but I could imagine it if they grew up around black people. Otherwise they can't really embrace the culture, like when hip-hop had a reason, a purpose, message, you know, "fight the power." Now it's all about gold teeth and profit. Non-blacks haven't embraced or experienced the culture. Dads are uptight Republicans, son is rebelling. Same as the 1950s with rock and roll (Justin).

["What do you think about the agent dancing at the end?"] I guess he was happy with the work that he let Pepsi can do, so he was in the mood with Pepsi can 'cause it was a number-one hit and everything, so he was in just the mood, like some people do. They just feel like, oh, everybody else is doing it, I can do it, too. Type a deal like that. ["Was he doing it, too?"] He was doing his OWN version [laughing] of it, like, he expressed himself differently than everyone else, so. ["If you had a chance to ask him, do you think he would say he was doing, that he was copying well?"] [Laughing] He was making an honest effort, I guess [laughing] (Alfonzo).

["At the end of the commercial, the agent dancing, what does that mean?"] He was happy, he got what he wanted, so he had, I mean, he had what he wanted, his client, the Pepsi can had the deal he made, with it kind of in his favor, the freedom the creativity to do what he wanted (Josh).

["What do you think about the agent dancing?"] He's funny, I mean, I've seen him on other shows, never have I seen him dancing or rapping like a hip-hop artist "come and get you some." It was funny. I know he has a great sense of humor, he was funny, I liked it. It seemed like he was probably out of his element but the video was funny. ["Would you say he could dance?"] I think so, if I knew him better, with the way things are nowadays, you can't count anybody out when it comes to dancing when it comes to hip-hop culture. It seems like a lot more people are interested in that kind of dancing now, the culture is cool, more accepted now, more so than it was two, three decades ago. I mean, when a rapper or artist has a hit, the statistics show its not African Americans who are buying, so it already shows that we are not the only people imitating, listening, learning. ["How do you feel about that?"] I don't mind it. I think it cool. I think he understands why we get so excited listening to our kind of music. ["Why do we?"] It relates to us, our personalities of what we think is fun, what excites us as a group, past history. ["How do you think the dance is related to consumption as far as a product?"] I'm not sure it's related to consumption. I'm sure it puts a thought in your brain to buy it even if you don't want it. "I haven't had a Diet Pepsi for a while; Diet Pepsi is doing something over there" (Kim).

Each of the respondents had a life long relationship with black social dance. It was in all cases a part of family and social life, and it extended into their personal histories as far as they could remember. All of the respondents used black social dance in their lives and identities, to build confidence in themselves, or to remember their African American diasporatic histories.

["Are you a dancer, dance socially?"] Yes. ["Have you danced all your life?"] As far back as I can remember.... ["Does your family dance?"] Yes, everyone in my family dances (Todd).

["Do you have any experiences with African American dance, social dance, hip-hop dance?"] Yeah, I have tons of experiences, I mean, it's a part of your life growing up, I mean, you know, at some point in the African American community you're gonna dance, I mean, it's how we socialize. We dance. I know, well, I started dancing to fit in. I wasn't much of a dancer, but I started dance 'cause I didn't want to be the guy at the party just sitting on the wall; I started dancing to fit in. ["Did it work?"] Yeah, it pretty much worked [laughing]. It was like the one thing, I mean, I could play basketball, I had decent grades and everything like that, but I couldn't dance so I kinda wanted to be well rounded. ["So did that change people's perception of you?"] It just felt like I can do it all. I mean, I don't think, it's a lot of stuff I can't do, but to me I felt like there's not someone where I lived where I can't do what they did. ["So it was like being accepted into the group?"] Yeah. ["How old were you?"] At that time, I was about 13? ["Did you keep up with dancing?"] Yeah, I been keeping up with dancing for a long time. ["Do your parents dance?"] Yeah, well, my parents used to dance, but most of my family dances. I mean, family reunions, everyone pretty much dances. I don't know too many people in my family that don't dance. ["Do you have anything else to add?"] Dance can be, I don't like dance with little kids, girls, 5 and 6 years old on music videos. I don't feel that's appropriate, but that's about it. I'm not saying it's, I mean, dancing provocative, I don't think kids should be doing that; it should be age appropriate. I wouldn't want my daughter out there doing that, preschool. ["Where do you see this?"] Social settings, little cheerleaders, social settings, recitals.... I don't think that's appropriate at all. ["Anything else?"] It was a good ad. It was hard not to pay attention to the ad; it was real catchy (Josh).

We don't dance at my house. It's not appealing. We do line dancing, like the electric slide at receptions, retreats. But friends and me from church go line dancing (Shiniqa).

When you dance it's not all the time you're dancing with yourself. It's always when you're social dancing, is more, there's a get together with a lot of people when you're dancing like that, whether it be guys and girls, or just a bunch of girls dancing with each other, bunch of guys, guys showing off moves, things like that. So it's always dancing with *someone* around, you don't really dance by yourself anymore ... in a social situation (Alfonzo).

In one case, the ability to dance was cause for a family rift, but the respondent still privately did black social dance. Her family's criticism of her caused her to move away from dancing publicly; however, it did not remove her longing to be able to fit in and be a part of the culture:

["So, do you dance, do African American social dance?"] Yeah [laughing]. ["Okay ... so did you start dancing when you were a little kid?"] Um, I do believe I started when I was about 5. I noticed everybody was dancing at our age, but then my mom said I couldn't dance and so kind of beat down on my dancing confidence. She was like, "You don't have any rhythm," and being a kid I was just like, I don't know what I was doing wrong, so I tried to imitate but so I gave up dancing early ... probably because of that; I'm not upset about it or anything like that, but it was just something that happened. ["From your point of view, was your mom, was she, did she want you to dance?"] For the fun of it, yes. As the years went by it was more of a "Oh, I didn't mean it like that; you can dance," but by then my confidence for dancing had left already and it starts then the people who are around you that you love, those are the people who help build your confidence in things like that and after that it wasn't there, I didn't really, if I danced, I was just joking but as far as being serious about dancing, it ended then. ["What do you think it meant to your mom that you're not dancing?"] I don't think she cared one way or the other; it was just dancing for her. You dance because you're having fun. It didn't mean much, and she thought I'd just come around and I'd start dancing. But I honestly think it ended there, for dances, proms, anything — I went to all those things but I didn't dance. ["But your mom dances?"] Uh huh, everybody in my family dances and they are always trying to get me to dance but I just don't have fun; I can't get into it anymore. ["Do you think it's natural for African Americans to dance?"] Sometimes I think it's natural; I try stuff like when I'm alone, I dance and I know I'm capable, some people just don't have it; they're not capable of that rhythm. I think it's based on just how you grew up I guess. ["So what do you mean by that?"] Your surroundings, who you grew up with, who you partied with, hung out with, all that stuff that helped make you what you are now. ["How rational is it that you would see a scene like that in real life?"] I'm leaning toward irrational. I doubt that I would ever see that; it won't happen. I just don't dance, I mean, my sister and I, we used to mess around. [Respondent related the question back to herself even after clarifying the question for her.] ["Is P Diddy a good dancer?"] People say he is. ["People say?"] I don't care for his dancing. He's not one of my favorites. I like Usher, he can dance. [Silence]. Do you have any questions? ["Yes, how long have you been dancing?"] A long time.... Yes, it's fun, it's freeing, and provides an escape, I agree. I'm 21, that would be the perfect time to go out, but it's hard, because dancing is a huge part, but when I get there, I'm sitting. I can't have fun, I can't let go, I can't dance. So that cuts out my social life. But I'm too old to learn or re-teach myself. I could say I would want to but I wouldn't. My grandma has a lot of basement parties, but when they start telling me to get up, I just go upstairs. I'm a party pooper. I guess I just blame my mom, and that whole, "You dance like a white girl," and she hit me. She was trying to teach me, but I took it the wrong way. So I don't want to dance like a white girl so I don't dance.... My sister, she's 18, she knows all the new dances, but dancing isn't like it used to be. It was fun when you were younger, the older you got, the more precise it got, and if you weren't doing it right, you shouldn't do it (Kim).

In closing, then, the following conceptualizations of black social dance from respondents' points of view include:

- Acceptance of media "making fun of" the dance
- Having a good time
- BSD in television ads are representations of the dance
- The representation is used to reflect Caucasian views of African American men
- Usurptation of valued cultural artifact that simultaneously furthers racism and sexism
- Signification of meanings and roles
- Society's acceptance of a representation of black social dance from African American culture
- The muting of black voices
- Continued separation of the races
- Deflation of power of black social dance and minimalizing its importance
- Black social dance as natural, interpretive, freeing, done in flow, relaxing
- The providing of expression of approval or triumph, knowledge of navigating the world

- Creation of a signature
- Knowledge of natural method of emotional release; it is done historically, and is genetic for African Americans
- Music makes you dance
- Caucasians want to be inside black culture but they can only imitate.
- Black social dance is a lifelong relationship, familial and social, and a way to write history
- Black social dance connects to personal history, identity, and confidence

These conceptualizations, I suggest, afford viewers connections with the dance to the brand. In chapter 5, these concepts and connections will be discussed in more detail.

In contrast to the respondents' relationships with black social dance and their ability to see its use in advertising as "just business" is the business of using it in a commercial. The next section discusses the role of cultural intermediaries in advertising and then summarizes an interview with an advertising agency professional, who functioned as a cultural intermediary (Cronin 2004) and his historical perception of using black social dance in television ads.

ADVERTISER'S CULTURAL INTERMEDIACY

Television ads have been shown to be socio-cultural and political artifacts that are also aesthetic objects paraded within a system of visual representations.[10] They are produced and used to their product's advantage as social signifiers, while individuals take from them symbolic value in regard to their consumption practices. There is no mistaking that difficult and often complex issues are addressed or at the minimum pointed to in television ads. In fact, "advertising imagery constitutes ubiquitous and influential bodily representations in public space, incorporating exercises of power, surveillance, and normativity within the consumer spectacle."[11]

Perhaps not intentionally, television ads provide a historical record, based on the historian's notion of what is important culturally at the point of product and cultural development. One important aspect of television advertising as part of post-postmodern society is that the product itself is not talked about but dancing images, celebrities, and ways of being are associated with it instead — "consumption is becoming 'more cultural,' that is, becoming more oriented around sign values and symbolic gains than use values and the satisfaction of needs."[12] Be that as it may, it is true that consumers often construct their identities based on what they see pandered in consumption markets or based on what they are rallying against as principles contained in those very markets.[13]

In order to accomplish deep knowledge structures like that, advertisers have to get inside the heads of the people in the culture.[14] The kind of knowledge they need is not what they can take from a few focus groups. As Holt (2003) has suggested, this kind of knowledge is had from engaging with cultural knowers — people who have lived it, experienced it, and take issue with it. Those people, for purposes of black social dance and the work at hand, are respondents, advertising executives and creatives who come from the culture, and certain anthropologists and dance historians.

Seriously, black people and white people are simply made-up categories based on skin color for purposes of capitalistic control and class manifestations. The same kinds of strife and struggles could just as easily been set up in opposite directions, as if the names of the identifiers had been earth and sky. Difference and dominance is in fact as fictional and made up as gender roles.[15] However, this is not to suggest that advertising does not exacerbate or even create critical issues because its employer is consumer capitalism. In fact, advertising keeps people looking in the mirror for preconceived boxes of identity, spawning consuming bodies trapped in race.

As it seems easy to point at advertisers as culpable in regard to cultural theft for less than altruistic motives,[16] there is some possibility that these allegations are without validity. Perhaps ad women are only trying to achieve their goals of profit and gain for the products they represent. Perhaps they do not, as some have argued extensively, sit and think sinisterly about how they can insult whole groups of people or alienate them from their sense of human identity. It is possible that advertising using dance as a carrier has done positive work in easing strife and minimizing racial hate, and prying open, by use of small wedges, the psyche of Americans. There are two points of view when it comes to advertising — some are relentlessly critical of it and claim that consumers are victims while others exonerate advertising. It can be placed in its own bipolar continuum with analogies of masculine versus feminine constructs — advertisers exert force over consumers who are passive and silent in their acquiescence.[17] Moreover, advertisers create, support, maintain, and absolve categories of taste through the morass of cultural change.[18]

In any event, executive white men who serve as ad executives — and, to a lesser extent, women and ethnic folks — are considered cultural intermediaries between producers and consumers. This tension has been addressed by Fowles (1996) and more recently by Cronin (2004), providing a balancing point that allows one to consider less of a villainous role for these executives, while spreading the net to assert that "account managers, account planners or media buyers" also play a significant role in ad development.[19] These individuals draw on their own experiences and use popular culture "as a *resource*" in developing ads:

> Practitioners strategically raid new cultural trends they see appearing across a range of sites (fashion, art, popular music, [dance,] design, television) and put selected elements of them to work in their campaigns.... Advertising is not the dynamic driver of cultural change.... Advertising [practitioners] ... feed off ... cultural changes.[20]

In addition, many employees in roles at advertising agencies are presenting ideas for ads that will make them rich and famous, and secondarily, in the process, hopefully make the brand or product successful within the limitations set by their client.

Remember too that ads are also created by ethnic individuals such as African Americans and, women, even though they are underrepresented historically and presently in advertising.[21]

Some of these tensions between advertisers and consumers will be borne out in the following interview with David Geeting. In chapter 6, I will return to the argument about the bipolar oppositions between advertisers and consumers.

An Agency/Client Perspective: Carla Stalling Huntington Interviews David Geeting[22]

DAVID GEETING: I'd like to speak frankly with you about everything. I started working with Joe Pytka in the mid–1980s he came out of Pittsburgh. I would say he's brilliant so you accept his personality. Underneath if you get to know him [and he respects you], and since I was fortunate enough to come out of Stanford with an education in film, communication theory, television, I knew what I was talking about and he and I got along very well. We did any number of commercials together, including Ringo Starr and his daughter, "It's not your father's Oldsmobile." Joe Pytka has done some interesting things, including the commercial where Michael Jackson's hair caught on fire. That wasn't Joe's fault, but he's unfortunately known as the director who got Michael Jackson's hair on fire. He's done a couple of movies — but as a commercials director he's brilliant. You go talk to him about your ideas, but the commercial comes out as his commercial but if you can accept that and work with Joe and get what you need in terms of client satisfaction, that's, well, what can I say, he's incredibly successful, incredibly wealthy.

Joe Pytka worked with Bob Giraldi, the master of the dance commercials out of New York, after having been a most highly successful

Young & Rubicam art director. He did the original *Thriller* commercial with Michael Jackson and set the standard for all dance commercials. He had great talent in being meticulous about the makeup and dance, but it was incredible.

CARLA HUNTINGTON: *Do you know how the decisions come about to use dance in a commercial?*

DAVID GEETING: Sure. Inside an agency, the beginning of any project is where the client expresses interest in selling a product, new or ongoing that needs new commercials. At the initial meeting the client expresses their desire, the creative director is assigned by a Group Creative Director or an executive creative director. The creative director has several teams under them, they work together to come up with ideas, then four or so emerge, and are sent to the client, with estimates for costs at a follow up meeting. The client would say yes, it goes back to the agency, and meets with the winning creative directors whose style or previous experience was suited to doing that kind of commercial, dance, special effects, experience with the product — some directors are considered universally good, in the area of food, automobiles, children, action — combining directing and special effects and even good dialog directors are specialists. After that we'd sort it out to three different companies, out for bids.

CH: *Is the commercial designed after that step? When is the decision made to use dance in the commercial?*

DG: No, the commercial is designed internally and presented to the client long before the director is chosen. The director is not in consideration at that point. The best creative presentations can incorporate dance if that's necessary or the team thinks it's a cool way they can appeal to people. You can do anything with anything. You have to decide what works with the great idea. The dancing raisins [are] a great example, because most people wouldn't think of raisins dancing; it requires quite a creative leap of faith for people to say, oh yeah, they will think this is cool.

CH: *Why will they think that?*

DG: Because it's different, that's mainly the thing, because it calls attention to the product. Leo Burnett — brilliant guy — always said look for the inherent drama in the product. That's a great example of taking inherent drama from the product, making it the center of the commercial, personifying but not to the point where you feel guilty about eating them. You have to decide if this is going to chill some people.

CH: *In my looking at the commercials over the time period, the dance is usually used in low involvement products, some are high involvement. Does that come into play at all?*

DG: Yes, of course. What is there you can say about sodas that hasn't already been said? In the raisin commercial it was exactly that: how do we make raisins popular, how do we make them interesting to people, how do we get consideration of raisins? Because they have personified it without making it something you don't want to eat. Take something that has no inherent drama and make it dramatic. The raisin commercial is probably the most successful.

CH: *What is inherent drama?*

DG: How do you take the product and use it in such a way that you don't take the interest away from the product? There are so many commercials where you don't remember the product. [You remember] the retro, it's cool, the fashion, etc., but you don't remember the product. Inherent drama focuses on the product and brings the drama out of the product. It's not easy to do; we spent years perfecting our ability to do that. In the 1950s Burnett became known for that kind of thing, and became fifth largest in the world with offices around the globe. They were purchased by Publicis as I was retiring.

CH: *Did you notice, at any time during your career, anything happening in the world that caused more or less dance to be used in advertising?*

DG: I don't think world events, but if dance appeared in a movie or TV show, or a show about dancing, like *So You Think You Can Dance*, that's popular right now, I would anticipate that commercials are built around what's popular. That's what creatives do is look at what's popular in culture. So as dance is more popular in the culture, more commercials will appear with dance or dance themes. I don't think it is world events, but cultural events in the sense that they are covered in the media. I remember African dance and singing groups worked their way into the commercials.

CH: *If I was to say, in the 1950s there was some dance with Dick Clark...*

DG: Yes, even with the Busby Berkeley musicals. Now you have to work with the ability of the client to pay for dance. Dance is an expensive proposition.

CH: *Why?*

DG: First of all you need people who can dance, you need a choreographer, a wardrober, and makeup, depending on how many are involved, usually quite a few. To do a Busby Berkeley–type commercial now with 30 dancers would be a major feat and no doubt would probably be done in South Africa, Czech Republic or Canada where labor is cheaper. The on-camera talent is most expensive, and the residuals, that's the hardest part. I did a couple of commercials, with the crash dummies, Vincent and Larry. When you saw it, it was simple, but executing it was complex. You could only shoot with them for only about 30 minutes for each hour. It's very complicated. They're sweating, and the dance music they can never start just where they left off, so they had to do a lot of repetition. It becomes very involved, need lights, lots of space.

CH: *What about dance commercials that don't have a lot of people? Is it still expensive?*

DG: Yes, there is generally a lot of pre-production, which involves dance training, even good dancers take time to learn the steps.

CH: *Commercials that have people dancing, like a Pepsi commercial with different snippets of slices of life, that still needs to be choreographed?*

DG: Everything is choreographed. You can't afford to take chances.

CH: *Or like one of Joe Pytka's commercials, with people dancing on the beach?*

DG: Yes, absolutely, it's choreographed. He doesn't like to do multiple takes. Joe does 2 or 3 takes and that's it. But in order to do that, he prepares ahead of time, and so you can bet his choreographer had those people ready. It's not "Go out there and dance around like you're at a club." Recreation of reality takes an enormous amount of work. And most people in a club are awful dancers; they haven't a clue. Anybody who would do a commercial with dance in it randomly would be a fool. Then you have principles and extras, where people have to stand, if they can or can't touch the product, background people have to stay in the background, and you don't want them doing things at random, especially too when it comes to residuals. So you tell them you have to dance right here, and not move out of this space.

CH: *Is there any thinking about getting the consumer to feel a certain way from the dance?*

DG: Yes, of course, sure, you're always thinking about the effects of the scenes you're filming. Before you go out and make a commercial, it's extensively researched, story boards or animatics, in focus groups or research sessions, people are asked which one they like and why. The more expensive and involved it is the more research you do. Burnett researched commercials extensively. So when I went out I knew exactly why we were shooting things so I could say to the director what we need. Public opinion or consumer feelings are important.

CH: *Is there a desire to have that person imagine they are in the dance?*

DG: Of course, you always want your consumer to identify with the heroine; you want to portray the experience they can expect if they use your widget or drive your car or eat your food. So yes, the goal is to make the consumer identify with your product to the exclusion of all other brands, similar or dissimilar.

CH: *There's a whole period of time in which advertising stayed away from segmenting African Americans but then there came a point in time when that changed. Is there anything about ethnic dance that is preferred or gives a way for people to identify with things?*

DG: Whatever we did, and I used to work on Hispanic market commercials for Burnett, I was the consultant with them and Foote Cone & Belding, but I understood the culture perhaps better, and, yes, there was no doubt that many agencies determined that not advertising to the black or Hispanic market, was a mistake.... There was definitely a cultural revolution in the 1980s when it became mandatory to integrate because they wanted to appeal to those groups. As far as using specific commercials that engaged dance, I didn't do any myself, but I saw many. We had a black creative director. She was great; she worked on McDonald's, and had a lot of opinions about what we should do to appeal to that market.

CH: *Since the '90s, do you think that dance used in ads appeals in segments or more mainstream?*

DG: Oh, definitely segmented, like the young people are influenced by black culture, they love hip-hop. There are more white kids that like hip-hop than black kids, but any cultural phenomenon is going to emerge in a commercial sooner or later, based on who they are targeting. McDonald's has a great ability to perceive cultural trends and segments of the population by age, income, location, not just skin color. When people in California wanted salads, they put salads in, or their Cafés. If it was something that would appeal to blacks, they would run it in shows that black people would watch.

CH: *If there is an ad that's run on the Super Bowl, that seems like it's a mixed-market segment, diverse.*

DG: So if you do a Super Bowl commercial, you want the commercial to appeal to everybody, but they're not afraid to appeal to different markets watching the Super Bowl.

CH: *Do you think there is a stereotype about who dances well and who doesn't in our society?*

DG: I suppose so, but I don't know. I would say people who are not post-racial would say yes, but I don't, I didn't grow up that way. But, yeah sure, there are people who say that. But I didn't understand this really until I went to work in Detroit, in 1967, when I started in the ad business there. But yes, there are always perceptions that certain people can dance better than others. But I must say to the credit of ad people, I've never heard a pejorative in relation to other cultures.

CH: *In many cases it looks like the agencies are in the position to frame a new world when it comes to social problems like racism. However, people have a desire to be cool, so because of that, when it comes to the issues the U.S., advertising has been a bridge over.*

DG: Yes, it's been a huge cultural developer; just look at McDonald's. There is no color or culture to a Big Mac or fries.

Advertising has become very much in the post-racial world,[23] as Martin Luther King [Jr.] said, about character and not skin. I think advertising is more interested in content, with culture and color mixed in to appeal to people. It's nothing if it doesn't appeal to people, as many as possible in any given commercial. I mean, you don't want to make it obnoxious for like a 50-year-old. But dance, when we've used it in commercials, it's been very specific about nostalgia appealing to certain groups, making it cool, without forgetting the product... To Joe Pytka's credit, he was one of the first to recruit blacks for working as technicians and crew, in the '70s; he asked me if I had any objections and I said no. So he was one wanting to get rid of whites-only culture in Hollywood... When I got to Burnett, there were certainly many people working there who were of different ethnic backgrounds.

Carol Williams, I used to work for, she was not removed from her culture and had insights about what would appeal. She would discuss things and was remarkably frank about everything and it was a wonderful thing because she was, in Burnett terms, very powerful, three-window office, big deal.... When we did a commercial when it had some cultural aspects, we listened to [people of color]. It would be silly not to, but also we listened to the research and the research was done appropriately by the research people who were also multicultural, and they wanted to see who was positively or adversely affected. So yes, dance will appear in commercials to the extent it appears is in the culture, maybe a smaller form of it because of the costs but...

CH: *Yes, we're past the dance video commercials.*
DG: Yes (laughing).

CH: *A couple of days ago I saw a hospital commercial with dance; that's not low involvement...*

DG: So that springs out of the inherent drama of the product; the hospital product is making them well. People think hospitals are gonna make them die, so they are trying to counter that perception. They want to change that, that's one of the motivations, so if you come to our hospital, you're going to be dancing.... Yes, the inherent drama is to make you happy and celebrate.

4. On Black Social Dance in Commercials in 2010 127

CH: *But advertising moves the culture along as well, doesn't it?*

DG: Yes, absolutely, there is a visceral response to dance. Dance is designed to evoke an emotional response, whether from an era or an event, or whatever.

In unpacking this interview about dance in advertising, we have a few themes that emerge. First of all, creative brilliance can often lead to wealth and success in the ad business, as in the case of Joe Pytka and Bob Giraldi. They are both quite successful. But success comes with client approval. In other words, the most creative and successful ad men and women are brilliant and work with commercial dance masters, but only after the client has approved a program with dance in it.

The creative director has several teams under him or her; they work together to come up with ideas, then four or so emerge, and are sent to the client, with estimates for costs of delivering the finished commercial within a given timeframe. The commercial is chosen not only for creativity but also taking cost to produce into consideration, along with what the client expects in terms of a return from airing the commercial. Clients select bids from creative providers based on content and cost. And, as Mr. Geeting suggested, the costs begin to add up and therefore you see fewer large groups of dancers in commercials, which has changed since the early decades of commercials, which used choreographed dance such as those discussed earlier in the book. It would require a major effort to do a huge Busby Berkeley–type of commercial probably being done in a country where labor is cheaper.

Interestingly, but simply stated, according to Mr. Geeting, the choreographed dance is used not to project an image of one or another group but it is used to appeal to people. What kind of dance and how much are cost factors. Dance in whatever format, though, is used because it showcases the item being advertised. Leo Burnett said to be mindful of the drama of the advertised item. Inherent drama becomes part of the tension between ad women and consumers. That has been going on since the 1950s. The goal is to make the product popular and appealing, interesting "without making it something you don't" want to consume. So while costs are a factor, for example, in making commercials with dance, and it could be argued that an idea for a commercial with dance in it will vary depending on if the dance is animated or done by humans, with the expertise of the dancers and choreographers. The fact remains that there is inherent drama in dance that becomes associated with the product. Inherent drama — centuries of it — lives within black social dance. However, commercials do not simply appear on television; they are extensively researched as are, in many cases, the very people to whom the target audience is made up, the focus groups and respondents who give the commercial a thumbs up.

The fact is that the ad men and women want that consumer to *feel something*, to identify with the product, and exclude others, as Mr. Geeting suggests. And, in particular dance provides a visceral response.

In the 1980s there was an increase of black social dance in television commercials. That no doubt was partially due to MTV's influence but also because of the cultural revolution in the 1980s: It was necessary to appeal to different markets, which increasingly targeted blacks.

What one has to take from this discussion is that the use of dance in television ads has been a growing force over the study period, and the motivators for that increase was a change in the cultural landscape around advertising to wider market segments. However, many people had a role to play in this and, as easy as it would be to assign causality to the advertising industry as a culprit, based on the literature and the interview, that would be an error of judgment. I will come back to this point in chapter 6 when I discuss what I conclude from this, and what I hope for future, research into dance and television advertising.

It was shown in chapter 3 that black social dance in television ads increased dramatically over the study period, particularly with the advent of the dance video concept. That the dance was increasingly removed from black people after that was evident from the commercials over time. In this chapter, respondents' views of black social dance were explored along with the production process of ads that contain dance. We have a historical view of black culture used in television advertising from a reputable ad man and in his view we have evolved to a post-racial society, a point which is itself arguable from at least two reference points. One, we have seen increased polarization in the political processes in the United States. And two, the reduction of affirmative action policy seems to be motivated along racial lines. These aspects of race in the United States will be discussed more fully when I turn to post-postmodernism in chapter 5. For purposes of this chapter, there is a meshing of the purpose of dance in television ads, and that is to evoke a visceral and emotional response from inherent fiction. Fiction drama, we know, is the drive of emotion generated through cognition.

Diet Pepsi, or any other product or brand, has no drama or emotion on its own. The use of black social dance in advertising definitely imbues the product with it, and perhaps makes the brand stable, and therefore live, for consumers in a shifting sand of too many consumption options.[24] As such, in chapter 5, the business of using black social dance in television commercials and the respondents' views are compared and contrasted. The conceptualizations of the dance along with the creation of dance and consumption connections are explored and interpreted, providing support for the framework described earlier for the theory of black social dance in television ads.

5. Interpretations

Instead, my interviews with advertising personnel reveal a belief that most advertising creatives, regardless of racial background, tend to reproduce what they see.[1]

Social dancing links African Americans to their past more strongly than any other aspect of their culture.[2]

INTRODUCTION

One thing must be kept in mind as this chapter progresses. That is simply that while advertising's purpose is to increase and predict consumers' consumption through brand loyalty, it has done so by evolving into a form of art,[3] and an aesthetic manifestation of its own.[4] As an art form, advertising has incorporated and commissioned various sources and creators of images, music, voices, and, as others have hinted at[5] but this book has shown, dance. As such I have argued that commercials also serve an hermeneutic anthropologic function.[6] The phenomenology of dance underpins this function when it is used in commercials. In this chapter I demonstrate this through interpreting the respondents' views presented in chapter 4. These relationships are graphically summarized in figure 5: "Conceptualizations of Dance."

The reader will readily recall that in chapter 4, voices of the respondents were presented regarding their thoughts, feelings, and opinions of black social dance used in the Diet Pepsi "Brown and Bubbly" commercial. Several theoretical concepts were honed from their remarks. They are schematically represented in figure 6: "Perceptual Map of Black Social Dance in Television Ads."

This chapter seeks to interpret the respondents' views of black social dance—created in the space between the screen and the body—within a

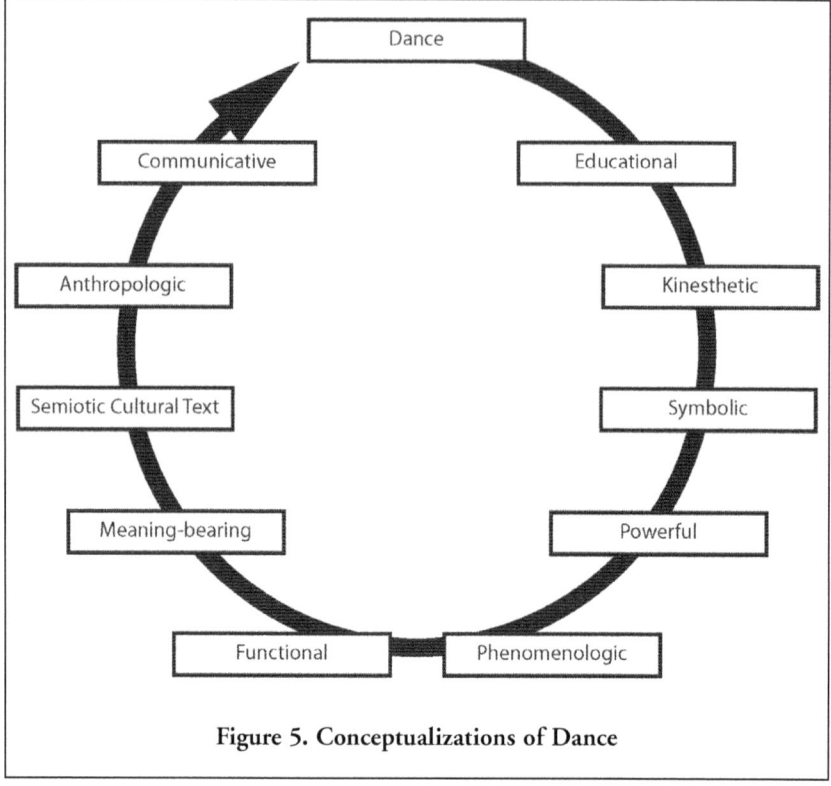

Figure 5. Conceptualizations of Dance

theoretical framework, as well as analyze and discuss relevant commercials over the study period. As has already been made apparent, I write from an African American woman's dance historian and interdisciplinary studies perspective. That perspective, in addition, includes that of a qualitative consumer researcher. Therefore, thick inscription[7] of the meanings of the dance in the text of the commercial and in daily life is provided, as I understand them. This methodology is in line with Royce's (1977) approach to an anthropological view. It should also be noted that while it is true that each respondent and their families were a part of black social dance culture, their belonging in these self-identified groups was purely coincidental — that is, there was no pre-screening of candidates for the research project. In addition I want to stress that there are many African Americans who, for a variety of reasons, do not dance. As Emery (1972, 1988) suggested in her historical survey of black dance from the 1600s through the 1970s, a belief system that supposes all black dance is stereotypical. However, that does not remove it from cultural productions and storage in an artifactual manner. As such, I want to avoid (a) suggesting that there are any essentializing attributes of any group of people,

5. Interpretations

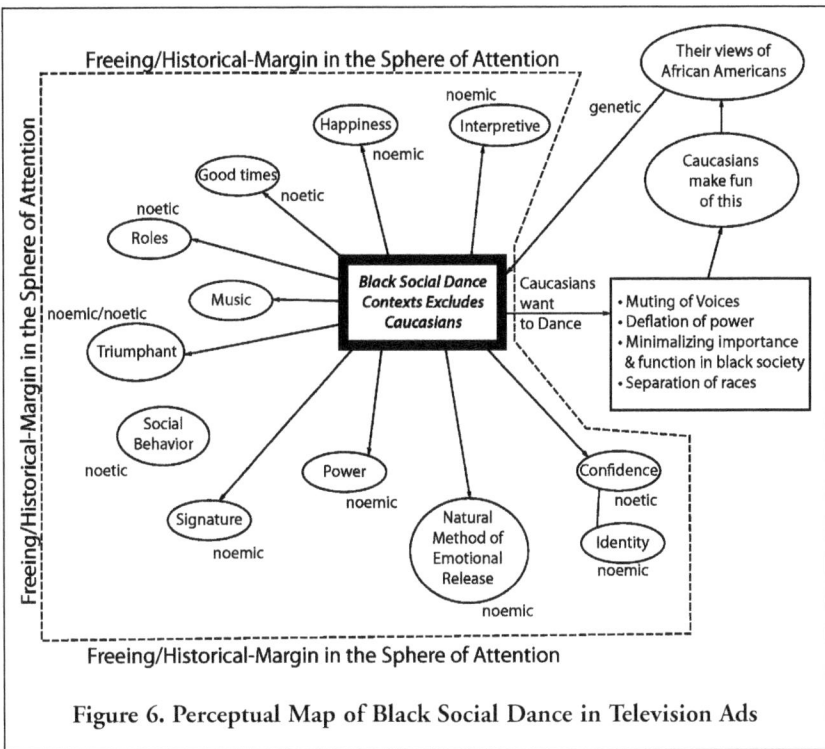

Figure 6. Perceptual Map of Black Social Dance in Television Ads

and (b) broad generalizations taken from the respondents' views. However, it is interesting that the non-black readings of black social dance in commercials seems to be in direct contrast to those of the African Americans. In Walter's (2011) analysis, the findings indicate that Euro Americans insist on participating in the culture in a way that allows them to maintain the point of view that Euro Americans remain in socio-economic control on a micro-level. In addition, individually, they feel included within the culture. What I want to do is bring these readings back to the effect that black social dance in television ads *vis à vis* consumption had on this group of respondents in a theoretical framework. Finally, I analyze the historical change over time of the use of black social dance during the study period, from modernity to postmodernity, and post-postmodernity. This point will be addressed in a section later on in the chapter. The other goal of this chapter is to extend and develop an explanatory theory of black social dance in television commercials, using the data at hand.

One point I want to make before beginning the overall analysis and interpretation is that some African American respondents in this research articulated a relationship between black social dance cataclysmically arising from feeling and hearing musical rhythms. We are reminded by dance scholars

Mandy's Ragtime Waltz. Rare Book, Manuscript, and Special Collections Library, Duke University, Durham, North Carolina.

Malone and Hazzard-Gordon that the historical relationship between music and dance in African American society is long standing,[8] to the point of it being embedded in African Americans' muscle memory. It is this kind of assertion that gives the respondents the idea that the dance is "genetic." And I have experienced something like this: hearing a song and remembering the dance, or hearing a new song and wanting to dance. This experience happens with black social dance and ballet for me—depending on the context, I may want to put on my toe shoes or get on up. In other words, the music makes you move. I suggest that this aspect of the effect of African American *music and dance* in television ads be taken up in a separate research project. Nevertheless, the interviews here focused on the dance, and that is what is interpreted here.

THE PERCEPTUAL MAP—WHAT IS ON RESPONDENTS' MINDS?

Respondents looking at the Diet Pepsi ad used in this research identified several areas of importance for them with regard to black social dance. I ask the reader to refer to figure 6. Placing black social dance as the center for purposes of interpretation, we find several radial noetic and noemic points. Circulating around the dance, first of all, respondents found it and themselves to be situated in a historical horizon within their spheres of attention,[9] linked with a concomitant and inseparable phenomenologically freeing sensation. As Josh said,

> I guess 'cause it's a different form of dance, it's more of a freedom of expression, guys spinning on they heads, girls dancing how they wanna dance.... It's more freedom of, in hip-hop dance you can do what you want.... It gives people freedom of expression. I mean, basically, that's what they feel like doing at the time; there don't have to be a name or something for the dance as long as it's what you feel like doing.... They're just expressing their selves, you can relieve, I mean, I know some people, I know my brother, when he stress, he goes outside and break dances in the grass, that's how he gets rid of his stress.

Black social dance is one thing African Americans have owned and found value in throughout their history. As Malone (1996, 23–24) writes,

> Even in the face of tremendous adversity, it evinces an affirmation and celebration of life. Furthermore, African American dance serves some of the same purposes of traditional dances in western and central African cultures: on both continents black dance is a source of energy, joy, and inspiration; a spiritual antidote to oppression; and a way to lighten work, teach social values, and strengthen institutions.

These meanings and messages come through the dance in television ads as well.

Moving into the margin of the experience with black social dance, we have several noetic (i.e., what they experience) and noemic (or what they see) elements as the essence or larger spiritual points to consider that arise from their experience and identities.[10] Noetically, we have black social dance as providing a good time, dictating social behaviors, building confidence, and defining roles and positions in society. But what do these mean in terms of black social dance? The phrase "having a good time" has several meanings imbedded within it, which on the surface may appear straightforward. First of all, it means being free from constraints, like financial, sexual, or racial pressures. One is in a social situation where people do not judge and everyone is allowed to let his or her guard down. So if you are the member of the family who is considered nonproductive, you can let that go. If you are the family member who is successful, you can rest from feeling responsible for taking care of the so-called non-productive family members. Or, one is in a social situation where black people understand each other's language, verbal and non-verbal, stemming from historical racial relationships. You can see this in black professional organizations as well, where the stress of being under the microscope from being non-black is removed. In terms of dictating behaviors, building confidence, and defining roles, the dance provides stable ground on which to stand since it has been with black people for centuries and carries historic success in survival and accomplishment. Noemically, the dance yields a life interpretive aspect, the ability to be triumphant in life and to leave a signatory and enduring mark on history with dance, creating a sense of power, a particular human identity and the generation of happiness. These noemic points also incorporate a seemingly innate bodily dancing ability to provide a method of natural emotional release, or theorizing.

These horizontal, marginal and focal points for the dance are seen in the commercial from the respondents' spheres of attention as reminders, for most of them positive ones, of black social dance performed in reality, in their private spaces. When the dance is placed in the commercial, particularly on non-black bodies, or discerned as being executed for non-noetic or -noemic purposes, the respondents find it problematic. First of all they interpret Caucasians as being outsiders to their spheres of attention in all aspects from the focal point to the horizon. This point was a finding shown in Walter's (2011) research. Secondly, they feel that the ability to dance and the meanings associated with it are genetically constituted such that a non-black person really cannot fathom the depth to which the dance speaks, a fact that has been documented by scholars such as Malone (1996), Emery (1988), and Hazzard-Gordon (1990). In taking the dance out of the context and placing a representation of it into the context of an advertisement, African American respondents suggest that their voices are muted, their power is deflated, and the importance of their dance as a key aspect to functioning historically and currently in American society is minimalized and ridiculed. What African American respondents considered as a cherished and sacred process of finding meaning and self-identity is instead used to continue racial separation *because* Caucasian Americans do not have the inherent capacity arising from the life experience and historical memory to dance. The anthropological reflection provided in the ads is what Caucasian Americans interpret, not what African Americans see. This is true even when blacks are controlling the commercial broadcasting; the question of whether blacks control these distribution channels is up for grabs. However, simultaneously, respondents suggested that use of the dance in advertisements pointed to an acceptance of African American culture through the mechanism of black social dance. Such acceptance was seen as an important and positive movement in the direction of needed critical social change to reduce continued racism. Todd put it this way:

> I kinda feel like us as a society is kinda moving towards that direction like seems like every commercial from McDonald's to anything else is kinda going towards the hip-hop, African American music or beat or dancing.... So generally it targeted African Americans but everyone else at the same time. You know what I mean? ["Why do you think the commercials are moving that direction?"] I don't know, I don't know if it is because, you know, us as a people [blacks], you know, has come a long ways or as barriers change, there's more open minds to, you know, the way we do things or the way we think or I think that over time, people, you know, other than black people, you know, they have come to find that our [black] culture is fun, you know, and fun is attractive.

Within this descriptive framework, dance can be shown to reside in a sphere of attention with noemic and noetic points. It attracts the viewer with the themes of having fun, having a good time, letting go of problems. At the viewer's horizon, the history of black social dance encircles the marginal current movement towards an acceptance of black culture as good, with the focal point being the product as it contributes to individual identity creation or reinforcement.

DIMENSIONAL ASPECTS OF BLACK SOCIAL DANCE IN COMMERCIALS

At the center of each of seven dichotomous dimensions, conceptual aspects of black social dance rotate like Mobius strips around the notion of awe.[11] As was discussed earlier in this study, awe provides a Piagetian process of accommodation. I explained this concept previously but, by way of reminder, the Piagetian process means that a given set of knowledge structures are interrupted and cause a change in the individual's view or understanding of some aspect of the world. Please refer to figure 7: "Dimensions of Black Social Dance in Commercials" for the ensuing analysis. I will start at the top of the diagram and work downward.

To begin, on the one hand, we have black social dance providing meaning for life within a capitalist culture in the United States when performed in private for personal reasons as they relate to an individual or group within the African American experience. This value has been evident since the advent of the new world. As we are told by Hazzard-Gordon (1990, 22),

> On the plantation, slaves danced for themselves as celebration, recreation, and mourning as well as for their masters' entertainment. As in the middle passage, dancers were sometimes rewarded.... Yet slave holders were well aware that dance could function as a form of social intercourse, cultural expression, assimilation mechanism, and political expression. Because it was a means of solidifying the slave community, dance could threaten white dominance.

On the other hand, there is that aspect of a representation of black social dance produced for sale where it is obvious that this was the case. The respondents put it this way. Todd said he thought the dancers were dancing the way they were

> mainly because I think they were getting paid to dance like that [laughing], um, trying to have a good time at the same time but I don't think it was merely off of emotion or anything.

While Kim and Josh respectively noted

> It was more of a, it wasn't really black social dance.... It was just, I don't know.
>
> I think the dance, was ... well they were going for a hip-hop–type vibe with the dance.

Alfonzo called it this way:

> The dancing. Actually, you know, it wasn't like a lot of hard dancing. I mean, it was more of things that are simple to do, easy. It was like, you know, so you know nothing that was too hard for anybody [non-black] to go out and learn.

This is the dance that is performed by non-blacks, but at the same time it too becomes its own capitalist production when placed in television ads where people consume as part of the American experience.

Moving down the spirals of figure 7, next identity and ability, though they seem to be different, are wrapped tightly together, circulating to create awe for black social dance. For non-blacks on one side of the endless strip, their identity is defined as not being able to dance, while on the other side, African Americans perceive themselves as defined by being able to dance or not but it is not always a positive choice. That is to say, the church as an

5. Interpretations

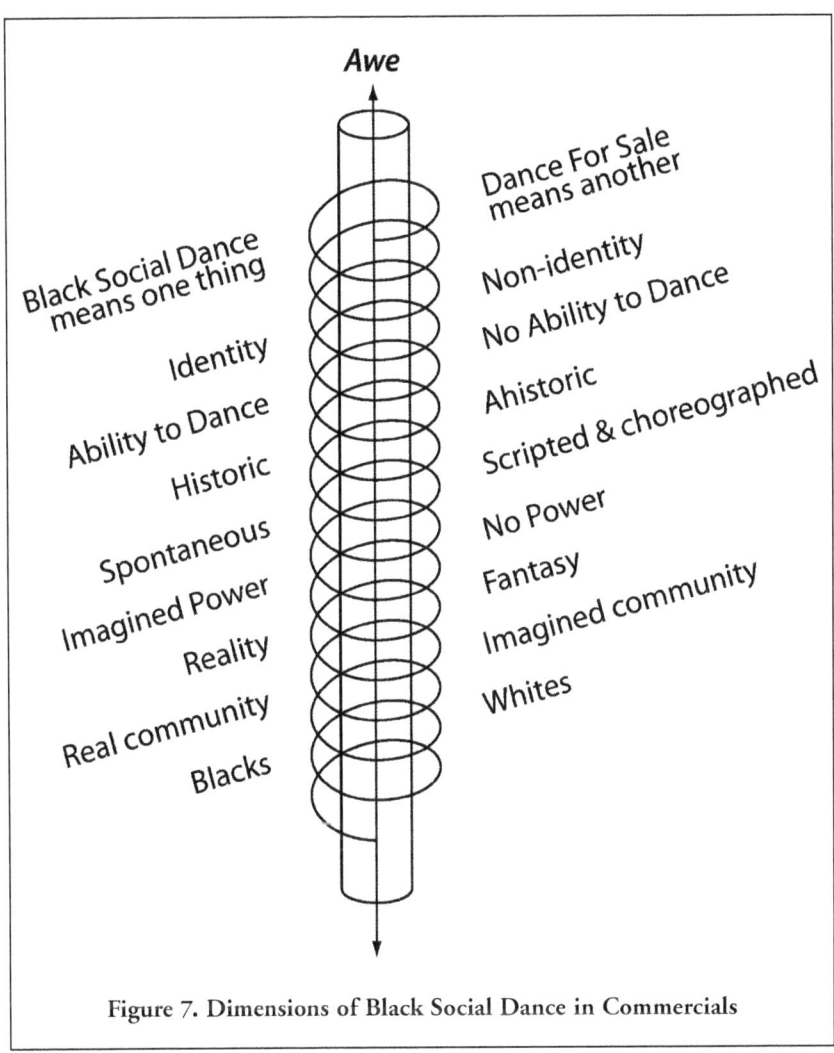

Figure 7. Dimensions of Black Social Dance in Commercials

adversary, or other hegemonic institution, can exert taboos over dance,[12] or people can be made to feel like they are not exceptional dancers, as respondent Kim shared:

> I do believe I started [black social dancing] when I was about 5. I noticed everybody was dancing at our age, but then my mom said I couldn't dance and so kind of beat down on my dancing confidence. She was like, "You don't have any rhythm," and being a kid I was just like, I don't know what I was doing wrong, so I tried to imitate but so I gave up dancing early ... probably because of that; I'm not upset about it or anything like that, but it was just something that happened.

Josh, on the other hand, had a different experience with the dance:

> I mean, it's a part of your life growing up, I mean, you know, at some point in the African American community you're gonna dance, I mean, it's how we socialize. We dance. I know, well, I started dancing to fit in. I wasn't much of a dancer, but I started dance 'cause I didn't want to be the guy at the party just sitting on the wall ... it pretty much worked [laughing]. It was like the one thing, I mean, I could play basketball, I had decent grades and everything like that, but I couldn't dance so I kinda wanted to be well rounded.... It just felt like I can do it all. I mean, I don't think, it's a lot of stuff I can't do, but to me I felt like there's not someone where I lived where I can't do what they did.

Nevertheless, one is transformed by the dance, be they onlookers, other performers, or dancers when no one is watching, as Kim said she did. When connecting ability or lack of ability with a brand, though, consuming the brand provided the imagined ability for whites[13] and reinforced the awe with the idea that blacks, and non-blacks according to Walter (2011) want to be included in black social dance, regardless. Here we see it reinforcing identity and awe in that it provoked a new level of learning.

Traveling from a personal meaning and identity perspective, the dimensions move to historic and spiritual levels. Let me say, too, before going on, that the order of these dimensions as presented here are purely arbitrary and they could be placed in any ranking. In any event, on the one hand, black social dance contains within it a collective history of the African diaspora of people to the New World, United States slavery, emancipation, segregation, desegregation, affirmative action, reduction of affirmative action, and globalization.[14] There is a sense of spirituality and spontaneity in the dance that draws on this history. On the other hand, when performed in television ads, the dance becomes ahistoric and choreographed perhaps, which seeks to make the viewer believe the dance as being created in that moment. With montage, dance sequence is "no longer limited to linear progression and, as a result, television has the capacity to restructure passage of events completely."[15] As such, through no fault of hers, the viewer perceives black social dance as connected with brands, sarcastically destablizing the dance and diminishing the historically critical aspects of it. The commercial draws only on an awe-inspiring, newly contextualized ahistorical rendition of the dance as meaning fun, cool, and easy to do for any non-black consumer. Perhaps, as Mr. Geeting suggested in his interview with me, this can be considered to be a level of the "inherent drama" of the dance that is connected to the brand. That is to say, one aspect of inherent drama is the fact that it is a historic, an aesthetic, and a cultural artifact, an anthropologic phenomenon, but no one really states it as such; rather, it is implicit within the commercial.

A consumer watching the dance in a commercial is not necessarily cued into the idea that the dance is choreographed,[16] as Mr. Geeting pointed out, and not spiritual, i.e., it does not appear to be non-spontaneous. It is true that respondents touched on the aspect of the dance as being done for money or being fake. But Justin put it this way as he read the choreography:

> I haven't seen a non-black person actually dance hip-hop but I could imagine it if they grew up around black people. Otherwise they can't really embrace the culture, like when hip-hop had a reason, a purpose, message, you know, "fight the power." Now it's all about gold teeth and profit. Non-blacks haven't embraced or experienced the culture.

In this dimension of the dance, then, on one end of the continuum, we have dance as spontaneous and dance as choreographed for the television ad. Here there are multiple aspects of choreographed dance, and I specifically address the choreography for advertising.[17] For the animated movies, many of the choreographed scenes are first designed within a stable venue such as a studio, encompassed by a linear time sequence. The dance is performed and taped, often with African American people doing the dancing, and then removed from those people and placed on digital Pixar renditions of chipmunks or rats. The same process happens in television ads, as was done for the Kia Soul hamsters, for example. In other dance motifs, like that being used in the Diet Pepsi commercial, dancers are instructed on what to do, either in replication of a club scene or party, or in this case, riding in a car. They are taped and the montage is placed in a nonlinear, non-temporal, non-stable context. As such, choreographed dance in commercials is really both, that which is non-spontaneous for the individual, and the group of black social dance scenes. And, as was learned from the interview with the advertising agency executive respondent, no dance is placed in a commercial without first choreographing it. As Mr. Geeting knows: "Everything is choreographed. You can't afford to take chances.... Anybody who would do a commercial with dance in it randomly would be a fool."

That said, the axial rotation of spontaneous versus choreographed black social dance means that awe is had at both levels: people, black or non-black, wish they could or already know they can do it.[18] Either way, as many respondents suggested they have fun with it, it reminds them of "a good time" and they simply feel good, and these feelings and memories are connected with the brand.

One of the most striking aspects of the dance as interpreted from the respondents' words is the notion that black social dance is powerful.[19] Being able to do the dance correctly allows one to fit in or be cast as a wallflower, tying the dancer to the history, while giving a means of current expression and release. On this rotating concept around the axis of awe, on one end we see dance as providing power to the individual and group while, on the other end, we see the rendering of the dance as powerless when one cannot effectively dance, but one can consume. The agent dancing, while seen as funny by the respondents, was only one aspect of this. At the beginning of the commercial he does not dance at all; at the end, when he is successful in his endeavors, he does. P Diddy does as well, although it is assumed that P Diddy can dance, however badly, at the outset by the respondents. To Jonathan and Kim especially, P Diddy is not a good dancer and this was something that "everybody knows." And even with that supposed stigma, he had the ability to make his own "signature dance," which placed him in an exalted category. But underlying this, there is the sense that when dancing in African American situations, there is a notion that they have power over the situation and the ability to control the environment rather than having the environment placed upon them. By environment I am talking specifically about the one containing historical and current hegemonic issues of race and problems associated with financial or resourceful lack arising from race situated within material capitalism. So while the dance is seen as providing and removing power from the two men in the commercial, there is also the removal of power from the dance when it is disseminated in these ahistorical projections, a lessening of its significance and a removal of a longstanding possession used as a coping device that is held, in a sense, as sacred. This is in line with Hanna's (1987) schema of dance as a communication device, shown in figure 2 earlier, in that dance is used for coping and organizing the world.

Finally we come to the dimension of reality versus fantasy: the imagined community[20] versus the real one, and I add, the mythical one[21] versus one's reality and the provocation of awe. It is one thing to imagine oneself as a part of a greater yet unseen community; it is another to create mythical worlds. Either way, black social dance is a documented commentary on life experiences and culture in the United States. The reality is that race plays a large role in identity in the United States and, as has been shown already, identity is wrapped up in black social dance regardless of whether one is black or nonblack. After all, as Malone (1988, 364) stated, black social dance is a heritage that is just as much a part of white America as it is black. One does not exist without the other.

In reality, African Americans experience racial strife and so do Caucasians. However, African American respondents know and are a part of the reality that generated black social dance. They indirectly acknowledged that Caucasians are part of that reality as well as the mirror image. The imagined ability to dance from their point of view allows them to be a part of the imagined community of Caucasians who can interpret black social dance and its myriad of cultural meanings. By crafting mythical worlds on the screen where Caucasians are placed on equal footing with African Americans, both groups are leveled and the issue of race is muted, at least for thirty seconds. The imagined community of life in the United States without racism as a result of being able to do black social dance emerges. One must only be completely awed by the possibility of this, as respondents suggested.

A question is begging to be asked, and that is what exactly does it mean to be African American? Nasir and colleagues (2009) have shown that for students in a predominately African American high school, this is not a simple question to answer. And nowadays it has become a sore subject, more so than before the election of Obama as president. However, Nasir and colleagues did find that being African American is connected with an historical and national media context along with immediate and local experiences. In short, the media renditions draw on negative histories and portrayals of African Americans, in a time when constructing positive identity is available to individual consumers. However, if one has brown skin, it is difficult to deny ethnicity, and in any event, "contemporary media tend to portray African Americans, particularly young males, most often as thugs, athletes or entertainers. The prevalence of this 'gangsta' identity is related to a consumer economy where gangsta rap is a multimillion dollar industry."[22] Gangstas are flanked by hypersexualized depictions of women so that not only are they gangsters, they are marked as sexual predators. True or not, verbal discussion of race in the post-affirmative action and what has become termed post-racial world becomes more and more marginalized while dance becomes more and more distributed around these difficult issues in American culture and history. Some respondents, particularly Justin, Shinqua and often Josh, suggest as much when black social dance was used in the Diet Pepsi ad. I will return to the post-racial discussion later in the chapter. The point is that the commercial documents the racial history[23] and static black and non-black identities, and I now assert that it is also done through black social dance.

While Nasir and colleagues (2009) did not address dance per se, they did address other aspects of life and cultural practices for African Americans, those "reoccurring, goal-directed activities that involve two or more people"[24] which include institutions and rituals, which I suggest embrace those that include black social dance. As was shown in chapter 4, respondents articulated the notion of an index of blackness: that if you can dance right, you are black, and simply you have to *be* African American or you will not be able to. Short of that there is no sign value[25] in it: Being-hereness[26] includes identifying with and living the life, wearing the clothes, feeling the music, and negotiating within the broad horizon of cultural history of the United States which is delivered in black social dance. Doing so does not mean or equate to negative stereotypes generated by the media, even if non-blacks interpret it that way. There is a sense of being able to decipher a real dance versus a fake one, and these all are related to the dimensions circulating around the discourse of awe, at least as it has been interpreted here.

MODERNITY, POSTMODERNITY, AND POST-POSTMODERNITY

In this book, when the terms "modernity," "post-modernity," and "post-post-modernity" are used, I am referring to the time periods that have marked consumer society. Specifically modernity and post-modernity as defined by Lyotard (1984) and Baudrillard (1995), followed by that of Fredric Jameson (1990) and other scholars critical of the effect of capitalist society on humanity. Modernity, post modernity and post–post-modernity have informed the arts, as defined in the continuum from modernism to post-postmodernism. I am suggesting that the dance in television ads reflects these ways of thinking and ways of creating art. While the boundaries between the time periods do blur, I work with the convention that post-modernity and postmodernism time period began at the end of World War II and ended with technological expansion of the information age. Post-postmodernism and post–post-modernity began, in my estimation, with the moment in time when images could be downloaded and disseminated, when it was normal to have a big screen and a personal digital device, and perhaps when dance performance began using digitized images in live performance, such that

> somewhere in the late 1990s or early 2000s, the emergence of new technologies re-structured, violently and forever, the nature of the author, the reader and the text, and the relationships between them ... and the "text" is characterized both by its hyper-ephemerality and by its instability. It is made up by the "viewer," if not in its content then in its sequence.[27]

What I am getting at is the progression of black social dance on the ground and its depiction in television commercials; as time plodded forward, advertising's reflection of black culture matches this progression. If I wanted to, I could upload a dance onto YouTube and then I could send it around the world on my personal device, and I could also use that device to control my television screen. As part of this progression, I would like to note that over the period under study, the trajectory was being paralleled by the employment of African American advertising executives and agencies. While more research may be needed to fully establish this relationship, it could be that the presentation of black social dance in television ads followed the rise and fall of blacks in creative roles in advertising agencies, to the usurping of their skill sets into non-black advertising creative divisions.[28] If that is shown to be true, then, how could intentionality be assigned? I think we have to exercise caution when asking why questions about black social dance over the period. As such, I walk closely next to the content of the commercials and published resources on them to make theoretical postulates.

"[T]here had to be an organic relation between design and cultural values.... [Advertising was] incorporating some designs more relevant to our life and needs by incorporating ... dancing."[29] During the modernist period in advertising, class distinctions gave rise to the use of art in advertising, and the view that life was somehow boring with massive industrialization. At that time, the elite Caucasian Americans held this view,[30] which was likely to be very different from black people regardless of their socio-economic standing in the 1950s; and in fact then, as now in the post-postmodern period, commercials reflected the views and anthropology of the dominant class. Even as that is true, television ads do function as a museum for folks, and just as curators decide what holdings to retain, individuals at the helms of media communications and consumer culture[31] decide what will be placed in the ephemeral museum of television ads. Moreover, the need to increase consumer purchases succeeded by using ads that incorporated artistic components, and at this juncture it is not necessary for me to further argue that point.

The use of dance in television ads was documented in chapter 3 and so was the rise of black social dance. As the consumer society progressed into the postmodern and post-postmodern eras, black social dance was shown briefly on black people, and then moved off of them over time for the most part and placed on non-black bodies, animals, and animated characters. This is not a new phenomenon as black social dance has been used for commercial gain over the course of American history. That is to say that white people learn dances from blacks until they can take control of them (Emery 1988, Malone 1996). Moreover, as of this writing, it was more interesting, then, to competitively compare and implicity bring up the idea that blacks dance and whites do not with respect to President Obama's and former President George W. Bush's dancing in the 2010 post-postmodern and post-racial era than it is to see black people doing black social dancing in commercials, as this is the way that the media's vision of the world has been characterized. However, this admittedly is a digression.

It is from within the post–post-modernity/-modernism thinking perhaps that the concept of post-racial society stems. I think the best way to look at post-racial society is said best by Ono (2010):

> *Mad Men, Avatar, Invictus,* and *Gran Torino* illustrate that we live in postracist times when representation is absolutely central to a racial project that both is an extension of colonial and neocolonial projects and also is a reinvented project of forgetting race and maneuvering and adjusting reality to deny historical and

contemporary reality. Examining media helps us to understand precisely how these politics are figured within the cultural landscape. Media participate in the construction of the racialized condition in which we live, and it is often through them that people negotiate identities, ideas, and relationships with other subjects.[32]

As the respondents claimed in this research, we are not post-racial, as advertisers, even those interviewed here, want us to believe. Some people do want to believe in the image,[33] and that is perhaps why Alonzo said it did not hit him at first when he watched the commercial: "The first time, I watched the commercial, it was funny, you know, you didn't pick up on a lot of things, you were just listening to the music, that was the first time."

Post-racist ideology is that which attempts to twist racism backwards onto the very people on which racism pressed, a "blame the victim" mentality, or worse, act like it never happened. It is similar to the feeling of wanting to go back to whatever good old days existed before a comfort zone was disturbed, when people used to boil water and not microwave it, or make a phone call and accept a busy signal. Black social dance used in this commercial, as interpreted by these respondents, and as depicted in the archives that were reviewed suggests that, as post-racism attempts, erasure of the meanings and disruption of the connection to the historical aspects of the dance will negate racism as a political and economic institution. However, as Mr. Geeting indicated, race is still considered in advertising:

> Carol Williams, I used to work for, she was not removed from her culture and had insights about what would appeal. She would discuss things and was remarkably frank about everything and it was a wonderful thing because she was, in Burnett terms, very powerful, three-window office, big deal.... When we did a commercial, when it had some cultural aspects, we listened to [people of color]. It would be silly not to, but also we listened to the research and the research was done appropriately by the research people who were also multicultural, and they wanted to see who was positively or adversely affected.

Cronin (2004) and Fowles (1998) articulated Mr. Geeting's point of view as well: what shows up in advertising is what people making the ads see.

CONNECTING BACK TO DOING DANCE AND THE CRITICAL ISSUES FOR CONSUMERS

How is this connected to the original proposition that dance is fleeting yet aesthetic, a social commentary, historically memorable, and spiritual? Where does the brand synaesthetic experience connect? I invite the reader to review the figures and tables for the following discussion, particularly figures 1 through 6, along with tables 1 and 2, from the previous chapters. I would suggest that the linkage arises with the dance as fleeting whereas we have black social dance as the defining central text. It is that aspect of the dance that is dually at each moment a socially critical commentary and spontaneously aesthetic. The feeling of wanting to dance comes from an emotional impetus while the feeling of not wanting to dance does as well. Even the desire to be an adversary of dance is based on an aesthetic response. The mechanism of meaning and comment, however, occurs whether the dance is executed by blacks or non-blacks. Readers are able to "cite" the dance, without consciously being aware of it. And the feeling of envy may cause both blacks and non-blacks to want to be able to perform black social dance. Connecting the envy with the brand, ads succeed at making it such that anyone can dance if he or she consumes the product. It provides powerful emotional connections between the brand and the viewer. An emotional connection to the brand is required for brand equity and brand loyalty. This is one of the purposes of using dance, in particular black social dance, in television ads: to increase both loyalty and, in turn, equity.

Dance in television ads are social *and* choreographed; however, the art form remains feminine but emerges from that categorization with this research in that dance as a carrier of consumer meaning has been under theorized yet theorized. It is an anthropology of ourselves. Sklar's (2001) premises allow binary oppositions of male and female, personal and corporate, art and non-art, social and choreographed, freeing and imprisoning. While we watch dance being used in these post-postmodern ways, dance has found value in producing awe, which is translated into brand equity value for the likes of Pepsi.

In chapter 1 I posited that dance played a part in forming identity and this has been shown with the respondents. It even provides an imagined identity for some, where people are goal oriented, as Josh said, learning to dance so that he could be a part of the social fabric. Each respondent suggested that dance ability was a part of their life's achievements and these achievements help to define them. This was in line with Klein and colleagues (1993) who claimed that a self-focus is always present in terms of defining identity and in turn, how one reads dance. Additionally, the reader will recall that it was McFee (1992) who suggested that goals and outcomes can be signaled with dance.

At the same time, the notion that blacks dance while whites do not was due to an adversarial relationship with dance,[34] one that was clearly articulated by the respondents. This was also true in another study.[35] Black social dance as seen by the respondents was not only a racial declaration, it was sexual manipulation, as Todd, Josh and Shiniqa stated, respectively:

> It was very suggestive. I mean, there's a saying "sex sells," and uh, a lot of the females were kissing up if you will, to the Pepsi can, and uh, that's the kind of dancing really going on.
>
> the females were doing some type of, I guess you can call it a sexy type dance [chuckle].... Basically [chuckle], I guess they were trying, I guess, like, they was really dancing like they were in a club, dancing with a guy, like, with a guy they wanted, but, I mean, they was dancing around a Pepsi can. So ... I guess the Pepsi can is like the player, that have, you know, the women all around him and stuff like that.
>
> [The dance] had nothing to do with Diet Pepsi. [They were] selling themselves, selling sex — the girls. To find a guy or a girl.

This validates a longstanding view, and the way it is portrayed in this ad, of the symbiotic relationship between dance's villanization due to its supposed power to seduce innocent people.[36] However, as I have defined aesthetics in this work, the evocation of emotion was all that was required for it to be classified this way.

That dance provides an educational component was clear through the views of respondents who thought the dance contained history, whether it was actually in the commercial or residing in their memories. In addition, dance in the commercial revealed effort as the respondents' suggested that the dance was not real but a representation of black social dance. In performing the dance, it gave respondents the illusion of power, though both Shiniqa and Justin immediately said that power presented in the commercial was illusory. And while Langer (1953) suggests that dance is not motivated by music, as was mentioned already, some respondents felt a strong connection between the music and the dance. It is possible that the connection increases and magnifies the sense of power that the dance holds. In the commercial, the scenes were set up, particularly the scene between P Diddy and the agent, to make people think black people had power. At the same time, other respondents believed that doing the dance in their private spaces was powerful; it generated the ability to fit in, and gave people a sense of being able to cope and deal with issues that arise in life.

Black social dance, according to these respondents on the topic, was phenomenologic.[37] That is, it is intertwined with experience, wrapped up in everyday negotiations of being in the world, over the course of time. Black social dance provided a time and space memory of dance in structuring the world. The dance, moreover, provided function in terms of creating a sense of value for the people who dance, a function that served to remind respondents that they had something of value that was inextricable from their bodies, which had historically been undervalued if not devalued. Within this phenomenologic reference, black social dance had meaning, and it was meaning bearing. Doing it meant one understood the need to be in community with people like oneself, and not doing it meant alienation and being separate, unable to enjoy having a good time.

As a cultural text both within the television advertisement and outside of it, black social dance communicates a stable structure of relating to the world for these respondents and those in previous research,[38] despite or in spite of the post–post-modernity of the commercialized choreography. Black respondents saw it as fragmented representations of something artistic while Walter (2011) revealed non-blacks saw it as something they gained access to by virtue of being able to replicate coolness. Included in the television commercial was anthropological knowledge transmission through an aesthetic. The knowledge was transmitted nonverbally and was known in the body kinesthetically. What I mean by this is that respondents suggested that they remembered being in the position of wanting to move, and that certain dance experiences are stored cognitively and affectively. Importantly, black social dance communicates instantly[39] to the viewer without there needing to be cognitive processing. This is not surprising given the neuroscience of dance, as studied by Calvo-Merino and colleagues in 2005. The critical issue is carrying this through to neuromarketing.[40]

For consumers and brands, in particular the brand covered in the research study, I want to emphasize that people recall experiences related to dancing as stored in their corporal memories that connect to the infusion of power, the illusion of freedom, the connection with something greater that transcends time and space. Dance is not simply an image that is entertaining. It is a synaesthetic phenomenon[41] when dance is done or connected with the brand, so much so that a consumer becomes the aesthetic subject.[42]

In asking permission to use the Diet Pepsi can in this work, I emailed the legal department at PepsiCo as I was directed after web inquiry and a phone call from the company. They wanted to know what the text was going to be around the trademark, and I replied that it was going to be the source of study because it had P Diddy, the agent and what has been defined as black social dance, and, because Pepsi had characteristically made its own market segments, such as the Pepsi Generation. The person from Pepsi wrote back to me and said that Pepsi had "always used popular culture in its DNA," and that they had used performers such as Michael Jackson, Madonna, and Britney Spears as well. In my mind, this is exactly what the respondents were saying to me, that black social dance progressively moved away from its contexts to be soaked up and absorbed in the mainstream of media flow. This was also evident in the commercials over the time period. The dance moved off of black bodies and onto non-blacks and then onto non-humans.

This leads us directly into the notion of aesthetics in advertising and why these issues are critical for consumers. I have stated that the dance is moved off the ground and onto the screen where people who watch are mesmerized — and sometimes awed. From a consumer culture theoretical view,[43] black social dance allows the culture of origin to be reconstructed through dance and consumption. None of the respondents suggested that they did not know the meanings of the dance, or that they were ashamed of their families for their connections to the dance. As Kim said, the one respondent with the most negativity about it and her experience with it, the commercial makes her want to go get a Diet Pepsi. This is because she sees something in the dance that is not available to her in real life. This is why black social dance is used.

In a television ad, the aesthetic of black social dance is operating as a source and non-source cue[44] connecting through to life themes and life projects via personal history and views of the world.[45] Whether a respondent such as Josh, Kim, or Jonathan says dance allowed him to fit in, or these representations of dance made him mad, they both motivate construction of and connections of themes and life projects. On the one hand, the consumer may want to distance him- or herself, like Josh for his children, Kim for her experience of being outcast, Justin for his readings of more of the same, or Shiniqa for her feeling that it is about sex and money, from the dance and therefore the brand. On the other hand, the consumer may choose to work harder to move away from these very deep-seeded negative feelings, through consuming some other branded good, or consuming something else that signifies success in changing the message they hear in their head, and know in their bodies.

Lakoff and Johnson (1995) suggest that people are empathetic with other people's experiences when watching other bodies move. The respondents exhibited an empathetic point of view when relating to the agent's attempt at black social dance. They recognized he was feeling successful and happy so he was dancing, but they noted his effort, as Laban (1974) indicated, was not the same as that of a black social dancer. The respondents were also empathetic with P Diddy in regard to feeling accepted and successful. They imagined what it was like for him in his position in that he was not a good dancer, but he had made his own form of black social dance. Between the two men, the respondents allowed P Diddy the cache of admission to the historical circle of black social dance, and applauded the agent for attempting to enter the circle, all the while indicating he was not able to due to his lack of experience.

Metaphorical meanings[46] are portrayed in this ad through the use of dance. Metaphors compare in an indirect way. In this commercial there are several metaphors that may not be explicit until the commercial is unpacked. For example, blacks and whites are compared with their dance abilities. Business acumen of black men versus white men is paraded. A white male agent who cannot dance will better serve a black artist than a black male music producer who cannot dance will. White men are honest and looking out for the best interest of the black artist; black businessmen are not and do not. Black social dance is equivalent to sexual expression. In this regard, an inanimate soda can moves as black men do, dancing and having fun. As part of the fun, they can attract white women and release pent-up sexual pressure. At the same time white women are bait for black men and the women who dance with them can be compared to harlots. In the end, with the correct maneuvering in the business world, a white guy can dance as well as a black one, or even better. An alternative metaphorical reading is that whites no longer control the entertainment industry but blacks do, and this is a positive change from the past. Either way, people want to do the right thing by the artist and this is a positive change from past usurping of cultural talent for profit. At the same time, interracial sexual relationships are accepted as normal, and there is no negative charge on riding in a hoopty; in fact it is sought after.

In the jumbled-up time sequence of this commercial, we have a black businessman music producer, which was brought into mainstream acceptance in the postmodern period, with black dancers being a major part of this, with dance from the 1960s. Next, we have the hip-hop dance and music era represented — dance from the 1970s through the 2000s — including the extraction of hip-hop dance from the context it was created in. There is the nearly timeless, unchanging representation of black social dance in the black neighborhood and this is silently and implicitly contrasted with what would be seen in a non-black neighborhood that the agent would live in.

The viewer is shown P Diddy in a personal space where he is dancing but it is not clear if he is in a wealthy or inner-city surrounding. His business conference room is decorated to the extreme, differently than a conservative business space but in the montage given in the commercial, there is no room to dance, and this is where he conducts his work. He does not dance here. The agent is never shown in a personal space but dances in P Diddy's business conference room though he does not leave his chair over the immediacy of the Pepsi can's success. The metaphor here is whites still dance around blacks in business ventures.

And while the respondents did not directly articulate these metaphors, they were implied in their comments. They said it is sex that sells, or that black people can dance because it is natural and genetic. It is about business, they said, or a separation of races. Shiniqa said the can pops his top and sprays the soda out of it. Or, as the male respondents suggested, guys would love to have beautiful women dancing around them. The dance metaphors are clearly working.

Remember, getting into people's heads in a commercial is accomplished through central and peripheral routes to persuasion.[47] In its simplistic forms, the reader may recall, central routes are direct forms of communication that require cognitive processing of information such as words and numbers. Peripheral routes are thought to conduct indirect forms of communication that utilize images and music to work through affective processing. Both forms are used, depending on the advertiser, the product, and the message. However, in this case where the Diet Pepsi can makes a rap song, the peripheral route to persuasion is being used with metaphors, images and music — aesthetic constructs. That is clearly articulated as this commercial functions in a post-postmodern image-producing timeframe. The benefits of the product are not discussed and no textual information is given as it relates to the product features. The only text given is that of the Diet Pepsi can and its title song, "Brown and Bubbly," as it works its way through the popular music charts.

That advertising is done through the peripheral route is not new but what is important for this research is that the aesthetic of black social dance is doing the silent communication. It is connecting the information shown through the dance to the brand, giving it currency as dance moves goods from the culturally constituted world that McCracken (1986) described. Is this a positive or negative for consumers? Does it do more than attain achievement of a branding strategy set forth by Diet Pepsi? Are consumers free and having fun as this commercial, as others that use black social dance in them suggest on their surfaces, or are consumers being driven somatoviscerally, affectively and cognitively to unnecessary consumption based on being trapped in race?

Ewen (1976) has argued that the changes in advertising methods and messages that occurred as the United States moved from modernity to postmodernity were made precisely because capitalism needed to be preserved. It was corporations that drove the advertising industry because they needed to constantly grow their profits and remain competitive. In doing so, advertising agencies hired artists of many sorts, and the artists were glad for the work. Advertisements have been entertaining and artistic, providing a diversion and a stable aesthetic to turn towards and grab onto in a hectic and post-postmodern world where everything changes constantly. However, as Jonathan and several other respondents surmised here, perhaps advertisers and corporations "have gone too" far with using black social dance in television commercials? The next section provides a theoretical answer to this musing.

THEORY OF BLACK SOCIAL DANCE IN TELEVISION COMMERCIALS

"Theory generating research identifies phenomena, discovers characteristics, and specifies relationships,"[48] which includes doing more than simply presenting research findings. They need to be explained.[49] As such, in this section, I draw on Strauss and Corbin's (1998) approach in developing an explanatory,[50] abstract, and substantive theory from the grounded theory tradition.[51] The purpose of doing this is to develop a broadly scoped pathway for a field of knowledge creation around the use of dance in television advertising. In this way, the theory itself has room for developing into a formal and predictive theory. Before doing so, it is important to explicitly state that in terms of setting forth a descriptive theory of black social dance in television ads, i.e., "what is this?,"[52] I have done so throughout this work. Namely, black social dance in television ads is a historical and current aesthetic that works through the consumer's sphere of attention. There, circulating concepts related to black social dance perform a continuous axial rotation around the concept of awe. Black social dance is a metaphoric cultural text and a communication vehicle. In using respondents and historical archived data, I am characterizing these phenomena of the use of black social dance in advertising over the study period.

Now the task is to develop an explanatory theory, that is, to ask "why is this?" using the descriptive theories I have set forth[53] and the descriptive theoretical framework that drove the research approach, namely Sklar's (2001) set of five interpretive dance premises. To remind the reader what those premises are, they are presented below:

Premise 1: Dance knowledge is a kind of cultural knowledge and

Premise 2: Dance knowledge is conceptual, and emotional, as well as kinesthetic. The dance embodies culture-specific ideas about nature, society, and the cosmos; beneath, these feelings are involved so that dance is associated with emotion.

Premise 3: Dance knowledge is intertwined with other kinds of cultural knowledge.

Premise 4: One has to look beyond dance to get at its meaning; concepts embodied in the dance are not necessarily evident in the dance itself.

Premise 5: Dance is always an immediate corporeal experience.

The first thing to note is that in this form, the premises have already been altered, by replacing the word "movement" with "dance." Next it should be

Table 3. Theory of Black Social Dance in Advertising

Theoretical anchors	Themes from respondents	Themes from ad agency	Themes from historical semiotic analysis	Change over time of black social dance in ads	Applied to Pepsi's brand over the study period
In a television ad, black social dance aesthetics communicates metaphorically historical and current socio-cultural behavior and knowledge regardless of which groups perform it, serving as a post-postmodern theatrical production.	Black social dance is historical.	Use an inherent drama of black social dance applied to products. Target the audience.	It is not said in words but dance forms (ballet, ballroom, black social dance, etc.); all have their own signifiers and signs.	No blacks in ads; blacks in ads dancing; non-blacks in ads doing black social dance.	PepsiCo was a pioneer in this aspect of dance utilization, applying ontological aspects of dance in consumption.
Communicating and understanding black social dance in commercials occurs in human beings through cognitive, emotional, and kinesthetic systems. Dance communicates imagined freedom and fun, through corporeal and non-verbal experience.	Black social dance means having a good time and expressing oneself.	Want the dance to communicate viscerally to the viewer so that they will identify with the dancer.	Television ads with dance in them depicted a celebratory and fun aspect as a result of consumption.	Tap dance, jazz dance, Motown, hip hop and black social dance. Repetitive cyclical use and discarding of black social dance for profit.	Over the study period, PepsiCo employed dance in an epistemological fashion to teach consumers physically about soda and what it can do for them.
Black social dance connected to brands is increasing over time, an anthropology of consumption as immediately celebratory, fun, and freeing. These meanings are not necessarily evident to the viewer.	Black social dance equates to fitting in and one fits in if one consumes.	To the extent that dance appears in culture, it appears in television ads.	Control of capital and expanding consumption increasing over time.	Black social dance is cool, easy; divorced from cultural context.	Axiologically, PepsiCo drew dance into its advertising strategy to make it a valuable brand.

Theoretical anchors	Themes from respondents	Themes from ad agency	Themes from historical semiotic analysis	Change over time of black social dance in ads	Applied to Pepsi's brand over the study period
In tandem, black social dance in advertisements allows an ever-increasing societal level directive, deflating power contained in dance. Instead of social commentary on the ground, people look on the screen and are mesmerized; on the ground people consume, either real or imagined consumption, products as social commentary.	Racial power relationships in society reinforced.	Post-racial society is promised through black social dance. Black creatives and choreographers are responsible as cultural intermediaries.	Increasing silent-level imperatives to consume products.	No change; the culturally constituted world of the United States is carried by black social dance.	Dance was used in reshaping the culturally constituted world over the study period as the issues in American society changed. PepsiCo pushes identity creation and uses dance spots now in post-post-modernity.

noted that the five premises have been consolidated into four[54] to arrive at the premises that served as the theoretical framework for the interviews:

1. Dance knowledge is a kind of cultural knowledge and it is conceptual, emotional, and kinesthetic. The dance embodies culture-specific ideas about nature, society, and the cosmos; beneath, these feelings are involved so that dance is associated with emotion.
2. Dance knowledge is intertwined with other kinds of cultural knowledge.
3. One has to look beyond dance to get at its meaning; concepts embodied in the dance are not necessarily evident in the dance itself.
4. Dance is always an immediate corporeal experience.

Grounded theory suggests that the approach to building theory be either to extend existing theory or to build theory from the data.[55] In this research I have done both. The interview data serves as a source for extending Sklar's theoretical framework, and the art historical and semiotic methods of data gathering and analysis, respectively, informs it as well. As such I propose the following abstract yet substantive and explanatory theory of black social dance in television ads:

- In a television ad, black social dance aesthetics communicates metaphorically historical and current socio-cultural behavior and knowledge regardless of which groups perform it, serving as a post-postmodern theatrical production. It works in the sphere of attention.
- Communicating and understanding of black social dance in commercials occurs in human beings through cognitive, emotional, and kinesthetic systems. Dance communicates imagined freedom and fun, through corporeal and non-verbal experience, setting up future expectations and drawing on memories or conditioned responses.
- Black social dance connected to brands portrays the increasing over time, anthropology of consumption as immediately celebratory, fun, and freeing. These meanings are not necessarily evident to the consumer, but build brand equity for the producer.
- In tandem, black social dance in advertisements allows an ever-increasing, societal level directive, deflating power contained in dance. Instead of social commentary on the ground, people look on the screen and are mesmerized; on the ground people consume, either real or imagined consumption, products as social commentary.

Therefore, black social dance is attached to both low- and high-involvement products so that people will buy more of them, and have a learned yet nonverbal muscle memory related to consumption of their products. This is the critical aspect of the use of black social dance in television ads. Please see table 3, "Theory of Black Social Dance," for a summary of the discussion. What the table shows is the theoretical component down the left side, with the readings from the respondents, the advertising agency executive, the analysis of the commercials over the study period, and finally, how PepsiCo fits within the theory.

This chapter has served to interpret, bring an analysis of change over time of black social dance in television advertisements, and build upon and present an extension of interpretive dance premises for explaining why dance is used in television commercials. The purpose of doing this was to pave the way for future research and these avenues are discussed fully in the next chapter.

Section Three

CONCLUSIONS AND FUTURE DIRECTIONS

Conclusions and Future Research

Along with spaces allocated for sacred purposes, the street is one of the oldest and most significant performance outlets in history.... Who would have dreamed that a people made captive and subjected to middle passage, slavery, torture, discrimination, and segregation could keep the force, roots, creativity and potential of their heritage so vital, intense, and immediate?[1]

IN CONCLUSION

In these proceeding pages, I have argued that black social dance is an artistic expression; its depiction in commercials is anthropologic and historical, and follows the modernity, post- and post–post-modernity pathways. The ebb and flow of black-dance aesthetic is plainly documented, and the lines between concert and social dance have clearly been blurred. This placement and performance of the dance on the screen has been choreographed by blacks and whites and presented on personal prosceniums held by blacks and whites. And this points out the symbiotic relationships between blacks and whites who supposedly can and cannot dance. The purpose of which, in terms of television advertising, is to get inside consumers' bodies and make them consume. I have adjudicated the argument of it being intentional versus unintentional manipulation of culture in a *Wag the Dog* (1997) and *Idiocracy* (2006) cinematic kind of way.

Did you know that there are rules to copyrighting dance? It has to be captured on a recording device and be of some length of time. Black social dance in my house is not copyrightable unless it is recorded this way, but does it belong to me? Does black social dance in the television advertisement designed for Diet Pepsi belong now to Diet Pepsi? In other commercials with dance in

A Little on the Rag-Time. Rare Book, Manuscript, and Special Collections Library, Duke University, Durham, North Carolina.

them, does the copyright belong to the ad men and women? With music, copyright is a big issue and people receive royalties when their music, even a small sound byte, is used in anything. Does dance not garner the same value? It should.

How does all the work discussed in the previous chapters relate to consumption and branding? Does it matter? Yes! I kept wanting it not to matter as I moved through this work, describing and explaining dance, and black social dance in commercials. At this point, two things matter, based on the research findings. One, people experience dance in advertising aesthetically as I have defined it; and two, there is something happening to them as a result and this is why dance is used in television ads. More research is needed to find out what is happening.

Over the study period, dance has evolved with the times and there has been an erasure of black bodies dancing to the point where Beyoncé was dancing for the Visio Television brand in front of a white guy sitting down on a couch watching television. She danced next to the television screen and the screen showed her dancing. While the man would not look at Beyoncé's "live" (reminiscent perhaps of strip tease) dancing in front of him, the commercial showed that he preferred looking at the televised image of her. In the televised and "real" image, Beyoncé was doing some kind of dance; she was completely dressed in a short dress and ultra brown, creamy smooth skin-bearing outfit and presented in a sexual manner. However, she was not doing black social dance; she was doing something else but marked in the objectified black woman sex object category. Is this the same story that Emery (1988) told us about of the decline of black social dance in African American night clubs where whites enjoyed themselves until they learned the music and the moves but only in commercials as whites have learned the way it works for them? There has been a historical ebb and flow of black social dance and this is now seen in television commercials. Still there is a continuing issue about how black social dance is borrowed from African American culture without "acknowledgement or appreciation," as Hazzard-Gordon (1990, xi) put it.

So who is responsible for that one with Beyoncé? Or for other commercials with dance?

I wanted it to be the advertising media, but as I researched and studied, I had to let that positionality go. First of all, I think it is inclusive of all of the cultural intermediaries, black agencies, white agencies, and the artists/choreographers who contribute to the use of dance in advertising in the ways that they do. Does it matter if you did not intend to set that fire? People are trying to make money, plain and simple. This is the way it has been in this country when it comes to artistic endeavor. In many cases, artists of all sorts turn to capitalistic devices in order to survive. It is no different with artists and advertising. That said, it does not diminish the fact that it is art that is included, no matter whether it has suffered extreme montage in an effort for the commercial itself to become a work of art. So you see, we have many concentric circles forming around this complex media. It is useless to point fingers to figure out blame. But we can examine the effect it has on consumers.

Dance studies needs to forge into writing predictive theories. My hypothesis is that when people are shown an ad with dance in it, they will prefer it over a similar one without dance. This was already shown in Walter and colleagues' (2011) study on a small scale. It was also shown there that dance in television ads influences purchase preference. What will happen on a large scale? Will respondents remember the brand? Will it influence their behavior or attitudes toward the brand or the ad? Consumer behavior studies can be and need to be empirically designed and tested for dance in advertisements, as well as how music is working in the ad.

The concern is that music and dance, as a multiple construct, and dance as its own construct are under-studied given the research findings on the effect that music in positive and negative valences have on consumers. This is also seriously begging for research given the integral connection between popular music and social dance, as Emery (1988) reminds us. This is also true for the research findings on movements for consumers. At issue, though, based on the research I have conducted, is the impact on black and white consumers. Are white consumers being driven to consume by using dance to assuage or minimize the history? For blacks, do the commercials perform a function just to make people feel good or to make people forget, imagine the past is not there when they consume the brand? Or is it none of these and something else?

Along with this, there needs to be a research stream from consumer studies that acknowledges the long history *of black social dance and music* as connected to capitalist consumption, as well as empirical studies about black social dance in post–post-modernity. In addition to this we would benefit from a research stream out of dance studies that examines choreography for commercials, not just bragging rights that somebody did some while complaining that people are just pimping dance. But how it is done, why it is done, how choreographers and dancers are solicited, and the business of choreography for television commercials needs further attention. In the interview with Mr. Geeting, we were told that even this aspect of commercial development has undergone capitalist interventions, with dancers employed in less developed nations, and scenes shot in cheap locations around the globe. We have this well documented for historical aesthetics and performing circuits, as researched by Malone (1996), Hazzard-Gordon (1990), and Emery (1972, 1988). Why not commercials?

Consumer culture theory needs to do more ethnography within social circles of dance, not hanging out with the trendsetters but with people who dance for social heritage and talk about what this does or does not do with and for consumption.

Mixed research approaches must be brought unbounded and simultaneously from dance and consumer research to study the effect of dance on consumption. And we have to ask: Does consumption have an effect on dance? What kinds and what effects? Before either of these occurs, however, a break from a mindset of where dance resides in its impact on consumption, i.e., as feminine or un-researchable, must be had.

A beginning could be made with effort theory, which suggests that dance is rife with effort and dynamic energy. Ways of measuring the effort a consumer makes (after viewing a commercial with dance in it) in seeking information about a product or the energy expended in the purchase process are within the realm of inquiry. Alternatively, we could consider applying dance (re)construction theory whereby dances are repeated by constructing them from notes, musical scores, artworks, and bodily operations of a particular period (i.e., showing consumers historical commercials and asking an array of questions). The goal of this research would be to look at forces or to conduct experiments that evaluate dance and the audience response. Alternatively, by using reconstruction theory in reconstructing consumers in the performance spaces they live in, or reconstructing the purchase process, consumer researchers can experiment with historical and therefore current responses from consumers to marketing messages that have dance in them.

Lastly, dance education theory provides two levels of transfer of dance knowledge and learning. Low-road transfers, according to Hanna (1999, 27–28), refers to the "automatic triggering of well practiced activities in new circumstances that are similar to the learning context ... [and] high road transfers depend on the intentional abstraction of the skill or knowledge from one context to a new one." Can consumers learn dances or be reminded of them or be made to imagine/believe that they can perform them, and link them to brands or product categories or behaviors? We know this already occurs in music from Scott's (1990) contributions. While it is true that movements could be linked to other cultural knowledges, I am focusing on the use of dance in consumption of goods, services, ideas, tangibles and intangibles.

The dance approaches described above provide for the entry of dance into consumption research. Of course, the suggestions are not meant to imply that they comprise the universe of possibilities, but rather to begin a dialog. Once the dialog begins, and these research projects are completed and findings discovered, the gendering of the two existing research domains becomes successfully deconstructed. A cognitive understanding of dance and how it relates to consumption may or may not result. Dance is not merely an expressive medium that is non-cognitive. That is the very point being made to argue that dance has not been historically considered in consumer research, and that it may be a gendered issue. New ways of understanding consumers evolves and our responsibilities as researchers are fulfilled.

At the beginning of this research project I asked questions about why dance was used in television ads. What did it mean? What was the effect this was having or did it have historically on consumers, if any? What about society as a whole? I wanted to come up with a theory, based on dance and consumer research approaches. I theorized that the consumption of certain brands and their related products had been connected to dance but was increasingly linked to black social dance, except sometimes the dances were not performed by black people.

In chapter 2 I argued that while dance studies encompasses a broad field, ranging from choreographic development to critical assessment and many points in between, for this research I utilized nine theories of dance. These in turn informed its use in television advertising. Specifically, dance is educational. It conveyed symbolic illusion and imagined power while being experiential and phenomenologic. Dance was functional, providing a vehicle for cultural anthropological knowledge transmission. As such, it is meaning-bearing and meaning-full, existing as a cultural text. Dance was aesthetic while being kinesthetic and communicative. I covered each of these areas to give background on the ways in which they inform dance in commercial advertisements. Next I discussed black social and concert dances as they have evolved over the study period, darkened by a historically negative relationship dance has had with humanity in this country. Finally, I discussed the use of black social dance as choreographed for television commercials, and showed how it is linked to the effects of dance from a theoretical perspective. In chapter 5 I demonstrated how black social dance was projected in commercials, teaching and guiding consumers through what some may argue was hegemonic control over the viewer in very important social, political, and economic arenas. Particularly, I offered synaesthetics as it allowed the understanding of dance to be something that cannot be put into words, an experience that is in line with Husserl's noema, and to experience dance in this fashion is to perceive details corporeally. Moreover, the imagination was placed within the body, and transcended the real and imaginary, so that the noetic process of engagement was undertaken as well. What we have is the lasting memory of an experience that is affective, and ignited each time the movement is encountered. This is what the television viewer experiences, perception and understanding without language that cannot be articulated verbally.

In looking back I find that the study provided a broad brush and contextual reference for dance in advertising, distancing itself as such from suggesting that dance had not been included in consumer research because it has never crossed anyone's mind. It was conjectured that it was absent from that body of study because of its feminine nature. Then, I walked through existing research literature that explained several nontraditional qualitative additions to the consumer research field, and argued that dance theory deserves an equal place alongside those approaches. I gave a view of dance theory's ontology, axiology and epistemology. From there, cultural meaning transfer in television ads was extended to include dance theory, and Husserl's phenomenology was regarded as a way to get into consumers' consciousnesses. Consciousness can be accessed in the use of metaphor, and clearly dance metaphors abound and will continue to. Rather than dismiss the power of dance metaphor, it was suggested that it in fact carries meaning by implied yet silent comparisons.

Next, a brief history of the discovery and use of music in advertising was given, with the supposition that dance could be providing similar effects on consumers, either through conditioned or unconditioned responses, through connections with information processing, and through somatovisceral pathways. A review of the historical basis for advertising in the American capitalistic landscape was drawn, showing that advertising has conducted several missions over the course of its lifetime in connection with products and brands. In fact, I suggested that television ads use dance in them to gain access to people's spheres of attention to help them focus on the product or brand. And finally, I showed how black people were not advertised to with any earnest as a market segment before certain point in time, but that black social dance played a role in getting both blacks' and non-blacks' attention. In chapters 4 and 5, I presented and analyzed television commercials, and interview materials. The voices of the respondents were given full exposure. Chapter 5 particularly served to interpret those voices, and to bring an analysis of change over time of black social dance in television advertisements, and to build upon and present an extension of interpretive dance premises for explaining why dance is used in television commercials.

PASSION FOR THE FUTURE

This study was motivated by my lifelong passion for dance. And I am able to state this explicitly without reservation or fear of reprisal from anybody — be it the institution of the church, a family member or colleague. The wonderful thing about using grounded theory as a research approach is that it allows the twists and turns that projects like this take us on. I spoke to many people over the course of this work, formally in interviews and at conferences and informally in discussions with colleagues, friends, family and students. In talking to respondents, they viewed the work of dance in ways that spoke to their culture and experiences, their economic and social standing, and their race and gender. Black respondents saw it as their historical and cultural heritage, an anchorage to the growth and development of African Americans as a race. It was seen as something unique to them. Euro Americans also saw black social dance as something that belonged to them. As was shown in Walter (2011), white respondents also discussed the notion of doing square dancing down on their farms in the south or Midwest, and that it would be equally difficult to people who did not grow up with it to execute the dance correctly. In short, two different American social dances, which have meaning, effort, and communication, exist side by side and have history embedded within them.

But returning to the African American respondents in this study, they spoke to me about how glad they were that "our culture and we as a people" are finally being accepted in American society and even though it was not "real" black social dance, in their minds it was a start to see television ads with black social dance in them. They also were willing to laugh about the fun being made of who dances well and who does not, and to shrug off the use of black social dance in commercials as "just business." After all we live in the United States, where everything has a value attached to it and people pay for the smallest increment of information.

I talked with a retired advertising executive who had been with one of the major advertising agencies through nearly the entire study period. I met this person through contacts within my professional circle. I was really appreciative of this because it is difficult to get to talk with famous advertising executives and creative people. In any event, this ad man began to quantify the costs of using dance in television ads. Over the time under study, dance in commercials had added value to products and brands by covering dancers' and choreographers' costs. In other words, a one-million-dollar cost to utilize dancers and choreographers, for example, could translate into millions of dollars in sales or brand equity if the consumer identified with the brand's inherent drama, saw it as believable, and could make that leap of faith transfer. And as I have stated, the copyright is up for grabs at best, and unattainable at worst when black social dance is in the mix.

The ad man also talked about the visceral effect that the producer hopes to deliver with the purpose of getting consumers to choose the brand over others, similar or dissimilar. I do not need to point out how serious this business is; it is the whole history of the need for corporate advertising in order for commodities to differentiate themselves as they dance with equally unnecessary commodities so that corporations survive.

I learned from the ad man that advertising reflects culture, and how, in his view, this is a unidirectional process. They use people of color and of varied ethnic backgrounds to help design campaigns to appeal to the target market. Who better to do this with black social dance than black choreographers and creatives? Besides, brilliance in creativity equals fame and fortune, and this was borne out in the winning creative ads, such as the California Raisins.

Some respondents thought black social dance in television advertisements was the same old tired and worn out commentary about black people designed by the man to keep us down, taking something, which in and of itself is good, and manipulating it for non-blacks to find an identity in.

At a conference I talked about dance aesthetics in a room full of consumer culture theory academics. When I brought up the notion of dance, the first thing out of some people's mouths was that dance had to be defined and how do you bind it so that it can be a subject of study? Where do you draw the line between dance and other movement like karate? I sighed, shook my head, and dropped my shoulders, and just looked up in exasperation. Dance scholars in their own conference venues really do not want to have their boats rocked when you start talking about dance aesthetics — what? You are kidding, right? In commercials? Oh no, that is NOT art! You are dancing around the wrong mulberry bush, sister!

But producers knew from the turn of advertisements as used for pressing unnecessary consumption that dance in television ads was going to affect people in some form or fashion. This study, along with the others that Walter (2011), Walter and Altamini (2010), and Walter and colleagues (2009), has collectively shown that dance does affect consumers and it affects each person in similar yet different ways, based on synaesthetics and their sphere of attention. Strong emotions are connected with it as is awe, whether one likes it or not — literally. This by itself points out the power of dance.

The approach I took to this research was to be an anthropologist who wandered through a museum of television advertisements and attempted to semiotically interpret what I found there. And using what I found, I developed a working theory of black social dance in television ads — which I fully expect to be criticized. On the one hand, we have dance over there written on the wall; on the other hand, we have dance in our bodies that we do or have done or wish we could do. The archives capture some of this, but, like fossils from different time periods, the record is incomplete and has to be pieced together. Or better yet, it is like the historian who writes from a privileged perspective — a person of color or varied background may choose something different to save for future reference.

The people who dance or do not dance use this in any event to identify themselves and identify the groups they belong to or do not belong to. And in consumption this is the key: mentally what does using and owning this product tell you about you? When it is connected to dance, what conscious and unconscious messages are you learning and associating with the product?

We live in a world where black social dance on the screen followed the trajectory of the rise and fall of black people. Segregation was followed by desegregation, and then by fragmentation. You can just call this modernity, post-modernity, and post–post-modernity. We are being told and expected to believe we live in a post-racial world where Beyoncé is doing some kind of dance and a white guy prefers to stare at her image without any reprisal and that black people can now freely choose an identity. They can get it from the media. Do you believe that? Can we? Is this a result of cultural intermediaries who are themselves trying this? Or is this a result of academic discourses in cultural studies?

What would happen if a product came along, a pill or what have you, that everyone took so that there were no racial differences? Would we be able to distinguish the meanings between ballroom dancing and square dancing? Would it matter in terms of consumption, especially if it was paired with a catchy jingle, appealing voice-over, lots of color, and some humor or sex? In my theory of black social dance in advertising, it does matter. This, however, can be applied to other dances and needs to be done.

The research needs to look at neuroscience, brand recall, attitude change, central versus peripheral route processing and elaboration, and classical and operant conditioning strategies. In addition clarification between what dance is doing and what music and dance do, and what kinds of dance do what to consumer behaviors is needed. That said, the theory of black social dance in television ads is available for use as a theoretical starting point for other types of dance in commercials.

Simply stated, everybody in this study had a passion for dance in some form or fashion, for a multitude of reasons, implicitly stated or metaphorically delivered.

Chapter Notes

Introduction

1. Fowles 1996, 77.
2. McFee 1992, 174, quoting David Best 1978, 115.
3. Joy and Sherry 2003.
4. Smyth 1984, Hanna 1987, and Francis 1996.
5. Smyth 1984, 19.
6. Adapted from the discussion with Fuat Firuat and Alladi Venkatesh at the "Heretical Consumer Research Conference," Andy Warhol Museum, Pittsburgh, Pennsylvania, USA, October 21, 2009; see also Charters 2006 and Aspara 2009.
7. Blair and Hatala 1992.
8. Hanna 1987.
9. Pham and colleagues 2001.
10. Sklar 2001.
11. Arvidson 2006.
12. Joy and Sherry 2003; Charter 2006.
13. Francis 1996.
14. Proctor and colleagues 2002, 247.
15. Sherry 1987.
16. Zakia and Nadin 1998.
17. Burrill 2006, 20.
18. Proctor and colleagues 2002; Cronin 2004; Schroeder 2002.
19. McCracken 1986; Mick and Buhl 1992.
20. Proctor and colleagues 2002.
21. Dodds 2004.
22. Pollay 1985; Belk and Pollay 1985; Scott 1994; Spears and Germain 2007; Pollay 1985.
23. Scott 1994, 261.
24. Spears and Germain 2007, 19.
25. Spears and Germain 2007.
26. Gorn 1982.
27. Scott 1990, 223.
28. Ibid., 227.
29. Hung 2000, 25.
30. Scott 1990, 228.
31. Walter and colleagues 2009.
32. Scott 1994.
33. Dodds 2004.
34. Blair and Hatala 1992.
35. Belk and Pollay 1985, 894.
36. Pollay 1985.
37. Spears and Germain 2007, table 2, 23.
38. Blair and Hatala 1992.
39. See Prevots 1998, for example.
40. Prevots 1998; Huntington 2004.
41. Zeigler 1994.
42. Sussman 1984; Rielly 2003.
43. Clarkson 1971; Cowley 1928; Emery 1972; Hartman 1997; Hazzard-Gordon 1998; Thorpe 1989.
44. Gottschild 1996; Hazzard-Gordan 1996; Hazzard-Gordan 1998; Malone 1996.
45. Gottschild 2005.
46. Banes 1994; Desmond 1997; Foster 1998; Rose 1994.
47. Hazzard-Gordan 1996; Huntington 2007; Orlando 2003; Osumare 1999.
48. Huntington 2007.
49. Rielly 2003.
50. Huntington 2007.
51. Dodds 2004.
52. Foucault 1970.
53. Schroeder 2002.
54. Spears and Germain 2007.
55. Barthes 1964.

56. Kvale 1983; Scott 1990; Prasad 2002.
57. Thompson and colleagues 1989.
58. Royce 1977.
59. Walter 2011.
60. Strauss and Corbin 1997.

Chapter 1

1. Davidson 1992, 125.
2. Turner 1987; Lears 1994; Painter 1994.
3. Kleine, Kleine, and Kernan 1993.
4. Ibid., 229.
5. Foucault 1970.
6. Langer 1953; Lange 1976; Synnott 1993; Joy and Venkatesh 1994; Goulding, Shankar, and Elliot 2002.
7. Descartes 1972, 1989.
8. Turner 1991.
9. Turner 1991 after Foucault 1975.
10. Synnott 1993.
11. Falk 1994.
12. Ibid., figure 5, 4, 137.
13. H'Doubler 1940, xxii, xxiii.
14. Lange 1976; Foster 1995 in Goellner and Shea Murphy 1995, 231–246.
15. H'Doubler 1940.
16. Ibid.; Synnott 1993, Wagner 1997.
17. H'Doubler 1940.
18. Ibid., xxv.
19. Kleine, Kleine, and Kernan 1993; Falk 1994.
20. H'Doubler 1940; Falk 1994.
21. H'Doubler 1940, 41.
22. Laban and Lawrence 1974, 1.
23. Ibid., 5.
24. Redfern 1965 and 1969, 25.
25. Langer 1953, 169.
26. Carroll 2001.
27. Langer 1953, 173.
28. Ibid., 175, italics original.
29. Ibid., 177.
30. Ibid., 177.
31. Ibid., 179 [quoting Curt Sachs 1937, 3].
32. Ibid., 180.
33. Ibid., 186.
34. Ibid., 183.
35. Sheets-Johnstone 1966, xv.
36. After Jean-Paul Sartre (1956) and Maurice Merleau-Ponty (1962), respectively; Sheets-Johnstone, 1966, 15, footnotes 1 and 2.
37. Sheets-Johnstone 1966, 22–23.
38. Ibid., xi.
39. Ibid., 11.
40. Lange 1976, 18.
41. Lange 1976.
42. See, for example, Kaeppler 1972; Barthes 1964, 80.
43. Barthes 1964, 30.
44. Barthes 1964.
45. Ibid., 42.
46. Barthes 1964.
47. Ibid., 55 (italics original).
48. Barthes 1964.
49. Barthes, italics original, 1964, 78.
50. Ibid., 83.
51. Ibid.
52. Ibid., 90.
53. Ibid., 91.
54. Geertz 1983, 120.
55. Lange 1976, 9.
56. Ibid., 45.
57. Ibid., 55.
58. Ibid., 54.
59. Ibid., 63.
60. Royce 1977, 16.
61. Ewen 1976.
62. Royce 1977, 14.
63. Ibid., 10.
64. Ibid., 84.
65. Ibid., 158.
66. Ibid., 159.
67. Ibid., 178.
68. Spencer 1985, 38.
69. Foster 1995.
70. Foster 1986, 98.
71. McFee 1992, 2.
72. Ibid., 168–169.
73. McFee 1992, 174, after Best 1978, 115.
74. Ibid., 291.
75. Not long after this or perhaps parallel and simultaneously to the emergence of McFee's work, film studies demonstrated the importance and value of non-written texts such as dance and their contribution to culture (Goellner and Shea Murphy 1994). Film and electronic media representation of dance posed significant change upon the non-ephemeral and repetitive reading of dance as well as the composition of dance. Undoubtedly, gaze theory (Rosen 1986) also informs dance in television advertising.
76. Croce 1965, xxv.
77. Ibid., 11.
78. Keltner and Haidt 2003.
79. Ibid., 300.
80. Ibid.
81. Ibid., 301.
82. Ibid., 302.

83. Ibid.
84. Ibid., 305, table 1, 310.
85. Walter 2011.
86. Machon 2009, 15.
87. Ibid., 19.
88. Ibid., 14.
89. Ibid., 16.
90. Ibid.
91. Ibid., 19, 20.
92. Ibid., 25.
93. Francis 1996; Burrill 2006.
94. Dodds 2004; Dunagan 2007.
95. Dodds 2004.
96. Joy and Sherry 2003.
97. Calvo-Merino and colleagues 2005.
98. Smyth 1984, 22.
99. Hanna 1987.
100. Ibid.
101. Ibid., 65–67.
102. Ibid., 68.
103. Foster 1986, 98.
104. Royce 1977, 112.
105. Ibid., 115.
106. Royce 1977.
107. Wagner 1997, 20.
108. Ibid., 73.
109. Wagner 1997.
110. Ibid., 253.
111. Huntington 2007.
112. Wagner 1997, 255.
113. Ibid., 255.
114. Ibid., 269–270.
115. Ibid., 274.
116. Ibid., 275.
117. Ibid., 331.
118. Ibid., 337, 349.
119. Ibid., 366.
120. See the following link for more details http://query nytimes com/gst/fullpage html?res=9C0CE7D81E3BF934A25757C0A966958260&n=Top/Reference/Times%20Topics/Subjects/C/Church-State%20Relations accessed December 18, 2010.
121. Cottle 1966.
122. Ibid.
123. Ibid., 196.

Chapter 2

1. Davidson 1992, 124.
2. Murray and Ozanne 1991, 129.
3. Ross 2000.
4. Hudson and Ozanne 1988, 508.
5. Ibid., 510.
6. Damasio 1999; Singer 2010.
7. Hudson and Ozanne 1988, 515.
8. Ibid., 518.
9. Ibid., 520.
10. Synnott 1993.
11. Locander and Pollio 1989, 144.
12. Scott 1990, 227.
13. Ibid., 228.
14. Goellner and Murphy 1995; Fraleigh and Hanstein 1999.
15. Mick and Buhl 1992, 319.
16. Ibid., 320.
17. Foucault 1977.
18. Desmond 1999, 313.
19. Desmond 1999.
20. According to Smith-Autard (2000, v), choreography is an art "commonly used to describe the activity of composing dances ... including themes, music or sound, design and lighting."
21. Butler 1993 states that "performativity must be understood ... as the reiterative and citational practice by which discourse produces the effects that it names" (2). This has everything to do with the gendered and historical exclusion of dance from consumer research and the gendered constructs of dance.
22. Desmond 1999, 317.
23. *Journal of Consumer Research* editors from the *Journal of Consumer Research* website (February 12, 2009) are as follows: John A. Deighton, 2005–present; Dawn Iacobucci, 2002–2005; David Glen Mick, 1999–2002; Robert Burnkrant, 1996–1999; Brian Sternthal, 1993–1996; Kent Monroe, 1990–1993; Richard Lutz, 1987–1990; James Bettman and Harold Kassarjian, 1982–1987; Seymour Sudman, 1981–1982; Robert Ferber, 1976–1981; Ronald Frank, 1972–1975. *Dance Research Journal* editors from JSTOR (February 12, 2009): Mark Franko, 2009–present; Ann Dils, 2003–2008; Jill Green and Ann Dils, 2003–2005; Julie Malnig, 2000–2003; Lynn Matluck Brooks, 1994–2000; Judy Van Zile, 1989–1994; Sally Banes, 1982–1989; Diane Woodruff, 1979–1982; Diane Woodruff, Nancy Reynolds, 1978–1979; Elizabeth Burtner, 1976–197; Lois Andreasen and Elizabeth Burtner, 1975–1976. These listings are not to suggest that associate editors or members of the respective editorial boards that are of opposite gender, or to say that academicians who publish in each of the journals, are of the same gender as their editors. The purpose of point-

ing to these two journals is to deconstruct how perhaps we are gendered in our respective constructs and judicial acceptances of knowledge structures, which we accept as implicitly natural. Also, these two journals have been purposely juxtaposed. There are other non-overlapping and distinct journals for dance and consumer research scholarship respectively.

24. Bristor and Fischer 1993.
25. Schroeder 2003, 1.
26. Bristor and Fischer 1993.
27. Derrida 1973.
28. An individual could record a dance and place it on YouTube. This does not alleviate the fact that historically and currently dance is not being theorized in consumption behavior. Actually, using recordings of consumers in motion could provide a basis of study. The effect of a dance in a television commercial on consumption, though, is what I am trying to drill down to; the absence of any historical study of it and the notion that the absence is due to gendered research inquiry is what I want to focus on.
29. Howard 1998, 4.
30. Hanstein 1999, 65.
31. This is true for other interpretive consumer behavior theories. However, interpretive theories can be used in tandem with positivist approaches to research and I am wondering whether this level of analysis can come to fruition for dance and consumer research.
32. Bristor and Fischer 1993.
33. McCracken 1986, 71.
34. Hirschman and Thompson 1997, after Randazzo 1993; Sherry 1987.
35. Proctor and colleagues 2002.
36. See Stern 1992; Thompson and Hirschman 1995; Joy and Venkatesh 1994, for examples.
37. McCracken 1986.
38. Nadir and colleagues 2009.
39. McCracken 1986, 75.
40. Holt 2004.
41. Joy and Sherry 2003, referencing Pine and Gilmore 1999.
42. Ibid., 259.
43. Ibid.
44. Arnould and Thompson 2005.
45. Ibid., 874.
46. Sherry 1987, 443–444.
47. McQuarrie and Mick 1999.
48. Ibid., 39.
49. Walter and colleagues 2009.
50. Bulmer and Buchanan-Oliver 2006, 57.
51. Husserl 1931, 110–111.
52. Husserl 1931, 260, to borrow from Husserl's description of the tree's noematic position.
53. Husserl 1931, 265–266; brackets added to replace "tree."
54. Stewart and Hecker 1988, 258.
55. Ibid., 257.
56. Stigal 2001.
57. Ibid., 323.
58. Ibid.
59. Ibid. 325.
60. Ibid., 326.
61. Ibid., 331.
62. Lawler 1951.
63. Lane and Marlow 1999, 362.
64. Neisser 2003, 29.
65. Ibid., 28.
66. Ibid., 35.
67. Ibid., 36.
68. Ibid., 40.
69. Ibid., 44.
70. Brown 1991; Brown 2004.
71. Kitayama and colleagues 2003.
72. Shiff 1979, 109.
73. Ibid., 113.
74. Ibid., 118.
75. Lakoff and Johnson 1999, 17.
76. Ibid.
77. Ibid.
78. Ibid., 16 and 555.
79. Ibid., 565.
80. Park and Young 1986, 13.
81. Humor, entertainment, surprise, excitement, self-recognition, and incongruity are examples; see Park and Young 1986; Alden and Hoyer 1993; Speck 1991; Alden and colleagues 1999, 2000; Faseur and Geuens 2006.
82. Gorn 1982; Kellaris and Cox 1989; Pitt and Abratt 1988; Mitchell 1988; Park and Young 1986.
83. Scott 1990, 223.
84. Dowling and Hardwood 1986.
85. Petty and colleagues 1983.
86. Zakia and Nadin 1987.
87. Fam 2008.
88. Petty and colleagues 1983.
89. Ibid.
90. Ibid.
91. Cacciopo and colleagues 1993; Strack and colleagues 1988; Wells and Petty 1980.

92. Wells and Petty 1980.
93. Petty and colleagues 2002; Brinol and Petty 2003.
94. Priester and colleagues 1996, 445.
95. Ibid.
96. Ibid., 446.
97. Strack and Neuman 1996, 302.
98. Forester 2004, 424.
99. Ibid., 419.
100. Berman 1981, 12–13.
101. Ibid., 42.
102. Ibid., 45–47.
103. Ibid., 109.
104. Venkatesh and Maember 2008.
105. Berman 1975, 101.
106. Ewen 1976, 6–12.
107. Ibid., 19.
108. Ibid., 27.
109. Ibid., 29.
110. Ibid., 31.
111. Ibid., 54.
112. Ibid., 34.
113. Royce 1977; Brown 1991; Wagner 1997.
114. Ewen 1976, 59.
115. Ibid., 61–62.
116. Venkatesh and Maember 2008.
117. Arvidson 2006.
118. Ibid., 4.
119. Ibid., 116.
120. Ibid., 128.
121. Ibid., 136.
122. Ibid., 136.
123. Ibid., 139.
124. Venkatesh and Maember 2008.
125. Salzman and colleagues 1996; Chambers 2008.
126. Friend and Kravis 1957; Bauer and Cunningham 1970.
127. Sexton 1972.
128. Bauer and Cunningham 1970.
129. Walter 2011.
130. Chambers 2008.
131. Salzman and colleagues 1996.
132. Low and Cliff 1981, 24.
133. Chambers 2008.
134. Scott 2001.

Chapter 3

1. Davidson 1992, 65.
2. Malone 1996, 7.
3. Fraleigh and Hanstein 1999.
4. Alasuutari 1995.
5. Royce 1977.
6. Schroeder 2002.
7. Barthes 1964.
8. Prasad 2005; Fraleigh and Hanstein 1999; Thomas 2003.
9. Royce 1977, 18.
10. Ibid., 34.
11. Ibid., 65.
12. The more difficult dances are left to the dance experts within the population.
13. Royce 1977, 81.
14. Schroeder 2002, 39, 115.
15. Ibid., 37.
16. Ibid., 116.
17. Schroeder and Zwick 2004, 23.
18. See tape with call numbers VA165M and VA1783T, respectively.
19. Alka Seltzer: http://www.youtube.com/watch?v=e85caXw_NG8 (accessed November 21, 2010).
20. Jax Beer: http://www.youtube.com/watch?v=tngNbodIq_M (accessed November 21, 2010).
21. Emery 1988.
22. See any introductory marketing principles textbook, such as R. Kerin, S. Hartley, and W. Rudelius. 2010. *Marketing*, 10th ed. New York: McGraw-Hill.
23. Frank 1997.
24. Paley Center Tape Number 115214.
25. UCLA Archives VA7690.
26. UCLA Archives VA1783T.
27. Sussman 1984; Huntington 2004.
28. In 1958 Pepsi was in a challenging situation as it needed to restructure its brand image. Pepsi begins to identify itself with young people who are linked into being fashionable consumers with the "Be Sociable, Have a Pepsi" theme. The design of the bottle was redone, providing a "swirl" bottle while divesting itself of the straight-sided bottle. See www.pepsico.com.
29. UCLA Archives VA12652T.
30. YouTube: http://www.youtube.com/watch?v=8ZRzBGpLsB8 (accessed November 21, 2010).
31. The Video Beat: http://www.thevideobeat.com/store/rock-roll-tv/1950s-teen-dance-shows-vol-1.html (accessed November 21, 2010).
32. The Video Beat: http://www.thevideobeat.com/store/rock-roll-tv/1950s-teen-dance-shows-vol-2.html (accessed November 21, 2010).
33. UCLA Archive VA5282, 1957.

34. AMC Filmsite: http://www.filmsite.org/50sintro.html (accessed November 21, 2010).
35. Black Classic Movies: http://www.blackclassicmovies.com/Movie_Feature/african_american_films_natl_registry.html (accessed November 21, 2010).
36. Salzman and colleagues 1996
37. http://en.wikipedia.org/wiki/List_of_African-American_firsts (accessed November 21, 2010).
38. Frank 1997.
39. Anderson 2005.
40. See, for example, http://www.pbs.org/hueypnewton/times/times_watts.html (accessed December 18, 2010) for a discussion of the riot and civil rights issues germane to the time.
41. Huntington 2004; Huntington 2007.
42. Black Classic Movies: http://www.blackclassicmovies.com/Movie_Feature/african_american_films_natl_registry.html (accessed November 21, 2010).
43. For a full reading list for the history of African Americans and critiques on film, see http://lib.berkeley.edu/MRC/AfricanAmBib.html (accessed November 21, 2010).
44. UCLA Archive VA5244T, 1964.
45. Hill 2010.
46. UCLA Archive VA14003T, 1968.
47. YouTube: http://www.youtube.com/watch?v=RLN5jdAyahU (accessed November 21, 2010).
48. Paley Center Tape Number 115214.
49. Paley Center 115427 — compilation of Pepsi commercials from 1951 until 1983.
50. UCLA Archives VA13543T, 1971.
51. UCLA Archives VA9836, 1969–1970.
52. UCLA Archives VA14061T, and VA 14061, 1970.
53. UCLA Archives VA12060T, 19 —.
54. UCLA Archives VA13543T, 1971.
55. YouTube: http://www.youtube.com/watch?v=KURYGzhQLa4 (accessed December 18, 2010).
56. UCLA Archives VA13849, 1970.
57. UCLA Archives VA13852 ,1970.
58. See Huntington 2004; Huntington 2007; Scott 2001; and Sussman 1984 for a discussion of classical ballet funding in the United States.
59. UCLA Archives VA3862, 1970.
60. Huntington 2007.
61. UCLA Archives VA 383, 1980–1981.
62. UCLA Archives VA12060T, is a collection of various advertisements dated from 19 —. It contained ads from the 1980s and before.
63. UCLA Archive VA13855T, 1980.
64. UCLA Archive VA14059T, 1982.
65. UCLA Archive VA13995T, 1981.
66. UCLA Archive VA14059T, 1982.
67. UCLA Archive VA5628, 1984.
68. Pepsi: www.pepsico.com (accessed December 18, 2010).
69. UCLA Archive VA15806, 1984.
70. UCLA Archive VA15807, 1984.
71. Paley Center Tape Number 113522.
72. Paley Center Tape Number 113498.
73. Paley Center Tape Number 115230.
74. UCLA Archives VA14773, 1989.
75. UCLA Archive VA13992, 1983.
76. UCLA Archive VA16736 T, 19 —. This tape contained advertisements from different years.
77. Paley Center Tape Number 115299.
78. Paley Center Tape Number 121218.
79. Paley Center Tape Numbers 121218 and 115226.
80. UCLA Archives VA163, Pytka Commercials 1984–1989 and VA7945, March 6, 1989; Paley Center Tape Number 113512.
81. Paley Center Tape Number 115226.
82. Paley Center Tape Number 115295, 1990 Trophy Video Awards.
83. Paley Center Tape Number 117219, 1995 Best in Ads.
84. YouTube: http://www.youtube.com/watch?v=Iqk492ovtSA (accessed November 28, 2010).
85. YouTube: http://www.youtube.com/watch?v=ypClEK0oqiU (accessed November 28, 2010).
86. YouTube: http://www.youtube.com/watch?v=ioQgA_Ej3pE (accessed November 28, 2010).
87. YouTube: http://www.youtube.com/watch?v=Qnqc8bQIv84 (accessed November 28, 2010).
88. YouTube: http://www.youtube.com/watch?v=Reiff9nPXWo (accessed November 28, 2010).
89. YouTube: http://www.youtube.com/watch?v=iQ3Yy0xcVNQ (accessed November 28, 2010).
90. YouTube: http://www.youtube.com/watch?v=m9Y0pMU9HmI (accessed November 28, 2010).

91. Kellough 2006.
92. Steps NYC: http://www.stepsnyc.com/faculty/bio/Donald-Byrd/ (accessed November 28, 2010).
93. Guggenheim: http://www.guggenheim.org/new-york/education/works-and-process/past-performances-1990 (accessed November 28, 2010).
94. Reuters: http://www.reuters.com/article/pressRelease/idUS193520+27-Feb-2009+BW20090227 (accessed November 28, 2010); there is a tremendous wealth of information on this topic, and this website is only given as a starting point.
95. The Numbers: http://www.the-numbers.com/movies/series/AfricanAmerican.php (accessed November 28, 2010).
96. Entertainment Weekly: http://www.ew.com/ew/article/0,,277033,00.html (accessed November 28, 2010).
97. Examiner: http://www.examiner.com/america-s-best-dance-crew-in-national/alex-bgirl-shorty-lends-her-dance-moves-to-alvin-the-chipmunks-the-squeakquel (accessed December 5, 2010).
98. Source: www.adcritic.com (accessed August 21, 2007).
99. YouTube: http://www.youtube.com/watch?v=RgHvtlgMc9E (accessed November 28, 2010).
100. YouTube: http://www.youtube.com/watch?v=becjk2__Q5M (accessed November 28, 2010).
101. YouTube: http://www.youtube.com/watch?v=1cNDSPutas8 (accessed December 18, 2010).
102. YouTube: http://www.youtube.com/watch?v=VQ3d3KigPQM (accessed November 28, 2010).
103. YouTube: http://www.youtube.com/watch?v=kfJnqbudMzs (accessed November 28, 2010); Kia: http://www.kiasoul.com/#/media (accessed November 28, 2010).
104. Holt 2004.
105. YouTube: http://www.youtube.com/watch?v=RsWpvkLCvu4 (accessed November 28, 2010).
106. YouTube: http://www.youtube.com/watch?v=rW3u4DugwRg (accessed November 28, 2010). See also the *Los Angeles Times*: http://latimesblogs.latimes.com/washington/2010/11/obama-boehner-pelosi-mcconnell.html (accessed November 28, 2010); CNN: http://articles.cnn.com/2010-11-19/politics/political.circus_1_president-obama-underwear-bush?_s=PM:POLITICS (accessed November 28, 2010).
107. Ads and History—Highlights from PepsiCo website: www.pepsico.com (accessed July 16, 2010). Pepsi's website has their account of their marketing and advertising history dating from the 1800s.
108. Klein 2009.
109. Frank 1997.
110. Holt 2004; Frank 1997.
111. Scott 2001.
112. Frank 1997.
113. Holt 2004.
114. Ibid.
115. Scott 2001, 120.
116. Fowles 1996.

Chapter 4

1. Royce 1977, 154.
2. Google Video: http://video.google.com/videoplay?docid=-4449065816181299003# (accessed December 18, 2010).
3. Portions of this chapter appear in "Moving Euro American Consumers in Mysterious Ways with African American Social Dance in Television Ads," in the 2011 *Consumption, Markets and Culture*.
4. Barthes 1977.
5. Sklar 2001.
6. Walter 2011.
7. Murray and Ozanne 1991.
8. Rose 1994.
9. See Frank 1997; Huntington 2007; Walter 2011.
10. Schroeder and Zwick 2004.
11. Ibid., 23.
12. Cronin 2004, 360.
13. See as an example, *Cool Hunting*, a documentary video discussing consumers' movement away from mainstream and from corporate advertising in http://www.pbs.org/wgbh/pages/frontline/shows/cool/etc/hunting.html (accessed October 15, 2010). See also Cronin 2004.
14. Hackley 2002.
15. Schroeder and Zwick 2004.
16. Adorno 1991; Goldman 1992; Leiss, Kline, and Jhally 1990; Wernick 1991.
17. This discussion is motivated by Jib Fowles' 1996 contribution, 60–76.
18. Schroeder and Zwick 2004.
19. Cronin 2004, 352.

20. Ibid., 354.
21. Chambers 2008.
22. David Geeting: "I went to work for Leo Burnett in 1971 after about 4–5 years with two other agencies in Detroit, Campbell Ewald, then, D'Arcy MacManus, John, & Adams, then Leo Burnett. I got moved to Chicago, then worked my way up to executive producer, and executive planning director, then went to another agency for five years, who wanted me to come to the west coast, Foote Cone & Belding. After five years, I went back to Leo Burnett, in LA then back to Chicago, where I became a VP, senior producer. The agency really expected me to be involved with projects from the beginning, working with clients and creatives, and account executives, so that everything was pointed to commercials we could deliver on budget."
23. See the *Washington Post*: http://www.washingtonpost.com/wp-dyn/content/article/2008/03/14/AR2008031401072.html (accessed November 28, 2010).
24. Cronin 2004.

Chapter 5

1. Chambers 2008, 269.
2. Hazzard-Gordan 1990, 3.
3. Bogart 1996.
4. Lears 1994.
5. Ibid.
6. Fowels 1996; Holt 2004.
7. Joy and Sherry 2003.
8. Hazzard-Gordan 1990, Malone 1996.
9. Arvidson 2006.
10. Husserl 1931; Arvidson 2006; Nasir and colleagues 2009.
11. Keltner and Haidt 2003.
12. Wagner 1977.
13. Walter 2011.
14. Hazzard-Gordan 1990; Malone 1996; Huntington 2007.
15. Dodds 2001, 33.
16. Smith-Autard 2000; Cooper 1998.
17. Dodds 2004.
18. Walter 2011.
19. Langer 1953.
20. Anderson 1993.
21. Holt 2004.
22. Nasir and colleagues 2009, 77.
23. Fredrickson 2002.
24. Nasir and colleagues 2009, 79.
25. Peirce 1991.
26. Sheets-Johnstone 1966.
27. Kirby 2010.
28. Chambers 2008.
29. Lears 1994, 312.
30. Ibid.
31. Cronin 2004; Dodds 2001.
32. Ono 2010, 232.
33. Cronin 2004.
34. Wagner 1997.
35. Walter 2011.
36. Wagner 1997.
37. Sheets-Johnstone 1966.
38. Walter 2011.
39. Lange 1976.
40. Singer 2010.
41. Machon 2009.
42. Venkatesh and Maember 2008.
43. Arnould and Thompson 2005.
44. Brumbaugh 2002.
45. Mick and Buhl 1992.
46. Shiff 1979.
47. Petty and colleagues 1983.
48. Horton and Fraleigh 1999, 65.
49. Strauss and Corbin 1998.
50. Horton and Fraleigh 1999.
51. Strauss and Corbin 1998.
52. Horton and Fraleigh 1999.
53. Ibid.
54. Walter 2011.
55. Strauss and Corbin 1998.

Conclusion

1. Emery 1972; Emery 1988, 341, 364.

Bibliography

Aaker, J., A. M. Brumbaugh, and S.A. Grier. 2000. Nontarget markets and viewer distinctiveness: The impact on target marketing and advertising attitudes. *Journal of Consumer Psychology* 9.3: 127–140.

Adorno, Theodor W. 1991. *The culture industry: Selected essays on mass culture.* London: Routledge.

Alasuutari, Pertti. 1995. *Researching culture: Qualitative method and cultural studies.* Thousand Oaks, CA: Sage Publications.

Alden, Dana L., Ashesh Mukherjee, and Wayne D. Hoyer. 2000. The effects of incongruity, surprise and positive moderators on perceived humor in television advertising. *Journal of Advertising* 29.2: 1–15.

———. 1999. Extending a contrast resolution model of humor in television advertising: The role of surprise. *HUMOR: International Journal of Humor Research* 12.1: 15–22.

———, and Wayne D. Hoyer. 1993. An examination of cognitive factors related to humorousness in television advertising. *Journal of Advertising* 22.2: 29–37.

Alexander, Alison, Louise M. Benjamin, Keisha Hoerrner, and Darrell Roe. 1998. Content analysis of advertisements in children's television in the 1950s. *Journal of Advertising*, 27.3: 1–9.

Allan, D. 2006. Effects of popular music in advertising on attention and memory. *Journal of Advertising Research* (Dec): 434–444.

Alpert, Judy I., and Mark I. Alpert. 1990. Music influences on mood and purchase intentions. *Psychology & Marketing* 7.2 (summer): 109–133.

Anderson, Benedict. 1983. *Imagined communities.* London: Verso.

Anderson, Terry. 2005. *The pursuit of fairness: A history of affirmative action.* New York: Oxford.

Arnould, Eric J., and Craig J. Thompson. 2005. Consumer culture theory (CCT): Twenty years of research. *Journal of Consumer Research* 31.4 (Mar): 868–882.

Arvidson, R. Sven. 2006. The sphere of attention, context and margin, contributions to phenomenology. *The Center for Advanced Research in Phenomenology* 54, n.p.

Banes, Sally. 1994. *Writing dancing in the age of postmodernism.* Middletown, CT: Wesleyan University Press.

Baudrillard, Jean. 1995. *Simulacra and simulation: The body, in theory: Histories of cultural materialism.* Ann Arbor: University of Michigan Press.

Barthes, Roland. 1977. *Image music text*. New York: Hill and Wang.

———. 1964. *Elements of semiology*. Trans. Annette Lavers and Colin Smith. New York: The Noonday Press.

Bauer, Raymond A., and Scott M. Cunningham. 1970. The Negro market. *Journal of Advertising Research* 10 (Apr): 3–13.

Baulac, Y., R. Bolden, and J. Moscarola. 2000. Interactive research: How internet technology could revolutionize the survey and analysis process. *Association for Survey Computing (ASC) Conference on Survey Research on the Internet*. London: Imperial College.

Belk, Russell W., and Richard W. Pollay. 1985. Images of ourselves: The good life in twentieth century advertising. *Journal of Consumer Research* 11 (Mar): 887–897.

Berman, Ronald. 1981. *Advertising and social change*. Beverly Hills, CA: Sage Publications.

Best, David N. 1978. *Philosophy and human movement*. London: George Allen & Unwin.

Blair, Elizabeth M., and Mark N. Hatala. 1992. The use of rap music in children's advertising. *Advances in Consumer Research*, 19: 719–724.

Boas, Franziska. 1944. *The function of dance in human society*. Brooklyn, NY: Dance Horizons.

Bogart, Michele H. 1995. *Artists, advertising, and the borders of art*. Chicago: University of Chicago Press.

Brinol, Pablo, and Richard E. Petty. 2003. Overt head movements and persuasion: A self-validation analysis. *Journal of Personality and Social Psychology* 84.6: 1123–1139.

Bristor, Julia M., and Eileen Fischer. 1993. Feminist thought: Implications for consumer research. *Journal of Consumer Research* 19 (Mar): 518–536.

Brown, Donald E. 2004. Human universals, human nature, and human culture. *Dædalus* (fall): 47–54.

———. 1991. *Human universals*. New York: McGraw Hill.

Brumbaugh, A. M. 2002. Source and nonsource cues in advertising and their effects on the activation of cultural and subcultural knowledge on the route to persuasion. *Journal of Consumer Research* 29 (Sep): 258–269.

Bryman, A. 2001. *Social research methods*. Oxford, UK: Oxford University Press.

Bulmer, S., and M. Buchanan-Oliver. 2006. Advertising across cultures: Interpretations of visually complex advertising. *Journal of Current Issues and Research in Advertising* 28.1: 57–71.

Burrill, D A. 2006. Check out my moves. *Social Semiotics* 16.1: 17–38.

Butler, Judith P. 1990. *Gender trouble: Feminism and the subversion of identity*. New York: Routledge.

———. 1993. *Bodies that matter: On the discursive limits of sex*. Stanford, CA: Stanford University Press.

Cacioppo, J. T., J. R. Priester, and G. G. Berntson. 1993. Rudimentary determinants of attitudes II: Arm flexion and extension have differential effects on attitudes. *Journal of Personality and Social Psychology* 65: 5–17.

Calvo-Merino, B., D. E. Glaser, J. Grezes, R. E. Passingham, and P. Haggard. 2005. Action observation and acquired motor skills: An fMRI study with expert dancers. *Cerebral Cortex* 15 (Aug): 1243–1249.

Carroll, N. 2001. Toward a definition of moving-picture dance. *Dance Research Journal* 33.1 (summer): 46–63.

Cass, Joan. 1993. *Dancing through history*. Upper Saddle River, NJ: Prentice Hall.

Cayla, J., and G. M. Eckhardt. 2008. Asian brands and the shaping of a transnational imagined community. *Journal of Consumer Research* 35 (Aug): 216–230.

Chambers, Jason. 2008. *Madison Avenue and the color line*. Philadelphia: University of Pennsylvania Press.

Charter, S. 2006. Aesthetic products and

aesthetic consumption: A review. *Consumption, Markets and Culture* 9.3 (Sep): 235–255.

Clarkson, Thomas. 1971. *An essay on the impolicy of the African slave trade in two parts.* 1789; Philadelphia: Francis Bailey.

———. 1787. *An essay on the slavery and commerce of the human species, particularly the African.* Philadelphia: Joseph Crukshank.

Clifford, James, and George E. Marcus. 1986. *Writing culture: The poetics and politics of ethnography.* Berkeley: University of California Press.

Cohen-Stratyner, B. 2001. Social dance: Contexts and definitions. *Dance Research Journal* 33.2 (winter): 121–123.

Conrad, F. G., M. P. Couper, and R. Tourangeau. 2003. Interactive features in web surveys. *Joint Meetings of the American Statistical Association.*

Copeland, Roger, and Marshall Cohen, eds. 1983. *What is dance? Readings in theory and criticism.* New York: Oxford University Press.

Cottle, Thomas J. 1966. Social class and social dancing. *The Sociological Quarterly* 7: 179 196.

Cowley, Malcolm, ed. 1928. *Adventures of an African slaver; being a true account of the life of Captain Theodore Canot, trader in gold, ivory & slaves on the coast of Guinea: His own story as told in the year 1984 to Brantz Mayer.* New York: Albert & Charles Boni.

Croce, Benedetto. *Guide to aesthetics.* Trans. Patrick Romanell. New York: The Bobbs-Merrill Company, 1965.

Cronin, Anne. 2004. Regimes of mediation: Advertising practitioners as cultural intermediaries? *Consumption, Markets, and Culture* 7.4 (Dec): 349–369.

Dake, Dennis. 2005. Aesthetic theory. In *Handbook of Visual Communication,* ed. Ken Smith et al. 3–42. Mahwah, MJ: Lawrence Erlbaum Associates.

Damasio, Antonio. 1999. *The feeling of what happens; body and emotion in the making of consciousness.* New York: Harcourt Brace & Company.

Davidson, Martin. 1992. *The consumerist manifesto: Advertising in postmodern times.* London and New York: Routledge.

Derrida, Jacques. 1973. *Speech and phenomena: And other essays on Husserl's theory of signs.* Evanston, IL: Northwestern University Press.

Descartes, Rene. 1989. *Discourse on method and the meditations.* New York: Prometheus Books.

Desmond, Jane C. 1997. Embodying difference: Issues in dance and cultural studies. In *Meaning in motion: New cultural studies of dance,* ed. Jane C. Desmond. 29–54. Durham, NC: Duke University Press.

———. 1999. Engendering dance: Feminist inquiry and dance research. In *Researching dance: Evolving methods of inquiry,* eds. Sondra Horton Fraleigh and Penelope Hanstein. 309–333. Pittsburgh: Pittsburgh University Press.

Dodds, Sherrill. 2004. *Dance on screen: Genres and media from Hollywood to experimental art.* New York and London: Palgrave MacMillian.

Dowling, W. Jay, and Dane L. Harwood. 1986. *Music cognition.* New York: Academic Press.

Dunagan, C. 2007. Performing the commodity-sign: Dancing in the gap. *Dance Research Journal* 39.2 (winter): 3–22.

Dunbar, D. S. 1990. Music, and advertising. *International Journal of Advertising* 9: 197–203.

Emery, Lynne Fauley. 1972. *Black dance in the United States from 1619 to today.* Washington, DC: National Press Books.

Ewen, Stuart. 1976. *Captains of consciousness: Advertising and the social roots of the consumer.* New York: McGraw-Hill Book Company.

Falk, Pasi. 1994. *The consuming body.* London: Sage Publications.

Fam, K-S. 2008. Attributes of likable television commercials in Asia. *Journal of Advertising Research* (Sep): 418–432.

Faseur, T., and M. Geuens. 2006. Different positive feelings leading to different ad evaluations: The case of coziness, excitement, and romance. *Journal of Advertising* 12.4 (winter): 129–142.

Featherstone, Mike, Bryan S. Turner, Mike Hepworth, eds. 1991. *The body: Social process and cultural theory*. Thousand Oaks, CA: Sage Publications.

Fontanille, J. 2004. *Soma et Séma, figures du corps*. Paris, France: Maisonneuve et Larose.

Forester, Jens. 2004. How body feedback influences consumers' evaluation of products. *Journal of Consumer Psychology* 14.4: 416–426.

Foster, Susan Leigh. 1986. *Reading dancing: Bodies and subjects in contemporary American dance*. Berkeley: University of California Press.

———. 1995. *Choreographing history*. Bloomington: Indiana University Press.

Foucault, Michel. 1970. *The order of things: An archaeology of the human sciences*. New York: Random House.

———. 1997. *Discipline & punish: The birth of the prison*. Trans. Alan Sheridan. New York: Random House.

Fowels, Jib. 1996. *Advertising and popular culture*. Thousand Oaks, CA: Sage Publications.

Fraleigh, Sondra Horton, and Penelope Hanstein. 1999. *Researching dance: Evolving modes of inquiry*. Pittsburgh: University of Pittsburgh Press.

Francis, S. T. 1996. Exploring dance as concept: Contributions from cognitive science. *Dance Research Journal* 28.1: 51–66.

Frank, Thomas. 1997. *The conquest of cool: Business culture, counterculture, and the rise of hip consumerism*. Chicago: University of Illinois Press.

Franko, Mark. 1993. *Dances as text: Ideologies of the Baroque body*. Cambridge: Cambridge University Press.

Frederickson, G. 2002. *Racism: A short history*. Princeton, NJ: Princeton University Press.

Friend, Irwin, and J. B. Kravis. 1957. New light on the consumer market. *Harvard Business Review* (Jan-Feb): 112–115.

Ganassali, S. 2008. The influence of the design of web survey questionnaires on the quality of responses. *Survey Research Methods* 2.1: 21–32.

Gao, Z. 2009. Beyond culture: A proposal for agent-based content analysis of international advertisements. *Journal of Current Issues and Research in Advertising* 31.1 (spring): 105–116.

Geertz, Clifford. 1983. *Local knowledge: Further essays in interpretive anthropology*. New York: Basic Books.

Goellner, Ellen W., and Jacqueline Shea Murphy. 1995. *Bodies of the text: Dance as theory, literature as dance*. Piscataway, NJ: Rutgers University Press.

Goldman, Robert. 1992. *Reading ads socially*. London: Routledge.

Gorn, G. J. 1982. The effects of music in advertising on choice behavior: A classical conditioning approach. *Journal of Marketing* 46 (winter): 94–100.

Gottschild, Brenda Dixon. 2005. *The African American dancing body: A geography from coon to cool*. New York: Palgrave Macmillan.

———. 1996. *Digging the Africanist presence in American performance: Dance and other contexts*. Westport, CT: Greenwood Press.

Goulding, C., A. Shankar, and R. Elliot. 2002. Working weeks, rave weekends: Identity fragmentation and the emergence of new communities. *Consumption, Markets and Culture* 5.4: 261–284.

Green, Jill, and Susan W. Stinson. 1999. Postpositivist research in dance. In *Researching dance: Evolving methods of inquiry*, eds. Sondra Horton Fraleigh and Penelope Hanstein. 91–123. Pittsburgh, PA: Pittsburgh University Press.

H'Doubler, Margaret N. 1940. *Dance: A*

creative art experience. Madison: University of Wisconsin Press.

Hackley, Chris. 2000. Silent running: Tacit, discursive and psychological aspects of management in a top UK advertising agency. *British Journal of Management* 11: 239–254.

Haley, R. I., J. Richardson, and B. Baldwin. 1984. The effects of nonverbal communications in television advertising. *Journal of Advertising Research* 24.4: 11–18.

Hall, Thomas Steel, trans. 1972. *Treatise of man: Rene Descartes*. Cambridge: Harvard University Press.

Hanna, Judith Lynne. 1987. *To dance is human: A theory of nonverbal communication*. Chicago: University of Chicago Press.

———. 1999. *Partnering dance and education*. Champaign, IL: Human Kinetics.

Hanstein, Penelope. 1999. Models and metaphors: Theory making and the creation of new knowledge. In *Researching Dance: Evolving Methods of Inquiry*, eds. Sondra Horton Fraleigh and Penelope Hanstein. 62–90. Pittsburgh: Pittsburgh University Press.

Hartman, Saidiya V. 1997. *Scenes of subjection: Terror, slavery, and self-making in nineteenth-century America*. New York: Oxford University Press.

Harwood, T. G., and T. Garry. 2003. An overview of content analysis. *The Marketing Review* 3.4: 479–498.

Hazzard-Gordan, Katrina. 1996. Dance in hip hop culture. In *Droppin' science: Critical essays on rap music and hip hop culture*, ed. William Eric Perkins. 220–237. Philadelphia: Temple University Press.

———. 1990. *Jookin': The rise of social dance formations in African-American culture*. Philadelphia: Temple University Press.

———. 1998. Dancing under the lash: Sociocultural disruption, continuity and synthesis. In *African dance: An artistic, historical, and philosophical inquiry*, ed.

Kariamu Welsh Asante. 101–130. Trenton, NJ: Africa World Press.

Hill, Constance Valis. 2010. *Tap dancing America: A cultural history*. Oxford: Oxford University Press.

Hirschman, E. C. 1993. Ideology in consumer research, 1980 and 1990: A Marxist and feminist critique. *Journal of Consumer Research* 19 (Mar): 537–555.

———, and C. J. Thompson. 1997. Why media matter: Toward a richer understanding of consumers' relationships with advertising and mass media. *Journal of Advertising* 26.1 (spring): 45–60.

———, L. S. Scott, and W. B. Wells. 1998. A model of product discourse: Linking consumer practice to cultural texts. *Journal of Advertising* 27.1 (spring): 33–50.

Holbrook, Morris B., and Robert M. Schindler. 1994. Age, sex, and attitude toward the past as predictors of consumers' aesthetic tastes for cultural products. *Journal of Marketing Research* (Aug): 412–422.

Holt, Douglas. 2004. *How brands become icons*. Boston: Harvard Business School Press.

hooks, bell. 2006. *Outlaw culture: Resisting representations*. New York: Taylor and Francis.

Horkheimer, Max. 1941. The end of reason. *Studies in Philosophy and Social Science* 9: 316–379.

Hudson, L. A., and J. L. Ozanne. 1988. Alternative ways of seeking knowledge in consumer research. *Journal of Consumer Research*, 14: 508–521.

Hung, Kineta. 2000. Narrative music in congruent and incongruent TV advertising. *Journal of Advertising* 29.1 (spring): 25–34.

Huntington, Carla. 2008. Choreographing the historical boundaries of dance and consumer research spheres, paper presented, Association for Consumer Research Gender Conference, Boston, MA.

_____. 2007. *Hip hop dance: Meanings and messages*. Jefferson, NC: McFarland.

_____. 2004. Moving beyond the Baumol and Bown cost disease in professional ballet: A pas de deux (dance) of new economic assumptions and dance history perspectives, diss., Riverside: University of California.

Husserl, Edmund. 1931. *Ideas*. Trans. W. R. Boyce Gibson. London: George Allen & Unwin.

Jameson, Fredric. 1990. *Postmodernism, or, the cultural logic of late capitalism (postcontemporary interventions)*. Durham, NC: Duke University Press.

Jones, D. G. Brian, and David D. Monieson. 1990. Early development of the philosophy of marketing thought. *Journal of Marketing* 54 (Jan): 102–113.

Joy, A., and J. F. Sherry. 2003. Speaking of art as embodied imagination: A multisensory approach to understanding aesthetic experience. *Journal of Consumer Research*, 30 (Sep): 259–282.

Joy, A., and A. Venkatesh. 1994. Postmodernism, feminism, and the body: The visible and the invisible in consumer research. *International Journal of Research in Marketing* 11, 333–357.

Kaeppler, Adrienne L. 1972. Method and theory in analyzing dance structure with an analysis of tongan dance. *Ethnomusicology* 16.2 (May): 173–217.

Kellaris, J. J., and A. D. Cox. 1989. The effects of background music in advertising: A reassessment. *Journal of Consumer Research* 16 (Jun): 113–118.

Kellough, J. Edward. 2006. *Understanding affirmative action: Politics, discrimination, and the search for justice*. Washington, DC: Georgetown University Press.

Keltner, Dacher, and Jonathan Haidt. 2003. Approaching awe, a moral, spiritual, and aesthetic emotion. *Cognition and Emotion* 17.2: 297–314.

Kirby, Alan. 2010. The death of postmodernism and beyond. *Philosophy Now* (Oct/Nov), http://www.philosophynow.org/issue58/58kirby.htm.

Kitayama, Shinobu, Sean Duffy, Tadashi Kawamura, and Jeff T. Larsen. 2003. Perceiving an object and its context in different cultures: A cultural look at new look. *American Psychological Society* 14.3: 201–206.

Kitwana, Bakari. 2003. *The hip hop generation: Young blacks and the crisis in African American culture*. New York: Perseus.

Klein, Bethany. 2009. *As heard on TV: Popular music in advertising*. London: Ashgate.

Kleine, R., S. S. Kleine, and J. B. Kernan. 1993. Mundane consumption and the self: A social-identity perspective. *Journal of Consumer Psychology* 2.3: 209–235.

Kvale, S. 1983. The qualitative research interview: A phenomenological and a hermeneutical mode of understanding. *Journal of Phenomenological Psychology* 14.2: 171–196.

Laban, Rudolf. 1966. *The language of movement*. London: Macdonald and Evans.

_____, and F. C. Lawrence. 1947, 1974. *Effort: Economy in body movement*. Boston: Plays.

Lakoff, George, and Mark Johnson. 1999. *Philosophy in the flesh: The embodied mind and its challenge to Western thought*. New York: Basic Books.

Lane, Lisbeth G., and Beth Marlow. 1999. Self as a verb and the metaphor of dance: An explanation of the self-discovery experience within a constructivist framework. *Asian Journal of Social Psychology* 2.3 (Dec): 357–365.

Lange, Roderyk. 1976. *The nature of dance: An anthropological perspective*. New York: International Publications Service.

Langer, Susan. 1953. *Feeling and form: A theory of art*. New York: Charles Scribner's Sons.

Laplantine, F. 2004. *Entretien par Alain Mons. MEI* 21: 15–30.

Lawler, Lillian B. 1951. The dance in metaphor. *The Classical Journal* 46.8 (May): 383–391.

Leiss, William, Stephen Kline and Sut Jhally. 1990. *Social communication in advertising: Persons, products and images of well-being.* London: Routledge.
Littlejohn, Stephen W., and Karen A. Foss. 2005. *Theories of human communication,* 8th ed. Belmont, CA: Thomson Wadsworth.
Lears, Jackson. 1994. *Fables of abundance: A cultural history of advertising in America.* New York: Basic Books.
Levi-Strauss, Claude. 1974. *Structural anthropology.* New York: Basic Books.
Leymore, Varda. 1975. *Hidden myth, structure & symbolism in advertising.* Englewood Cliffs, NJ: Harper & Row.
Loewenstein, George. 1996. Out of control: Visceral influences on behavior. *Organizational Behavior and Human Decision Processes* 65.3: 272–292.
Low, W. Augustus, and Virgil A. Clift. 1981. *Encyclopedia of black America.* New York: McGraw-Hill Higher Education.
Lyotard, Jean-François. 1984. *The postmodern condition: A report on knowledge.* Minneapolis: University of Minneapolis Press.
Machon, Josephine. 2009. *(Syn)aesthetics* New York: Palgrave MacMillan.
Macinnis, D. J., and C. W. Park. 1991. The differential role of characteristics of music on high- and low-involvement consumers' processing of ads. *Journal of Consumer Research* 18 (Sept): 161–173.
Malone, Jacqui. 1996. *Steppin' on the blues: The visible rhythms of African American dance.* Champaign: University of Illinois Press.
Maxwell, Richard, ed. 2001. *Culture works: The political economy of culture.* Minneapolis: University of Minnesota Press.
McCracken, G. 1986. Culture and consumption: A theoretical account of the structure and movement of the cultural meaning of consumer goods. *Journal of Consumer Research* 13 (Jun): 71–84.
McFee, Graham. 1992. *Understanding dance.* London: Routledge.

McQuarrie, E. F., and D. G. Mick. 1999. Visual rhetoric in advertising: Text-interpretive, experimental, and reader-response analyses. *Journal of Consumer Research* 26 (Jun): 37–54.
Merleau-Ponty, Maurice. 1945. *Phenomenologie de la Perception.* Paris: Librarie Gallimard.
Mick, D. G., and C. Buhl. 1992. A meaning-based model of advertising experiences. *Journal of Consumer Research* 19 (Dec): 317–338.
Mick, D. G., and L. G. Politi. 1989. Consumers' interpretations of advertising imagery: A visit to the hell of connotation. *Interpretive Consumer Research, Association for Consumer Research,* 85–96.
Miller, W. L., and B. F. Crabtree. 2004. Depth interviewing. In *Approaches to Qualitative Research,* eds. Dans S. N. Hesse-Biber and P. Leavy. 185–202. New York: Oxford University Press.
Mitchell, Andrew A. 1988. Current perspectives and issues concerning the explanation of "feeling" advertising effects. In *Nonverbal Communication in Advertising,* eds. Sidney Hecker and David W. Stewart. 127–143. Lanham, MD: Lexington Books.
Moriarty, Sandra. 2005. Visual semiotics theory. In *Handbook of Visual Communication,* eds. Ken Smith et al. 227–241. Mahwah, NJ: Lawrence Erlbaum.
Moscarola, J. 2002. Contribution of qualitative methods to research in work and organizational psychology: Sphinx lexica and MCA. *ISSWOV 2002* (June), VARSAW.
_____, and R. Bolden. 1998. From the data mine to the knowledge mill: Applying the principles of lexical analysis to the data mining and knowledge discovery process. Paper presented at the 2nd European Symposium on Principles of Data Mining and Knowledge Discovery, Nantes, France.
Murray, J. B., and J. Ozanne. 1991. The critical imagination: Emancipatory in-

terests in consumer research. *Journal of Consumer Research* 18 (Sep): 129–144.

Nasir, Na'ilah Suad, Milbrey W. McLaughlin, and Amina Jones. 2009. What does it mean to be African American? Constructions of race and academic identity in an urban public high school. *American Educational Research Journal* 26.1: 73–144.

Neisser, Joseph U. 2003. The swaying form: Imagination, metaphor, embodiment. *Phenomenology and the Cognitive Sciences* 2: 27–55.

Oakes, S. 2007. Evaluating empirical research into music in advertising: A congruity perspective. *Journal of Advertising Research* 47.1 (Mar): 38–50.

Ono, Kent A. 2010. Postracism: A theory of the "post"—as political strategy. *Journal of Communication Inquiry* 34.3: 237–234.

Orlando, V. 2003. From rap to rai in the mixing bowl: Beur hip-hop culture and Banlieue cinema in urban France. *Journal of Popular Culture* 36.3 (winter): 395–414.

Osumare, Halifu. 1999. African aesthetics, American culture: Hip hop in the global era, diss., University of Hawaii.

Painter, Andrew A. 1994. On the anthropology of television: A perspective from Japan. *Visual Anthropology Review* 10.1 (Mar): 70–84.

Park, C. W., and S. M. Young. 1986. Consumer response to television commercials: The impact of involvement and background music on brand attitude formation. *Journal of Marketing Research* 23 (Feb): 11–24.

Peirce, Charles Sanders. 1991. *Peirce on signs: Writings on semiotic by Charles Sanders Peirce*. Chapel Hill: University of North Carolina Press.

Petty, Richard E., John T. Cacioppo, and David Schumann. 1983. Central and peripheral routes to advertising effectiveness: The moderating role of involvement. *Journal of Consumer Research* 10 (Sep): 135–146.

Petty, Richard, Pablo Brinol, and John Priester. 2008. Mass media attitude change: Implications for the elaboration likelihood model of persuasion. In *Media effects: Advances in theory and research*, eds. Jennings Bryant and Mary Beth Oliver. 155–198. New York: Routledge.

Pham, Michel Tuan, Joel B. Cohen, John W. Pracejus, and G. David Hughes. 2001. Affect monitoring and the primacy of feelings in judgment. *Journal of Consumer Research* 28.2 (Sep): 167–188.

Phillips, B. J. 1997. Thinking into it: Consumer interpretation of complex advertising images. *Journal of Advertising* 26.2 (summer): 77–87.

Pitt, L., and R. Abratt. 1988. Music in advertisements for unmentionable products—A classical conditioning experiment. *International Journal of Advertising* 7.1: 130–137.

Pollay, Richard W. 1985. The subsidizing sizzle: A descriptive history of print advertising, 1900–1980. *Journal of Marketing* 49 (summer): 24–37.

Poppelaars, Caelesta. 2009. *Steering a course between friends and foes: Why bureaucrats interact with interest groups*. Delft, Neth.: Eburon Academic Publisher.

Prasad, Pushkala. 2005. *Crafting qualitative research: Working in the postpositivist traditions*. Armonk, NY: ME Sharpe.

Prevots, Naima. 1998. *Dance for export: Cultural diplomacy and the Cold War*. Middleton, CT: Wesleyan University Press.

Priester, J. R., J. T. Cacioppo, and R. E. Petty. 1996. The influence of motor processes on attitudes toward novel versus familiar semantic stimuli. *Society for Personality and Social Psychology* 22.5: 442–447.

Proctor, S., I. Papasolomou-Doukakis, and T. Proctor. 2002. What are television advertisements really trying to tell us? A postmodern perspective. *Journal of Consumer Behaviour* 1.3 (Feb): 246–255.

Randazzo, Sal. 1993. *Mythmaking on Madison Avenue*. Chicago: Probus Press.

Redfern, Betty. 1965. *Introducing Laban art of movement*. London: MacDonald & Evans.

Ricoeur, Paul. 1979. The metaphorical process as cognition, imagination, and feeling. In *On metaphor*, ed. Sheldon Sacks. 141–157. Chicago: University Press.

Rielly, Edward J. 2003. *The 1960s, American Popular Culture through History*. Westport, CT: Greenwood Press.

Ross, Janice. 2000. Moving lessons: Margaret H'Doubler and the beginning of dance in American education. Madison: University of Wisconsin Press.

Rose, Tricia. 1994. *Black noise: Rap music and black culture in contemporary America*. Middletown, CT: Wesleyan University Press.

Rosen, Philip, ed. 1986. *Narrative, apparatus, ideology: A film theory reader*. New York: Columbia University Press.

Royce, Anya Peterson. 1977. *The anthropology of dance*. Bloomington: Indiana University Press.

Roztocki, N., and N. A. Lahri, 2003. Is the applicability of web-based surveys for academic research limited to the field of information technology? Proceedings of the 36th Hawaii International Conference on System Sciences (HICSS).

Sachs, Curt. 1937. *World history of the dance*. New York: W.W. Norton.

Sacks, Sheldon, ed. 1979. *On metaphor*. Chicago: University of Chicago Press.

Sagert, Kelly Boyer. 2007. *The 1970s, American popular culture through history*. Westport, CT: Greenwood Press.

Salzman, Jack, David Lionel Smith, and Cornel West, eds. 1996. *Encyclopedia of African American culture and history*. New York: Simon and Schuster.

Samaritter, Rosemarie. 2009. The use of metaphors in dance movement therapy. *Body Movement and Dance in Psychotherapy: An International Journal for Theory, Research and Practice* 4.1 (April): 33–43.

Sartre, Jean Paul. 1956. *Being and nothingness*. New York: Philosophical Library.

Schechner, Richard. 1985. *Between theater & anthropology*. Philadelphia: University of Pennsylvania Press.

Schmidt, W. C. 1997. Worldwide web survey research: Benefits, potential problems, and solutions. *Behavior Research Methods, Instruments and Computers* 29.2: 274–279.

Schroeder, Jonathan E. 2003. Guest editor's introduction: Consumption, gender and identity. *Consumption, Markets and Culture* 6.1: 1–4.

———. 2002. *Visual consumption*. London: Routledge.

———, and Detlev Zwick. 2004. Mirrors of masculinity: Representations and identity in advertising images. *Consumption, Markets and Culture* 7.1 (Mar): 21–52.

Sckiles, Howard. 1998. *The politics of courtly dancing in early modern England*. Amherst: University of Massachusetts Press.

Scott, Anna Beatrice. 2001. Dance. In *Culture works: The political economy of culture*, ed. Richard Maxwell. 107–130. Minneapolis: University of Minnesota Press.

Scott, Linda M. 1990. Understanding jingles and needledrop: A rhetorical approach to music in advertising. *Journal of Consumer Research* 17 (Sep): 223–236.

———. 1994. Images in advertising: The need for a theory of visual rhetoric. *Journal of Consumer Research* 21 (Sep): 252–273.

Sexton, Donald E., Jr. 1972. Black buyer behavior. *Journal of Marketing* 36 (Oct): 36–39.

Sheets-Johnstone, Maxine. 1966. *The phenomenology of dance*. London: Dance Books.

Sherry, John F. 1987. Advertising as a cultural system. In *Marketing and semiotics*, ed. Jena Umiker-Sebeok. 442–461. Berlin: Mouton de Gruyter.

Shiff, Richard. 1979. Art and life: A metaphoric relationship. In *On metaphor*, ed. Sheldon Sacks. 105–120. Chicago: University of Chicago Press.

Shilling, C. 1993. *The body and social theory*. London: Sage Publications.

Singer, Natasha. 2010. Making ads that whisper to the brain. *The New York Times*, 14 Nov 2010, www.nytimes.com.

Sklar, Deidre. 2001. Five premises for a culturally sensitive approach to dance. In *Moving history/dancing cultures: A dance history reader*, eds. Ann Dils and Ann Cooper Albright. 30–22. Middletown, CT: Wesleyan University Press.

Smith, Ken, ed. 2005. *Handbook of visual communication*. Mahwah, NJ: Lawrence Erlbaum.

Smith-Autard, Jaqueline M. 2000. *Dance Composition*, 4th ed. New York: Routledge.

Smyth, M. M. 1984. Kinesthetic communication in dance. *Dance Research Journal* 16.2: 19–22.

Spears, Nancy, and Richard Germain. 2007. The shifting role and face of animals in print advertisements in the twentieth century. *Journal of Advertising* 36.3: 19–33.

Speck, Paul S. 1991. The humorous message taxonomy: A framework for the study of humorous ads. In *Current Issues in Research in Advertising*, eds. James H. Leigh and Claude R. Martin Jr. 1–44. Ann Arbor: Michigan Business School.

Spencer, Paul, ed. 1985. *Society and the dance*. New York: Cambridge University Press.

Sperber, Dan, and Deirdre Wilson. 1986. *Relevance: Communication and cognition*. Oxford, UK: Blackwell.

Stern, Barbara B. 1992. Feminist literary theory and advertising research: A new reading of the text and the consumer. *Journal of Current Issues and Research in Advertising* 14 (spring): 9–22.

Stewart, David W., and Sidney Hecker. 1988. The future of research on nonverbal communication in advertising. In *Nonverbal communication in advertising*, eds. David W. Stewart and Sidney Hecker. 253–263. Lexington, MA: Lexington Books.

Stigel, Jorgen. 2001. TV advertising virtually speaking: The invisible voice elaborating on the space between screen and viewer. In *The aesthetics of television*, eds. Gunhild Agger and Jens F. Jensen. 321–348. Aalborg, Den.: Aalborg University Press.

Strack, F., and R. Neuman. 1996. The spirit is willing but the flesh is weak: Beyond mind-body interactions in human decision making. *Organizational Behavior and Human Decision Processes* 65.3: 300–304.

Strack, F., L. Martin, and S. Stepper. 1988. Inhibiting and facilitating conditions of the human smile: A non-obtrusive test of the facial feedback hypothesis. *Journal of Personality and Social Psychology* 54: 768–777.

Strauss, Anselm, and Juliet Corbin. 1998. *Basics of qualitative research: Techniques and procedures for developing grounded theory*. Thousand Oaks, CA: Sage Publications.

Sussman, Leila. 1984. Anatomy of the dance company boom, 1958–1980. *Dance Research Journal* 16.2: 23–28.

Synnott, Anthony. 1993. *The body social: Symbolism, self and society*. New York: Routledge.

Tate, Greg. 2003. *Everything but the burden: What white people are taking from black culture*. New York: Broadway Books.

Thomas, Helen. 2003. *The body, dance and cultural theory*. New York: Palgrave MacMillan.

Thompson, Craig J., and E. Hirschman. 1995. Understanding the socialized body: A poststructuralist analysis of consumers' self-conceptions, body images, and self-care practices. *Journal of Consumer Research* 22 (Sep): 139–153.

Thompson, Craig J. 1997. Interpreting consumers: A hermeneutical approach for deriving marketing insights from the texts of consumers' consumption stories. *Journal of Marketing Research*, 34: 438–455.

Thompson, Craig J., W. B. Locander, and H. R. Pollio. 1989. Putting consumer experience back into consumer research: The philosophy and method of existential-phenomenology. *Journal of Consumer Research* 16: 133–146.

Thompson, Craig J., and Elizabeth C. Hirschman. 1995. Understanding the socialized body: A poststructuralist analysis of consumers' self-conceptions, body images, and self-care practices. *Journal of Consumer Research* 22 (Sep): 139–153.

Thorpe, Edward. 1989. *Black dance*. Woodstock, NY: The Overlook Press.

Turner, Bryan S. 1991. Recent developments. *The body: Social process and cultural theory*, ed. Mike Featherstone, Bryan S. Turner, Mike Hepworth. 1–35. Thousand Oaks, CA: Sage Publications.

Turner, Bryan S. 1996. *Body and society: Explorations in social theory*. Thousand Oaks, CA: Sage Publications.

Turner, Victor. 1987. *The anthropology of performance*. New York: PAJ Publications.

Venkatesh, Alladi, and Laurie A. Maember. 2008. The aesthetics of consumption and the consumer as an aesthetic subject. *Consumption, Markets and Culture* 11.1 (Mar): 45–70.

Wagner, Ann. 1977. *Adversaries of dance: From the Puritans to the present*. Urbana: University of Illinois Press.

Walter, Carla. 2011. Moving (Euro) American consumers in mysterious ways with African American social dance in commercials. In *Consumption, Markets, and Culture* 3 or 4. N.p. London: Routledge.

_____, L. Altamimi, J. J. Moscarola, and J. Ibanez-Bueno. 2009. Research design: Exploring dance in advertising and its influence on consumption and culture. *Consumer Culture Theory Conference 4*, paper presented, Ann Arbor, MI.

_____, and Loay Altamini. 2010. Consumers prefer television ads with dance: Researching the effects of dance on consumer behavior. *Advances in Consumer Research*, Provo, UT.

Watts, E. K., and M. P. Orbe. 2002. The spectacular consumption of "true" African American culture: "Whassup" with the Budweiser guys? *Critical Studies in Media Communication* 19.1 (Mar): 1–20.

Wells, G. L., and R. Petty. 1980. The effects of overt head movements on persuasion: Compatibility and incompatibility of responses. *Basic and Applied Social Psychology* 1.3: 219–230.

Wernick, Andrew. 1991. *Promotional culture: Advertising, ideology and symbolic expression*, London: Sage Publications.

Wright, K. B. 2005. Researching internet-based populations: Advantages and disadvantages of online survey research, online questionnaire authoring software packages, and web survey services. *Journal of Computer-Mediated Communication* 10.3 [online journal, Article 11].

Wyatt, J. C. 2000. When to use web-based surveys. *Journal of the American Medical Informatics Association* 7.4: 426–430.

Young, C. E., and M. Robinson. 1989. Video rhythms and recall. *Journal of Advertising Research* (Jun/Jul): 29.3: 22–25.

Zakia, R. D., and M. Nadin. 1987. Semiotics, advertising and marketing. *Journal of Consumer Marketing* 4.2: 5–12.

Zeigler, Joseph Wesley. 1994. *Arts in crisis: The National Endowment for the Arts versus America*. Chicago: Chicago Review Press.

Index

advertising: as aesthetic events 56; black social dance 18; effectiveness 66; foreground and background 17; uses 59; virtual space 60; visceral affects of dance 166
aesthetics: in advertising 147; appeal and self-reflection 68; black social dance 148; and creativity 34; defined 37; mass industrialism 69
affirmative action 12; policy reversals 14
American National Theater and Academy 13
anthropologic approaches to research 77
art: as advertising 80; historical method 17, 77
Arvidson, David 70
attitude: formation 66; somatovisceral explanations 66
awe 37
axiological assumptions 53

Barthes, Roland 29
being-hereness 141
black dance aesthetic 159
black social dance: collective history 138; conceptualizations 118; dimensions 137; impact 79; perceptual map 131; in television advertising theory 151
blackface minstrelsy 14, 43
break dancing 14
Bush, George W. 98

Cartesian method of scientific analysis 25
Checker, Chubby 14
choreography for television commercials, business of 162
civil rights movement 14
Clark, Dick 14
Cold War 13

consumer culture theory 50, 167
consumption 68
consumption research, feminist approaches 53
cool identity 14
critical semiosis 17
Croce, Benedetto 36–37
cross-cultural variation 34
cultural artifacts 80
cultural intermediaries 81
cultural research design 77
cultural semiotic contexts 9
cultural studies 35
culturally constituted world 56

Damasio, Antonio 32
dance: in advertising 81, 134; affective and cognitive 41; assemblies 43; childhood memories 41; as communication device 140; conceptualizations of 130; consumer research 53; copyright 159; critical function in society 15; as cultural artifact 16; as education 44, 163; influence on product valence 67; as linguistic approach to communication 60; memories 79; metaphors 15, 59, 61–62; neutralization 31; as nonverbal communication device 8; proscenium, new 69; prototype 38; as psychological outlet 80; as social fabric of production and consumption 53; structure 34, 79; theory in 52
dancing hamsters 96
dancing master 43
digitized representations 9
discourse theory in advertising 11

effort theory 163
embodied agents 61

embodied spiritual experiences 63
epistemological assumptions 53
epistemological structures 25
executional element, advertising contexts 11
existential phenomenology 11

field of attention 70

Geertz, Clifford 32
gendered spheres 55
Gestalt-coherence 70
Great Recession 12
grounded theory 18, 154
Gulick, Luther Haley 44

Hanna, Judith Lynn 40
Hart, Oliver 43
H'Doubler, Margaret 26
hegemonic dance 15
hermeneutical method 17
high and low dance forms 43
hip-hop 14, 15
the hitch-hike 14
human universals 62
Husserl, Edmund 29, 58, 164

identity marker 34
ideology of reason 63
illusion created by dance 28
imagined spiritual experiences 63
implicature 57
indexicality 10
intertextuality 9

Jackson, Michael 14, 122, 147
The Jackson 5 14
the jitterbug 14
Journal of Consumer Research 48
judgment formation and body reaction 67

Laban, Rudolph 27
Lange, Roderyck 29
Langer, Susanne K. 27
Luther, Martin 42

Machon, Josephine 38
mass communication model 68
Mather, Increase 43
McCracken, Grant 50, 150
McFee, Graham 35
Merleau-Ponty, Maurice 30
metaphoric approaches to dance 59, 61–62
multi-sensory approach and consumption study 11
Murray, Arthur 45

National Endowment for the Humanities and Arts 13
Negro Revolution 72
neurobiological aspects 32
neuromarketing 51
noesis and noema 59

Obama, Barack 98
Obama, Michelle 98
ontological assumptions 53

participant observer research method 79
persuasion, central and peripheral routes 10
phenomenologic interviews 17
Piagetian process of accommodation 38
plane of content 32
plane of expression 32
populist worlds 56
post-racial society 143, 153
print advertising methods of analysis 17
Puritan 69

qualitative research design 77

ragtime 14, 44
reason as separate from embodiment 63
reflection, authentic and inauthentic 71
Ricoeur, Paul 62
Royce, Anya Peterson 33

Savoy Ballroom, Harlem 45
semiotic analysis 77
Sheets-Johnstone, Maxine 29
signification 9, 29–31
Sklar, Deidre 8
Smith, Adam 32
Smith, Herbert 32
socialized body 11
societal elements in dance research 12
Spencer, Paul 34, 35
sphere of attention 8, 62, 70, 134
synaesthesia 38
synaesthetic phenomenon 147
syntagms 31

tap dance 14, 44
Thomas, Helen 55
the twist 14

United States Information Agency 13
University of Wisconsin, Madison 45

vastness 38
Vietnam War 12
visual rhetoric 11, 57

Williams, Carol 144

www.ingramcontent.com/pod-product-compliance
Ingram Content Group UK Ltd.
Pitfield, Milton Keynes, MK11 3LW, UK
UKHW042010140426
5217IPUK00015B/1091